HERSHEY'S®
Chocolate Cookbook

PUBLICATIONS INTERNATIONAL, LTD.

Contents

All recipes developed and tested by the Hershey Kitchens.

This edition published by
Publications International, Ltd.
7373 North Cicero Avenue
Lincolnwood, Illinois 60646

Library of Congress Catalog Card Number 88-82162

ISBN: 0-88176-488-4

Pictured on the front cover: Crème de Cacao Torte
(*see page 6*).

Printed in the U.S.A.

h g f e d c b a

All About Chocolate

An "original American," the cacao bean was one of the treasures Columbus brought back from the New World. But neither he nor his patrons, Ferdinand and Isabella of Spain, understood its potential pleasures. It took Cortez, while conquering Mexico for Spain, to realize that there must be something very special about this *chocoatl* if Emperor Montezuma and his Aztec court sipped it from golden goblets.

Golden goblets notwithstanding, the rich chocolate liquid was not to Spanish tastes until someone added a bit of sugar and a drop or so of vanilla, heated the mixture and topped it with a cinnamon stick. With that, chocolate became the "in" drink of the day in Spain. Eventually, chocolate fever spread to Italy, then to France and Holland and finally to England. There its popularity was so great that there were actually Chocolate Houses, where meeting, greeting and sipping were the order of the day.

Chocolate, however, was still considered exotic. It was also quite expensive, as the cacao beans were still grown, picked and processed much as they had been in Cortez's time. During the Industrial Revolution, methods were developed to make chocolate finer and smoother. But perhaps the biggest step toward chocolate as we know it today was taken in Switzerland in the 1800s, when Daniel Peter added milk to basic chocolate. He also developed the formula for making the first solid chocolate. Chocolate finally sailed back across the Atlantic, and it was Milton S. Hershey who made it a true All-American.

Chocolate and Hershey have been virtually synonymous since the turn of the century, when Milton Hershey built his chocolate factory amid the rich dairylands of Pennsylvania's Lebanon Valley. It's an association that's even stronger today, and one that we're very proud of.

Over the years, thousands upon thousands of chocolate recipes have been developed and tested in the Hershey Kitchens. The following pages feature more than 150 of the recipes that we deem to be the very best. Many of them will doubtless remind you of your favorite childhood chocolate treats; others will introduce you to imaginative new ways to enjoy chocolate and cocoa in all their delicious forms. We hope you will enjoy sampling the wide variety of recipes offered for every taste and for every occasion.

Chocolate Is Chocolate...or Is It?

Purists would limit the use of the word "chocolate" to just two forms: solid unsweetened chocolate or its liquid form, chocolate liquor. They're right, of course. But the rest of the world is happily willing to accept a much broader definition. Here's a little background on chocolate in its various phases and forms:

Cacao (Cocoa) Beans are the starting point. They are the fruit of the cacao tree, which grows in a very limited climate zone—only 20 degrees north and south of the Equator—and mainly in West Africa and Latin America.

Cacao Nibs are the "meat" of the beans. The beans are cleaned and then roasted at carefully controlled temperatures to bring out their full flavor and aroma. When the outer shells are removed, the nibs are ready to go on to greater things. (They contain more than 50% cocoa butter, and that's rich treasure indeed.)

Chocolate Liquor is what makes all real chocolate products possible. The nibs are ground by a process that generates enough heat to liquefy the cocoa butter, thus creating the liquor. (The term "liquor" is used in its true sense, that of liquid essence—it has nothing to do with alcohol.)

Cocoa Butter is the vegetable fat that's extracted when the chocolate liquor is "pressed" under high pressure. This butter has a distinctive melting quality that gives chocolate products their unique texture.

Cocoa Powder made by the American process (such as HERSHEY'S Cocoa) is the marvelous by-product that remains after most of the cocoa butter has been extracted from the liquor. It has no additives and no preservatives, so it's 100% pure. And because most of the cocoa butter has been removed, it has the lowest fat content of any chocolate product. Stored in a tightly closed container, cocoa will retain its freshness and quality almost indefinitely—and without refrigeration.

Dutch-Process Cocoa Powder is made from chocolate liquor that has been treated with an alkali agent. This makes a darker powder, with a flavor that differs from that of American-process cocoa.

Bitter Chocolate, commonly referred to as unsweetened, baking or cooking chocolate, is chocolate *au naturel*. It is pure chocolate liquor, cooled and molded, usually in blocks.

Semi-Sweet Chocolate is a combination of chocolate liquor with added cocoa butter and sugar. To qualify for this term, the product must contain at least 35% chocolate liquor. Available in bars, this form is more popularly available in chips.

Sweet (Dark) Chocolate combines the same ingredients as semi-sweet, but the balance is different. This form must contain at least 15% chocolate liquor, but it has a higher sugar level.

Milk Chocolate also uses the same ingredients but with the addition of milk or cream. At least 10% chocolate liquor is required in milk chocolate products.

White Chocolate, also called confectioners' chocolate, is known in the chocolate industry as compound chocolate. It isn't really chocolate at all. Most or all of the cocoa butter has been removed and replaced by another vegetable fat, and it contains no chocolate liquor. Also called confectioners' coating, it is available in a range of colors, from dark to white and even pastels.

Chocolate-Flavored is the term applied to food products that derive their flavor from cocoa and/or chocolate liquor but do not contain a sufficient quantity of these ingredients to meet the government's definition of "true" chocolate. Chocolate-flavored syrups, which combine chocolate liquor or cocoa, sugar, water, salt and sometimes other flavorings, are among the products in this category.

Artificial Chocolate is a product of the chemical industry, not chocolate-makers. Such products contain no ingredients derived from the cacao bean—and, at the extreme, contain no sugar or milk.

Storing Chocolate

Chocolate products will stay fresh for well over a year if stored in a cool, dry place (65°–70°F). It's a good idea to keep an eye on the temperature and humidity.

Temperatures above 78°F will cause chocolate to melt. The cocoa butter then rises to the surface and forms a grayish discoloration called "cocoa butter bloom." Condensation on milk or semi-sweet chocolate may cause the sugar to dissolve and rise to the surface as "sugar bloom." Neither "bloom" affects the quality or flavor of chocolate and, once melted, the chocolate will regain its original color. Thus, it's a good idea to keep chocolate (well wrapped, of course) in as cool a place as possible during prolonged periods of heat and high humidity.

Melting Chocolate

Using a Double Boiler: This is the preferred method for melting all types of chocolate, avoiding both scorching and the formation of steam droplets. Simply place the chocolate in the top of a double boiler over hot, not boiling, water.

Using Direct Heat: Because chocolate scorches so easily, this method is not strongly recommended. There are three "musts": very low heat; a heavy saucepan; constant stirring.

Using a Microwave Oven: See page 86 for detailed directions.

For Small Amounts: If melting less than 2 ounces, place in a small heatproof cup and place in a shallow pan with a small amount of warm water; stir until smooth. (Or use a microwave oven.)

Tips from the Experts
• Wash and dry the melting utensil thoroughly after each use. Any residue will affect the taste of chocolate.
• A wet utensil or the condensation of steam droplets can cause chocolate to get stiff and grainy. Don't panic. As an emergency measure, simply stir in 1 teaspoon solid vegetable shortening (not butter) for every 2 ounces of chocolate.
• Stir the melting chocolate periodically with a wire whisk to help blending and discourage scorching.
• Break chocolate into 1-inch pieces to speed the melting process.

Using Cocoa Instead of Chocolate

Cocoa is so convenient to use that many cooks use it as a substitute for chocolate in their favorite recipes. Here's an easy formula:

For unsweetened baking chocolate: 3 level tablespoons cocoa plus 1 tablespoon shortening (liquid or solid) equals 1 block (1 ounce).

For semi-sweet chocolate: 6 tablespoons cocoa plus 7 tablespoons sugar plus 1/4 cup shortening equals one 6-ounce package (1 cup) semi-sweet chocolate chips or 6 blocks (1 ounce each) semi-sweet chocolate.

For sweet baking chocolate: 3 tablespoons cocoa plus 4 1/2 tablespoons sugar plus 2 2/3 tablespoons shortening equals 1 bar (4 ounces).

A Note About Butter or Margarine

Regular butter or margarine in sticks should be used in Hershey recipes. Diet, soft, "light," and vegetable oil spread products act differently in cooking and baking than regular butter or stick margarine and may cause unsatisfactory results.

Showstoppers

Deluxe Ice Cream Cocoa Roll

6 egg yolks, at room
   temperature
$^3/_4$ cup sugar
1 teaspoon vanilla
6 egg whites, at room
   temperature
$^1/_3$ cup HERSHEY'S Cocoa
3 tablespoons flour
1 quart ice cream (any flavor),
   softened
   Hot Fudge Sauce or
   confectioners' sugar

Grease $15^1/_2 \times 10^1/_2 \times 1$-inch jelly roll pan; line with wax paper and lightly grease paper. Set aside. Beat egg yolks in small mixer bowl on high speed; gradually add $^1/_4$ cup of the sugar and the vanilla, beating until thick and lemon-colored. Beat egg whites in large mixer bowl; gradually add $^1/_4$ cup of the sugar, beating until stiff but not dry. Carefully fold egg yolk mixture into beaten egg whites. Combine remaining $^1/_4$ cup sugar, the cocoa and flour; fold about 2 tablespoons at a time into egg mixture just until blended.

Spread batter evenly in prepared pan. Bake at 375° for 15 to 18 minutes or just until cake springs back when touched lightly in center. Invert onto slightly dampened towel; carefully peel off wax paper. Immediately roll cake and towel together starting from narrow end; place on wire rack to cool completely.

Carefully unroll cake; remove towel. Quickly spread with softened ice cream. Reroll; wrap and freeze completely. At serving time, drizzle with Hot Fudge Sauce or sprinkle with confectioners' sugar; slice and serve with additional sauce, if desired.

8 to 10 servings

HOT FUDGE SAUCE

$^3/_4$ cup sugar
$^1/_2$ cup HERSHEY'S Cocoa
$^1/_2$ cup plus 2 tablespoons
   (5-ounce can) evaporated
   milk
$^1/_3$ cup light corn syrup
$^1/_3$ cup butter or margarine
1 teaspoon vanilla

Combine sugar and cocoa in saucepan; blend in evaporated milk and corn syrup. Cook over medium heat, stirring constantly, until mixture boils; boil and stir 1 minute. Remove from heat; stir in butter and vanilla. Serve warm.

Crème de Cacao Torte

2/3 cup butter or margarine, softened
12/3 cups sugar
3 eggs
1/2 teaspoon vanilla
2 cups unsifted all-purpose flour
2/3 cup HERSHEY'S Cocoa
11/4 teaspoons baking soda
1/4 teaspoon baking powder
11/3 cups milk
2 tablespoons crème de cacao
Crème de Cacao Filling
Chocolate Ganache Glaze

Cream butter, sugar, eggs and vanilla in large mixer bowl until light and fluffy. Combine flour, cocoa, baking soda and baking powder; add alternately with milk to creamed mixture, blending just until combined.

Pour into two greased and floured 9-inch layer pans. Bake at 350° for 30 to 35 minutes or until cake tester comes out clean. Cool 10 minutes; remove from pans. Sprinkle each layer with 1 tablespoon crème de cacao; cool completely.

Meanwhile, prepare Crème de Cacao Filling. Split each cake layer horizontally into 2 layers. Place one layer on serving plate; spread with one-third of the filling. Repeat layering with remaining cake and filling, ending with cake layer. Cover tightly; chill at least 8 hours. Prepare Chocolate Ganache Glaze; spoon on top of chilled cake, allowing glaze to drizzle down side. Chill. Garnish as desired.

10 to 12 servings

CRÈME DE CACAO FILLING

1 cup heavy or whipping cream
2 tablespoons crème de cacao
1 tablespoon HERSHEY'S Cocoa

Beat cream, crème de cacao and cocoa until stiff. Cover; chill.

CHOCOLATE GANACHE GLAZE

1 HERSHEY'S SPECIAL DARK Sweet Chocolate Bar (8 ounces), broken into pieces
1/4 cup heavy or whipping cream
1 tablespoon butter or margarine
11/2 teaspoons crème de cacao

Combine chocolate bar pieces, cream and butter in medium saucepan. Cook over low heat, stirring constantly, until mixture is melted and smooth. Stir in crème de cacao. Cool to lukewarm (glaze will be slightly thickened).

Crème de Cacao Torte

Chocolate Peach Charlotte with Peach Melba Topping

4 eggs, separated
1/2 cup plus 1/3 cup sugar, divided
1 teaspoon vanilla extract
1/2 cup all-purpose flour
1/3 cup HERSHEY'S Cocoa
1/2 teaspoon baking powder
1/4 teaspoon baking soda
1/8 teaspoon salt
1/3 cup water
Chocolate Peach Filling
Peach Melba Topping
Peach slices, fresh* or canned

Line 15 1/2 × 10 1/2 × 1-inch jelly-roll pan with foil; generously grease foil. In large mixer bowl beat egg whites until soft peaks form; gradually add 1/2 cup sugar and beat until stiff peaks form; set aside. In small mixer bowl beat egg yolks and vanilla on high speed about 3 minutes; gradually add remaining 1/3 cup sugar. Continue beating 2 additional minutes until mixture is thick and lemon-colored. Combine flour, cocoa, baking powder, baking soda and salt; on low speed add to egg yolk mixture alternately with water, beating just until batter is smooth. Gradually fold chocolate mixture into egg whites; spread evenly in prepared pan. Bake at 375° for 12 to 15 minutes or until top springs back when touched lightly in center. Immediately loosen cake from edges of pan. Place foil over cake; invert cake onto countertop. Remove pan; allow to cool. Prepare Chocolate Peach Filling. Peel foil off cake. When completely cool cut a circle from one end of cake to fit bottom of 9-inch springform pan. Divide remaining cake into 3 equal vertical strips. Cut across strips forming sticks approximately 3 × 1 inch. Place sticks vertically around inside edge of springform pan; pour filling into cake-lined pan. Refrigerate 4 to 6 hours or until firm. Prepare Peach Melba Topping. To serve, remove rim of springform pan. Spoon on topping. Arrange peach slices on top. Cover; refrigerate leftovers.

12 to 14 servings

*To keep fresh peaches from turning brown, dip in mixture of 1 cup water, 1/2 teaspoon lemon juice and 1/8 teaspoon salt; drain before placing on top of dessert.

Chocolate Peach Filling

2 envelopes unflavored gelatin
3/4 cup cold water
1 cup sugar
1/3 cup HERSHEY'S Cocoa
1/4 cup butter or margarine
2 1/4 cups milk, divided
1 teaspoon vanilla extract
1 cup chilled whipping cream
1 cup pureed peaches, fresh or canned

In small bowl sprinkle gelatin over water; let stand 3 or 4 minutes to soften. In medium saucepan place sugar, cocoa, butter and 1/2 cup milk; cook over low heat, stirring constantly, until mixture is smooth and very hot. *Do not boil.* Add gelatin mixture, stirring until gelatin is completely dissolved. Remove from heat; add remaining 1 3/4 cups milk and vanilla. Pour into bowl; chill, stirring occasionally, until mixture mounds when dropped from a spoon. In small mixer bowl, beat whipping cream until stiff; fold with pureed peaches into chocolate mixture.

Peach Melba Topping

1/3 cup seedless red raspberry preserves
1/4 teaspoon lemon juice
1 teaspoon cornstarch
2 tablespoons water
1/4 teaspoon almond extract

In small saucepan combine raspberry preserves and lemon juice. In small bowl or cup mix cornstarch with water; add to raspberry mixture. Cook over medium heat, stirring constantly, until mixture begins to boil. Continue cooking until mixture thickens slightly; remove from heat. Stir in almond extract. Cool.

Georgia Peach Shortcake

Georgia Peach Shortcake

4 egg yolks
¹/₂ cup sugar
¹/₂ cup unsifted all-purpose flour
¹/₃ cup HERSHEY'S Cocoa
¹/₄ cup sugar
¹/₂ teaspoon baking soda
¹/₄ teaspoon salt
¹/₃ cup water
1 teaspoon vanilla
4 egg whites
2 tablespoons sugar
2 cups heavy or whipping cream
³/₄ cup confectioners' sugar
1 teaspoon vanilla
3 cups sliced peaches, well drained*

Grease bottom of two 9-inch square or layer pans. Line with wax paper; grease paper. Set aside. Beat egg yolks 3 minutes on medium speed in large mixer bowl. Gradually add ¹/₂ cup sugar; continue beating 2 minutes. Combine flour, cocoa, ¹/₄ cup sugar, the baking soda and salt; add alternately with water and 1 teaspoon vanilla on low speed just until batter is smooth. Beat egg whites in small mixer bowl until foamy; add 2 tablespoons sugar and beat until stiff peaks form. Carefully fold beaten egg whites into chocolate mixture.

Spread batter evenly in prepared pans. Bake at 375° for 14 to 16 minutes or until cake springs back when touched lightly. Cool 10 minutes; remove cakes from pans. Peel off wax paper; cool completely.

Beat cream, confectioners' sugar and 1 teaspoon vanilla in large mixer bowl until stiff. Place one cake layer upside down on serving plate; frost with about 1 cup of the whipped cream. With pastry tube or spoon, make a border of whipped cream ¹/₂ inch high and 1 inch wide around edge of layer. Fill center with peach slices, reserving 12 peach slices for top of cake. Carefully place second layer, top side up, on filling. Gently spread all but 1 cup whipped cream on top of cake. With pastry tube or spoon, make a border of whipped cream around edge of top layer of cake. Arrange remaining peach slices in center. Chill about 1 hour before serving.

10 to 12 servings

*Use fresh peaches or 16-ounce package frozen or 29-ounce can peach slices.

Choco-Coconut Cake Roll

4 egg whites, at room
    temperature
1/2 cup sugar
4 egg yolks, at room
    temperature
1/3 cup sugar
1 teaspoon vanilla
1/2 cup unsifted all-purpose flour
1/3 cup HERSHEY'S Cocoa
1/2 teaspoon baking powder
1/4 teaspoon baking soda
1/8 teaspoon salt
1/3 cup water
    Cherry-Coconut Filling
    Confectioners' sugar

Line 15 1/2 × 10 1/2 × 1-inch jelly roll pan with aluminum foil; generously grease foil. Set aside. Beat egg whites in large mixer bowl until foamy; gradually add 1/2 cup sugar and beat until stiff peaks form. Set aside.

Beat egg yolks in small mixer bowl 3 minutes on high speed. Gradually add 1/3 cup sugar and the vanilla; continue beating 2 additional minutes. Combine flour, cocoa, baking powder, baking soda and salt; add alternately with water to egg yolk mixture, beating on low speed just until batter is smooth. Gradually fold chocolate mixture into beaten egg whites until mixture is well blended.

Spread batter evenly in prepared pan. Bake at 375° for 12 to 15 minutes or until cake springs back when touched lightly. Invert onto towel sprinkled with confectioners' sugar; carefully peel off foil. Immediately roll cake and towel together starting from narrow end; place on wire rack to cool completely.

Prepare Cherry-Coconut Filling. Carefully unroll cake; remove towel. Spread cake with filling; reroll and chill. Sprinkle with confectioners' sugar just before serving.

8 to 10 servings

CHERRY-COCONUT FILLING

1 cup heavy or whipping cream
3 tablespoons confectioners'
    sugar
    Few drops red food color
    (optional)
1/3 cup chopped maraschino
    cherries, well drained
1/2 cup flaked coconut

Beat cream until slightly thickened. Add confectioners' sugar and food color; beat until stiff. Fold in cherries and coconut.

Choco-Coconut Cake Roll

Peanut Butter Shells
with Chocolate-Almond Cream

2 cups REESE'S Peanut Butter
   Chips
2 tablespoons shortening*
   Chocolate-Almond Cream
   Filling

Melt peanut butter chips and shortening in top of double boiler over hot, not boiling, water; stir until smooth. Remove from heat; cool slightly. Place 15 paper baking cups (2¾ inches in diameter) in muffin pans. Using a narrow, soft-bristled pastry brush, thickly and evenly coat the inside pleated surface and bottom of each cup with peanut butter mixture. (Reserve any remaining peanut butter mixture for touch-up.) Chill 10 minutes; coat any thin spots. (If peanut butter mixture thickens, stir over hot water until mixture becomes fluid again.) Cover; chill at least 1 hour or until firm.

Remove only a few peanut butter shells from refrigerator at a time; carefully peel paper from each cup. (Unfilled cups will keep for weeks in an airtight container in the refrigerator.) Fill each cup with Chocolate-Almond Cream Filling; chill several hours or overnight.

15 desserts

*Do not use butter, margarine or oil.

CHOCOLATE-ALMOND CREAM FILLING

1 HERSHEY'S Milk Chocolate
   Bar with Almonds
   (7 ounces)
1½ cups miniature or 15 large
   marshmallows
⅓ cup milk
1 cup heavy or whipping cream

Cut chocolate bar in pieces, chopping almonds into small pieces. Place in top of double boiler and melt with marshmallows and milk over hot, not boiling, water. Stir until chocolate and marshmallows are melted and mixture is smooth. Remove from heat; cool. Whip cream until stiff and fold into chocolate mixture. Cover; chill until ready to use.

Tip: You may prepare the shells weeks in advance of use, but for best results make the filling no earlier than a day ahead of serving time.

Chocolate Sundae Pizza

¾ cup shortening
1 cup packed light brown sugar
1 egg
2¼ cups unsifted all-purpose
   flour
¼ teaspoon baking soda
¼ teaspoon cinnamon
¼ teaspoon salt
½ cup (5.5-ounce can)
   HERSHEY'S Syrup
1 quart ice cream (any flavor)
   Chocolate Caramel Sauce
   (recipe follows)
   Fresh fruits

Cream shortening and brown sugar in large mixer bowl; add egg and blend well. Combine flour, baking soda, cinnamon and salt; add alternately with syrup to creamed mixture, blending well. Pat dough evenly onto greased 12-inch pizza pan, forming a thicker 1-inch-wide edge against rim of pan. Bake at 375° for 10 to 12 minutes or until top springs back when touched lightly. Cool completely.

Cut crust into 10 to 12 wedges, but do not remove from pan. Place small scoops of ice cream around edge. Wrap tightly; freeze until firm.

When ready to serve, prepare Chocolate Caramel Sauce. Arrange assorted fruits on "pizza." Pour warm sauce over ice cream. Serve immediately.

10 to 12 servings

CHOCOLATE CARAMEL SAUCE

(Continued from page 12)

1/2 cup (5.5-ounce can)
    HERSHEY'S Syrup
20 unwrapped light caramels
3 tablespoons milk
2 tablespoons butter or
    margarine

Combine syrup, unwrapped caramels and milk in top of double boiler over hot, not boiling, water; stir until caramels are melted and mixture is smooth. Blend in butter. Keep sauce warm until serving time.

Pears au Chocolat

4 fresh pears
1/2 cup sugar
1 cup water
1 teaspoon vanilla
6 tablespoons finely chopped
    nuts
2 tablespoons confectioners'
    sugar
1 teaspoon milk
    Chocolate Sauce

Core pears from bottom, leaving stems intact. Peel pears. Slice piece off bottom to make a flat base. Combine sugar and water in medium saucepan; add pears. Cover; simmer over low heat 10 to 20 minutes (depending on ripeness) or just until pears are soft. Remove from heat; add vanilla. Cool pears in syrup; chill. Combine nuts, confectioners' sugar and milk in small bowl. To serve, drain pears; spoon nut mixture into cavities. Place pears on dessert plates. Prepare Chocolate Sauce; pour or spoon sauce onto each pear. Serve with remaining sauce.

4 servings

CHOCOLATE SAUCE

6 tablespoons water
6 tablespoons sugar
1/4 cup butter or margarine
1 1/3 cups HERSHEY'S MINI
    CHIPS Semi-Sweet
    Chocolate

Combine water, sugar and butter in small saucepan; bring to full boil. Remove from heat; stir in MINI CHIPS Chocolates. Stir until chocolate has completely melted; beat or whisk until smooth. Cool.

Pears au Chocolat

Heavenly Heart Cake

Heavenly Heart Cake

³/₄ cup HERSHEY'S Cocoa
²/₃ cup boiling water
³/₄ cup butter or margarine,
    softened
2 cups sugar
1 teaspoon vanilla
2 eggs
2 cups unsifted cake flour or
    1³/₄ cups unsifted all-
    purpose flour
1¹/₄ teaspoons baking soda
¹/₄ teaspoon salt
³/₄ cup buttermilk or sour milk*
    Glossy Chocolate Sour Cream
    Frosting (recipe follows)
    Creamy Buttercream Frosting
    (recipe follows)

Stir together cocoa and boiling water in small bowl until smooth; set aside. Cream butter, sugar and vanilla in large mixer bowl until light and fluffy; beat in eggs and cocoa mixture. Combine flour, baking soda and salt; add alternately with buttermilk to creamed mixture.

Line bottoms of two heart-shaped pans with wax paper. Pour batter into prepared pans. Bake at 350° for 30 to 35 minutes or until cake tester comes out clean. Cool 10 minutes; remove from pans. Cool completely. Frost with Glossy Chocolate Sour Cream Frosting and decorate as desired with Creamy Buttercream Frosting.

8 to 10 servings

*To sour milk: Use 2 teaspoons vinegar plus milk to equal ³/₄ cup.

Note: If you don't have heart-shaped pans, bake cake as directed in two greased and floured pans: a 9-inch square and a 9-inch round. Slice round layer in half; arrange halves beside square layer to form heart shape.

GLOSSY CHOCOLATE SOUR CREAM FROSTING

(Continued from page 14)

1½ cups HERSHEY'S Semi-Sweet
    Chocolate Chips
¾ cup sour cream
2 cups confectioners' sugar
1 teaspoon vanilla

Melt chocolate chips in top of double boiler over hot, not boiling, water, stirring constantly until completely melted. Remove from heat; beat in sour cream, confectioners' sugar and vanilla.

CREAMY BUTTERCREAM FROSTING

2 cups confectioners' sugar
¼ cup butter or margarine,
    softened
2½ tablespoons milk
½ teaspoon vanilla
    Few drops red food color

Combine confectioners' sugar, butter, milk, vanilla and food color in small bowl until smooth and creamy.

Chocolate Cream Crepes

    Chocolate Cream
    Apricot Sauce
½ cup milk
2 eggs
½ teaspoon vanilla
½ cup plus 2 tablespoons
    unsifted all-purpose flour
1 tablespoon sugar
⅛ teaspoon salt
2 tablespoons butter or
    margarine, melted
    Vegetable oil

Prepare Chocolate Cream and Apricot Sauce. Combine milk, eggs and vanilla in small mixer bowl; beat slightly. Combine flour, sugar and salt in small bowl; add to egg mixture, beating until smooth. Blend in butter. Heat crepe pan or small omelet pan over medium heat; brush lightly with oil. Pour about 2 tablespoons batter into pan for each crepe; quickly tilt and spread batter evenly over bottom. Cook about 1 minute or until underside is golden brown. Loosen edges; turn and cook until lightly browned. Remove from pan. Place 3 tablespoons Chocolate Cream on each crepe; fold. Top with Apricot Sauce. Refrigerate leftovers.

About 10 crepes

CHOCOLATE CREAM

⅓ cup HERSHEY'S Cocoa
¼ teaspoon salt
1⅓ cups (14-ounce can) sweetened
    condensed milk*
¼ cup hot water
2 tablespoons butter or
    margarine
½ teaspoon vanilla
1 cup heavy or whipping cream

Combine cocoa and salt in top of double boiler; gradually stir in sweetened condensed milk. Place over boiling water and cook, stirring constantly, until mixture is very thick. Gradually stir in hot water. Continue cooking 5 minutes, stirring frequently, until mixture thickens again. Remove from heat; stir in butter and vanilla. Cool to room temperature. Whip cream; fold into chocolate mixture. Chill thoroughly.

*Do not use evaporated milk.

APRICOT SAUCE

1½ cups (17-ounce can) apricot
    halves
¼ cup sugar
4 teaspoons cornstarch
¼ cup water
½ teaspoon lemon juice
1 tablespoon orange-flavored
    liqueur

Drain and slice apricots (reserve ½ cup syrup). Combine sugar and cornstarch in 2-quart saucepan; gradually stir in reserved syrup and the water. Cook over low heat, stirring constantly, until mixture thickens and just begins to boil. Add apricots and lemon juice; heat until fruit is warm. Remove from heat; stir in liqueur. Serve warm. (Sauce can be reheated over low heat.)

Chocolate-Filled Boston Cream Pie ⌇⌇⌇⌇⌇⌇⌇⌇⌇⌇⌇⌇⌇⌇

2 cups unsifted all-purpose
    flour
1½ cups sugar
3½ teaspoons baking powder
1 teaspoon salt
¼ cup butter or margarine,
    softened
¼ cup shortening
1 cup milk
3 eggs
1 teaspoon vanilla
    Chocolate Cream Filling
    Chocolate Glaze

Combine all ingredients except Chocolate Cream Filling and Chocolate Glaze in large mixer bowl. Blend 30 seconds on low speed; beat 3 minutes on high speed. Pour into two greased and floured 9-inch layer pans. Bake at 350° for 30 to 35 minutes. Cool 10 minutes; remove from pans. Cool completely.

Meanwhile, prepare Chocolate Cream Filling. Place one cake layer on serving plate; spread with filling. Top with second cake layer; chill. Prepare Chocolate Glaze. Spoon hot glaze on top of cake, allowing glaze to drizzle down side. Chill before serving. Refrigerate any remaining dessert.

10 to 12 servings

CHOCOLATE CREAM FILLING

⅔ cup sugar
2 tablespoons cornstarch
⅛ teaspoon salt
1½ cups milk
2 egg yolks, slightly beaten
1 bar (1 ounce) HERSHEY'S
    Unsweetened Baking
    Chocolate, broken into
    pieces
2 teaspoons vanilla

Combine sugar, cornstarch and salt in medium saucepan; gradually add milk and egg yolks. Add baking chocolate. Cook over medium heat, stirring constantly, until mixture boils; boil and stir 1 minute or until chocolate flecks disappear. Remove from heat; stir in vanilla. Pour into bowl; press plastic wrap directly onto surface. Cool; chill.

CHOCOLATE GLAZE

¼ cup sugar
1 tablespoon cornstarch
    Dash salt
⅓ cup water
1 bar (1 ounce) HERSHEY'S
    Unsweetened Baking
    Chocolate
1 tablespoon butter or
    margarine
½ teaspoon vanilla

Combine sugar, cornstarch, salt and water in small mixing bowl; set aside. Melt baking chocolate with butter in small saucepan over low heat. Add sugar-water mixture and bring to a boil, stirring constantly. Remove from heat; stir in vanilla.

Mexican Cocoa Torte

Mexican Cocoa Torte

1 cup sugar
1/2 cup HERSHEY'S Cocoa
1/4 teaspoon cinnamon
1/3 cup shortening
1/2 cup strong coffee
1 package (11 ounces) pie crust mix
2 cups heavy or whipping cream
HERSHEY'S MINI CHIPS Semi-Sweet Chocolate (optional)

Combine sugar, cocoa, cinnamon, shortening and coffee in small saucepan. Cook over very low heat, stirring constantly, until smooth and creamy. Cool to room temperature. Place pie crust mix in medium mixing bowl; stir in 3/4 cup of the cocoa mixture, blending thoroughly. Shape into smooth ball; chill 1 hour.

Divide dough into 4 pieces. Line two cookie sheets with aluminum foil; mark two 8-inch circles on each. Place balls of dough on foil; press with fingers into marked circles. Bake at 375° for 10 to 12 minutes or until almost set; cool on cookie sheets.

Add remaining cocoa mixture to cream in small mixer bowl; beat until stiff. Place one pastry round on serving plate; spread with one-fourth of the whipped cream mixture. Repeat layering with remaining three rounds and whipped cream mixture, ending with whipped cream. Chill several hours. Garnish with MINI CHIPS Chocolates.

8 to 10 servings

Cakes & Cheesecakes

Strawberry Chocolate Chip Cheesecake

Pastry Crust
3 packages (8 ounces each)
    cream cheese, softened
³/₄ cup sugar
1 package (10 ounces) frozen
    sliced strawberries with
    syrup, thawed
²/₃ cup unsifted all-purpose flour
3 eggs
1 teaspoon strawberry extract
4 or 5 drops red food color
1 cup HERSHEY'S MINI
    CHIPS Semi-Sweet
    Chocolate
Sweetened whipped cream
    (optional)
Fresh strawberries (optional)

Prepare Pastry Crust; set aside. Beat cream cheese and sugar in large mixer bowl until smooth. Puree strawberries with syrup in food processor or blender; add to cream cheese mixture. Blend in flour, eggs, strawberry extract and food color. Stir in MINI CHIPS Chocolates.

Pour into prepared crust. Bake at 450° for 10 minutes; without opening oven door, decrease temperature to 250° and continue to bake for 50 to 60 minutes or until set. Cool; loosen cake from side of pan. Cover; chill several hours or overnight. Serve topped with sweetened whipped cream and strawberries.

10 to 12 servings

PASTRY CRUST

¹/₃ cup butter or margarine,
    softened
¹/₃ cup sugar
1 egg
1¹/₄ cups unsifted all-purpose
    flour

Cream butter and sugar in small mixer bowl; blend in egg. Add flour; mix well. Spread dough on bottom and 1¹/₂ inches up side of 9-inch springform pan. Bake at 450° for 5 minutes; cool.

Top: No-Bake Chocolate Cheesecake (see page 20)
Bottom: Strawberry Chocolate Chip Cheesecake

No-Bake Chocolate Cheesecake

Crumb-Nut Crust
1 1/2 cups HERSHEY'S Semi-Sweet
    Chocolate Chips
1 package (8 ounces) plus 1
    package (3 ounces) cream
    cheese, softened
1/3 cup sugar
1/4 cup butter or margarine,
    softened
1 1/2 teaspoons vanilla
1 cup heavy or whipping cream
    Peach Topping
    Grated chocolate (optional)

Prepare Crumb-Nut Crust; set aside. Melt chocolate chips in top of double boiler over hot, not boiling, water, stirring until smooth. Combine cream cheese and sugar in large mixer bowl; add butter, beating until smooth. Blend in vanilla. Beat in melted chocolate all at once. Whip cream until stiff; fold into chocolate mixture.

Spoon into prepared crust; chill while preparing Peach Topping. Spoon topping onto chocolate layer and chill thoroughly. Garnish with grated chocolate.

10 to 12 servings

CRUMB-NUT CRUST

5 ounces almonds or pecans
3/4 cup vanilla wafer crumbs
    (about 25 wafers)
1/4 cup confectioners' sugar
1/4 cup butter or margarine,
    melted

If using almonds, toast in shallow baking pan at 350° for 8 to 10 minutes, stirring frequently; cool. Chop nuts very finely in food processor or blender (you should have 1 cup). Combine nuts with wafer crumbs and confectioners' sugar in medium bowl; drizzle with melted butter. Press onto bottom and 1 1/2 inches up side of 9-inch springform pan.

Note: You may substitute 1 3/4 cups graham cracker crumbs for the nuts and vanilla wafer crumbs.

PEACH TOPPING

1 teaspoon unflavored gelatine
1 tablespoon cold water
2 tablespoons boiling water
1 cup heavy or whipping cream
2 tablespoons sugar
1 teaspoon vanilla
1/2 cup sweetened peaches,
    drained and diced

Sprinkle gelatine onto cold water in small glass dish; allow to stand a few minutes to soften. Add boiling water and stir until gelatine is dissolved. Whip cream and sugar until stiff; beat in gelatine mixture and vanilla. Fold in diced peaches.

Devil's Food Cake

3/4 cup butter or margarine,
    softened
1 1/2 cups sugar
1 1/2 teaspoons vanilla
2 eggs
1 3/4 cups unsifted all-purpose
    flour
1/2 cup HERSHEY'S Cocoa
1 teaspoon baking soda
1/4 teaspoon salt
1/2 cup buttermilk or sour milk*
1/2 cup boiling water

Cream butter, sugar and vanilla in large mixer bowl until light and fluffy. Add eggs; beat well. Combine flour, cocoa, baking soda and salt; add alternately with buttermilk to creamed mixture. Add boiling water; beat until smooth.

Pour into wax paper-lined 13×9-inch pan. Bake at 350° for 35 to 40 minutes or until cake tester comes out clean. Cool 10 minutes; remove cake from pan. Cool completely; frost as desired (see pages 88–93).

8 to 10 servings

*To sour milk: Use 1 1/2 teaspoons vinegar plus milk to equal 1/2 cup.

Chocolate Syrup Swirl Cake

Chocolate Syrup Swirl Cake

1 cup butter or margarine,
    softened
2 cups sugar
2 teaspoons vanilla
3 eggs
2³/₄ cups unsifted all-purpose
    flour
1 teaspoon baking soda
¹/₂ teaspoon salt
1 cup buttermilk or sour milk*
1 cup HERSHEY'S Syrup
¹/₄ teaspoon baking soda
1 cup flaked coconut (optional)

Cream butter, sugar and vanilla in large mixer bowl until light and fluffy. Add eggs; beat well. Combine flour, 1 teaspoon baking soda and the salt; add alternately with buttermilk to creamed mixture. Combine syrup and ¹/₄ teaspoon baking soda. Measure 2 cups batter into small bowl; blend in syrup mixture.

Add coconut to remaining batter; pour into greased and floured 12-cup Bundt pan or 10-inch tube pan. Pour chocolate batter over vanilla batter in pan; *do not mix*. Bake at 350° about 70 minutes or until cake tester comes out clean. Cool 15 minutes; remove from pan. Cool completely; glaze or frost as desired (see pages 88–93).

12 to 16 servings

*To sour milk: Use 1 tablespoon vinegar plus milk to equal 1 cup.

Chocolate-Strawberry Chiffon Squares

Chocolate-Strawberry Chiffon Squares

1½ cups unsifted cake flour
1 cup sugar
½ cup HERSHEY'S Cocoa
¾ teaspoon baking soda
½ teaspoon salt
1 cup buttermilk or sour milk*
½ cup vegetable oil
2 egg yolks
2 egg whites
½ cup sugar
Berry Cream
Fresh strawberries

Combine cake flour, 1 cup sugar, the cocoa, baking soda and salt in large mixer bowl. Add buttermilk, oil and egg yolks; beat until smooth. Beat egg whites in small mixer bowl until foamy; gradually add ½ cup sugar, beating until very stiff peaks form. Gently fold egg whites into chocolate batter. Pour into greased and floured 13×9-inch pan. Bake at 350° for 30 to 35 minutes or until cake springs back when touched lightly in center. Cool in pan on wire rack. Just before serving, prepare Berry Cream; frost top of cake. Cut into squares and garnish with strawberry halves. Refrigerate leftovers.

10 to 12 servings

*To sour milk: Use 1 tablespoon vinegar plus milk to equal 1 cup.

BERRY CREAM

1 cup sweetened sliced
    strawberries
1 cup heavy or whipping cream
1 teaspoon vanilla
2 or 3 drops red food color
    (optional)

Mash or puree strawberries in blender or food processor (you should have ½ cup). Whip cream until stiff; gently fold in puree, vanilla and food color.

Cocoa Medallion Cake

3/4 cup HERSHEY'S Cocoa
3/4 cup boiling water
1/4 cup butter or margarine, softened
1/4 cup shortening
2 cups sugar
1 teaspoon vanilla
1/8 teaspoon salt
2 eggs
1 1/2 teaspoons baking soda
1 cup buttermilk or sour milk*
1 3/4 cups unsifted all-purpose flour

Stir together cocoa and boiling water until smooth; set aside. Cream butter, shortening, sugar, vanilla and salt in large mixer bowl until light and fluffy. Add eggs; beat well. Stir baking soda into buttermilk; add alternately with flour to creamed mixture. Blend in cocoa mixture.

Pour into two greased and wax paper-lined 9-inch layer pans or 8-inch square pans. Bake at 350° for 30 to 35 minutes for 9-inch pans or 40 to 45 minutes for 8-inch pans, or until cake tester comes out clean. Cool 10 minutes; remove from pans. Cool completely; frost as desired (see pages 88–93).

8 to 10 servings

*To sour milk: Use 1 tablespoon vinegar plus milk to equal 1 cup.

VARIATION
Picnic Medallion Cake: Prepare batter as directed above; pour into greased and floured 13×9-inch pan. Bake at 350° for 40 to 45 minutes or until cake tester comes out clean. Cool completely; frost as desired.

Party Chocolate Cheesecake Cups

Graham Shells
2 packages (8 ounces each) cream cheese, softened
1 cup sour cream
1 1/4 cups sugar
1/3 cup HERSHEY'S Cocoa
2 tablespoons flour
3 eggs
1 teaspoon vanilla
Sour Cream Topping
Cherry pie filling

Prepare Graham Shells; set aside. Combine cream cheese and sour cream in large mixer bowl. Combine sugar, cocoa and flour; add to cream cheese mixture, blending well. Add eggs, one at a time, beating well after each addition. Blend in vanilla.

Fill each prepared cup almost full with cheese mixture (mixture rises only slightly during baking). Bake at 350° for 15 to 20 minutes. Turn off oven; let cheese cups remain in oven 45 minutes without opening door. Prepare Sour Cream Topping; spread heaping teaspoonful on each cup. Cool completely; chill thoroughly. Garnish with dollop of cherry pie filling just before serving.

2 dozen desserts

GRAHAM SHELLS

1 1/2 cups graham cracker crumbs
1/3 cup sugar
1/4 cup butter or margarine, melted

Line 24 muffin cups (2 1/2 inches in diameter) with paper baking cups. Combine graham cracker crumbs, sugar and melted butter. Press about 1 tablespoon onto bottom of each cup.

SOUR CREAM TOPPING

1 cup sour cream
2 tablespoons sugar
1 teaspoon vanilla

Combine sour cream, sugar and vanilla; stir until sugar is dissolved.

Chocolatetown Special Cake

½ cup HERSHEY'S Cocoa
½ cup boiling water
⅔ cup shortening
1¾ cups sugar
1 teaspoon vanilla
2 eggs
2¼ cups unsifted all-purpose flour
1½ teaspoons baking soda
½ teaspoon salt
1⅓ cups buttermilk or sour milk*

Stir together cocoa and boiling water in small bowl until smooth; set aside. Cream shortening, sugar and vanilla in large mixer bowl until light and fluffy. Add eggs; beat well. Combine flour, baking soda and salt; add alternately with buttermilk to creamed mixture. Blend in cocoa mixture.

Pour into three greased and floured 8-inch or two 9-inch layer pans. Bake at 350° for 25 to 30 minutes for 8-inch pans or 35 to 40 minutes for 9-inch pans, or until cake tester comes out clean. Cool 10 minutes; remove from pans. Cool completely; frost as desired (see pages 88–93).

8 to 10 servings

*To sour milk: Use 4 teaspoons vinegar plus milk to equal 1⅓ cups.

Mocha Cheesecake

Chocolate Cookie Crust
4 packages (3 ounces each) cream cheese, softened
2½ tablespoons butter or margarine, softened
1 cup sugar
2 eggs
5 tablespoons HERSHEY'S Cocoa
¾ teaspoon vanilla extract
1 tablespoon powdered instant coffee
1 teaspoon boiling water
1 cup sour cream

Prepare Chocolate Cookie Crust; set aside. In large mixer bowl beat cream cheese and butter until smooth and fluffy. Gradually beat in sugar. Add eggs, one at a time, beating well after each addition. Beat in cocoa and vanilla. Dissolve instant coffee in water; stir into cheese mixture. Add sour cream; blend well. Pour mixture into pan. Bake at 325° for 30 minutes. Turn off oven; leave cheesecake in oven 15 minutes without opening door. Remove from oven. Cool in pan on wire rack. Cover; chill. Garnish as desired.

10 to 12 servings

CHOCOLATE COOKIE CRUST

22 chocolate wafers (½ of 8½-ounce package)
¼ cup cold butter or margarine, cut into ½-inch slices
⅛ teaspoon cinnamon

Crush wafers in food processor or blender to form fine crumbs. In medium bowl mix crumbs, butter and cinnamon until evenly blended. Press mixture evenly on bottom of 9-inch springform pan.

Chocolatetown Special Cake with Chocolate Fudge Frosting (see page 92)

Marble Cheesecake

Marble Cheesecake ⟡⟡⟡⟡⟡⟡⟡⟡⟡⟡⟡⟡⟡⟡⟡⟡⟡⟡⟡⟡⟡⟡⟡

Graham Crust (page 31)
3 packages (8 ounces each)
   cream cheese, softened
³/₄ cup sugar
¹/₂ cup sour cream
2 teaspoons vanilla
3 tablespoons flour
3 eggs
¹/₄ cup HERSHEY'S Cocoa
¹/₄ cup sugar
1 tablespoon vegetable oil
¹/₂ teaspoon vanilla

Prepare Graham Crust; set aside. Combine cream cheese, ³/₄ cup sugar, the sour cream and 2 teaspoons vanilla in large mixer bowl; beat on medium speed until smooth. Add flour, 1 tablespoon at a time, blending well. Add eggs; beat well. Combine cocoa and ¹/₄ cup sugar in small bowl. Add oil, ¹/₂ teaspoon vanilla and 1¹/₂ cups of the cream cheese mixture; mix until well blended.

Spoon plain and chocolate mixtures alternately into prepared crust, ending with dollops of chocolate on top; gently swirl with knife or spatula for marbled effect. Bake at 450° for 10 minutes; without opening oven door, decrease temperature to 250° and continue to bake for 30 minutes. Turn off oven; let cheesecake remain in oven 30 minutes without opening door. Remove from oven; loosen cake from side of pan. Cool completely; chill thoroughly.

10 to 12 servings

Cocoa-Spice Snackin' Cake

1/4 cup butter or margarine, melted
1/4 cup HERSHEY'S Cocoa
3/4 cup applesauce
1 1/4 cups unsifted all-purpose flour
1 cup sugar
3/4 teaspoon baking soda
1/2 teaspoon cinnamon
1/4 teaspoon nutmeg
1/4 teaspoon salt
1 egg, beaten
1/2 cup chopped nuts

Combine melted butter and cocoa; blend in applesauce. Combine flour, sugar, baking soda, cinnamon, nutmeg and salt in large bowl. Blend in cocoa mixture and egg until dry ingredients are moistened. Stir in nuts.

Spread in greased 9-inch square pan. Bake at 350° for 30 to 35 minutes or until cake tester comes out clean. Cool in pan.

8 to 10 servings

Chocolate Peanut Butter Marble Cake

1/4 cup HERSHEY'S Cocoa
2 tablespoons confectioners' sugar
2 tablespoons butter or margarine, softened
2 tablespoons hot water
1 cup REESE'S Peanut Butter Chips
1 tablespoon shortening
1 package (18 1/2 ounces) white cake mix (pudding-in-the-mix type)
1/2 cup packed light brown sugar
1 1/4 cups water
3 eggs

Combine cocoa, confectioners' sugar, butter and 2 tablespoons hot water in small bowl until smooth; set aside. Melt peanut butter chips and shortening in top of double boiler over hot, not boiling, water; set aside. Combine dry cake mix, brown sugar, 1 1/4 cups water, the eggs and melted peanut butter mixture in large mixer bowl; beat on low speed until moistened. Beat 2 minutes on medium speed until smooth. Add 1 1/2 cups batter to reserved cocoa mixture; blend well. Pour remaining batter into greased and floured 13 × 9-inch pan; spoon dollops of chocolate batter on top. Swirl with knife or spatula for marbled effect. Bake at 350° for 40 to 45 minutes or until cake tester comes out clean. Cool; frost as desired (see pages 88–93).

10 to 12 servings

Lickety-Split Cocoa Cake

1 1/2 cups unsifted all-purpose flour
1 cup sugar
1/4 cup HERSHEY'S Cocoa
1 teaspoon baking soda
1/2 teaspoon salt
1 cup water
1/4 cup plus 2 tablespoons vegetable oil
1 tablespoon vinegar
1 teaspoon vanilla

Combine flour, sugar, cocoa, baking soda and salt in large bowl. Add water, oil, vinegar and vanilla; stir with spoon or wire whisk just until batter is smooth and ingredients are well blended.

Pour into greased and floured 9-inch layer pan or 8-inch square pan. Bake at 350° for 35 to 40 minutes or until cake tester comes out clean. Cool in pan; frost as desired (see pages 88–93).

6 to 8 servings

Mousse-Filled Cocoa Chiffon Cake

1³/₄ cups sugar
1¹/₂ cups unsifted cake flour
²/₃ cup HERSHEY'S Cocoa
2 teaspoons baking powder
1 teaspoon salt
¹/₂ teaspoon baking soda
¹/₂ cup vegetable oil
7 egg yolks
³/₄ cup cold water
2 teaspoons vanilla
7 egg whites, at room temperature
¹/₂ teaspoon cream of tartar
¹/₄ cup sugar
  Mousse Filling
  Chocolate Cream Frosting

Combine 1³/₄ cups sugar, the cake flour, cocoa, baking powder, salt and baking soda in large mixing bowl. Make a "well" in mixture and add in order: oil, egg yolks, water and vanilla. Beat until smooth. Beat egg whites and cream of tartar in large mixer bowl until foamy. Gradually add ¹/₄ cup sugar and beat until stiff peaks form. Gradually pour chocolate batter over beaten egg whites, gently folding just until blended. Pour into ungreased 10-inch tube pan. Bake at 325° for 1 hour and 20 minutes or until cake springs back when touched lightly. Meanwhile, prepare Mousse Filling and Chocolate Cream Frosting.

Invert cake over heat-proof funnel or bottle until completely cool. Loosen cake from pan; invert onto serving plate. Slice ³/₄-inch-thick layer from top of cake; set aside. Being careful to leave 1-inch-thick walls and base, cut a neat cavity in cake. With fork, remove section of cake between the cuts. Spoon Mousse Filling into cavity. Replace top of cake; press gently. Frost cake with Chocolate Cream Frosting. Chill several hours. Refrigerate leftovers.

12 to 16 servings

MOUSSE FILLING

1 envelope unflavored gelatine
2 tablespoons cold water
¹/₃ cup water
¹/₃ cup HERSHEY'S Cocoa
²/₃ cup sugar
1¹/₂ cups heavy or whipping cream
2 teaspoons vanilla

Sprinkle gelatine onto 2 tablespoons water in small glass dish; set aside to soften. Bring ¹/₃ cup water to boil in small saucepan; stir in cocoa over low heat until smooth and thickened. Add softened gelatine, stirring until dissolved. Remove from heat; stir in sugar. Cool to room temperature. Whip cream with vanilla until stiff peaks form. Gradually add chocolate mixture while beating on low speed just until well blended. Chill 30 minutes.

CHOCOLATE CREAM FROSTING

³/₄ cup confectioners' sugar
6 tablespoons HERSHEY'S Cocoa
1¹/₂ cups heavy or whipping cream
³/₄ teaspoon vanilla

Combine confectioners' sugar and cocoa in small mixer bowl. Add cream and vanilla; beat until stiff. Cover; chill.

Top: Mousse-Filled Cocoa Chiffon Cake
Bottom: Marble Chiffon Cake (see page 30)

Marble Chiffon Cake

1/3 cup HERSHEY'S Cocoa
2 tablespoons sugar
1/4 cup water
2 tablespoons vegetable oil
2 cups unsifted all-purpose flour
1 1/2 cups sugar
3 teaspoons baking powder
1 teaspoon salt
1/2 cup vegetable oil
7 egg yolks, at room temperature
3/4 cup cold water
2 teaspoons vanilla
7 egg whites, at room temperature
1/2 teaspoon cream of tartar
Cocoa Glaze

Combine cocoa, 2 tablespoons sugar, 1/4 cup water and 2 tablespoons oil in small bowl until smooth; set aside. Combine flour, 1 1/2 cups sugar, the baking powder and salt in large mixer bowl; add 1/2 cup oil, the egg yolks, 3/4 cup cold water and the vanilla. Beat on low speed until combined. Beat 5 minutes on high speed. With clean beaters, beat egg whites and cream of tartar in another large mixer bowl until stiff peaks form.

Pour batter in thin stream over entire surface of egg whites; fold in lightly, using rubber spatula. Remove one-third of the batter to another bowl; gently fold in chocolate mixture. Pour half the vanilla batter into ungreased 10-inch tube pan; spread half the chocolate batter over vanilla. Repeat layers; gently swirl with spatula or knife for marbled effect. Bake at 325° for 65 to 70 minutes or until cake springs back when touched lightly. Invert cake over heatproof funnel or bottle until completely cool. Loosen cake from pan; invert onto serving plate. Spread top with Cocoa Glaze.

12 to 16 servings

COCOA GLAZE

2 tablespoons butter or margarine
1/4 cup HERSHEY'S Cocoa
3 tablespoons water
1/2 teaspoon vanilla
1 1/4 cups confectioners' sugar

Melt butter in small saucepan over low heat. Stir in cocoa and water. Cook, stirring constantly, until mixture thickens; *do not boil.* Remove from heat. Stir in vanilla. Gradually add confectioners' sugar; beat with wire whisk until smooth.

Cocoa Cheesecake

Graham Crust
2 packages (8 ounces each) cream cheese, softened
3/4 cup sugar
1/2 cup HERSHEY'S Cocoa
1 teaspoon vanilla
2 eggs
1 cup sour cream
2 tablespoons sugar
1 teaspoon vanilla

Prepare Graham Crust; set aside. Beat cream cheese, 3/4 cup sugar, the cocoa and 1 teaspoon vanilla in large mixer bowl until light and fluffy. Add eggs; blend well. Pour into prepared crust. Bake at 375° for 20 minutes. Remove cheesecake from oven; cool for 15 minutes.

Combine sour cream, 2 tablespoons sugar and 1 teaspoon vanilla; stir until smooth. Spread evenly over baked filling. Bake at 425° for 10 minutes. Cool; chill several hours or overnight.

10 to 12 servings

GRAHAM CRUST

1 1/2 cups graham cracker crumbs
1/3 cup sugar
1/3 cup butter or margarine, melted

Combine graham cracker crumbs, sugar and melted butter. Press mixture onto bottom and halfway up side of 9-inch springform pan.

Chocolate Ricotta Cheesecake with Glazed Fruit

Graham Crust
3 cups ricotta or low-fat cottage
   cheese
1 cup sugar
4 eggs
1 cup heavy or whipping cream
1/3 cup HERSHEY'S Cocoa
1/4 cup unsifted all-purpose flour
1/8 teaspoon salt
1/2 teaspoon vanilla
Glazed Fruit
Sweetened whipped cream
   (optional)

Prepare Graham Crust; set aside. Place ricotta cheese, sugar and eggs in food processor or blender container; process until smooth. Add cream, cocoa, flour, salt and vanilla; process until smooth.

Pour into prepared crust. Bake at 350° about 1 hour and 15 minutes or until set. Turn off oven; open door and let cheesecake remain in oven 1 hour. Cool completely; chill thoroughly. Just before serving, arrange Glazed Fruit on top of cheesecake. With pastry tube, make a border of sweetened whipped cream around edge.

10 to 12 servings

GRAHAM CRUST

1 cup graham cracker crumbs
2 tablespoons sugar
1/4 cup butter or margarine,
   melted

Combine graham cracker crumbs, sugar and melted butter. Press mixture onto bottom and 1/2 inch up side of 9-inch springform pan. Bake at 350° for 8 to 10 minutes; cool.

GLAZED FRUIT

1/2 cup sliced nectarines*
1/2 cup blueberries*
1/4 cup apricot preserves

Stir together fruit and preserves until fruit pieces are well coated.

*You may substitute peaches, pitted sweet cherries, strawberries or canned pineapple chunks for the nectarines and blueberries.

Chocolate Ricotta Cheesecake with Glazed Fruit

Orange Cocoa Cake

½ cup HERSHEY'S Cocoa
½ cup boiling water
¼ cup butter or margarine, softened
¼ cup shortening
2 cups sugar
⅛ teaspoon salt
1 teaspoon vanilla
2 eggs
1½ teaspoons baking soda
1 cup buttermilk or sour milk*
1¾ cups unsifted all-purpose flour
3 tablespoons buttermilk or sour milk*
⅛ teaspoon baking soda
¾ teaspoon grated orange peel
¼ teaspoon orange extract
Orange Buttercream Frosting

Grease three 8- or 9-inch layer pans and line with wax paper; set aside. Stir together cocoa and boiling water in small bowl until smooth; set aside. Cream butter, shortening, sugar, salt and vanilla in large mixer bowl until light and fluffy. Add eggs; beat well. Stir 1½ teaspoons baking soda into 1 cup buttermilk; add alternately with flour to creamed mixture.

Measure 1⅔ cups batter into small bowl. Stir in 3 tablespoons buttermilk, ⅛ teaspoon baking soda, the orange peel and orange extract; pour into one prepared pan. Blend cocoa mixture into remaining batter; divide evenly among remaining two prepared pans. Bake at 350° for 25 to 30 minutes or until cake tester comes out clean. Cool 10 minutes; remove from pans. Cool completely. Place one chocolate layer on serving plate; spread with some of the Orange Buttercream Frosting. Top with orange layer and spread with frosting. Top with remaining chocolate layer and frost entire cake.

10 to 12 servings

*To sour milk: Use 1 tablespoon vinegar plus milk to equal 1 cup; use ½ teaspoon vinegar plus milk to equal 3 tablespoons.

ORANGE BUTTERCREAM FROSTING

⅔ cup butter or margarine, softened
6 cups confectioners' sugar
2 teaspoons grated orange peel
1½ teaspoons vanilla
4 to 6 tablespoons milk

Cream butter, 1 cup confectioners' sugar, the orange peel and vanilla in large mixer bowl. Add remaining confectioners' sugar alternately with milk, beating to spreading consistency.

Hershey Bar Cake

1 HERSHEY'S Milk Chocolate Bar (8 ounces), broken into pieces
¼ cup butter or margarine
1⅔ cups boiling water
2⅓ cups unsifted all-purpose flour
2 cups packed light brown sugar
2 teaspoons baking soda
1 teaspoon salt
2 eggs
½ cup sour cream
1 teaspoon vanilla

Combine chocolate bar pieces, butter and boiling water in medium bowl; stir until chocolate is melted. Combine flour, brown sugar, baking soda and salt in large mixer bowl; gradually add chocolate mixture, beating until thoroughly blended. Blend in eggs, sour cream and vanilla; beat 1 minute on medium speed.

Pour into greased and floured 13 × 9-inch pan. Bake at 350° for 35 to 40 minutes or until cake tester comes out clean. Cool completely; frost as desired (see pages 88–93).

8 to 10 servings

Orange Cocoa Cake

Center top: Creme-Filled Cupcakes. Left to right: Chocolatetown Cupcakes with Chocolate-Coconut Frosting (see page 88) and Chocolate Buttercream Frosting (see page 93).

Creme-Filled Cupcakes ∿∿∿∿∿∿∿∿∿∿∿∿∿∿∿∿∿∿∿∿∿∿∿

3/4 cup shortening
1 1/4 cups sugar
2 eggs
1 teaspoon vanilla
1 3/4 cups unsifted all-purpose
    flour
1/2 cup HERSHEY'S Cocoa
1 teaspoon baking soda
1/2 teaspoon salt
1 cup milk
    Vanilla Creme

Cream shortening and sugar in large mixer bowl. Add eggs and vanilla; blend well. Combine flour, cocoa, baking soda and salt; add alternately with milk to creamed mixture. Fill paper-lined muffin cups (2 1/2 inches in diameter) two-thirds full with batter. Bake at 375° for 20 to 25 minutes or until cake tester comes out clean. Cool completely.

Prepare Vanilla Creme; spoon into pastry bag with open star tip. Insert tip into center of top of cupcake; gently squeeze until cupcake begins to peak. Cover top with swirl of filling. (Or cut a 1 1/2-inch cone from top of cupcake. Fill; replace cone. Swirl filling over top.)

About 2 dozen cupcakes

VANILLA CREME

1/4 cup unsifted all-purpose flour
1/2 cup milk
1/4 cup butter or margarine,
    softened
1/4 cup shortening
2 teaspoons vanilla
1/4 teaspoon salt
4 cups confectioners' sugar

Combine flour and milk in small saucepan; cook over low heat, stirring constantly with wire whisk, until mixture thickens and just begins to boil. Remove from heat; chill. Cream butter and shortening in large mixer bowl; blend in vanilla, salt and the chilled flour mixture. Gradually add confectioners' sugar; beat to spreading consistency.

Double Chocolate Snack Cake

1²/₃ cups all-purpose flour
1 cup packed light brown sugar
¹/₄ cup HERSHEY'S Cocoa
1 teaspoon baking soda
¹/₄ teaspoon salt
1 cup water
¹/₃ cup vegetable oil
1 teaspoon white vinegar
³/₄ teaspoon vanilla extract
¹/₂ cup HERSHEY'S Semi-Sweet
   Chocolate Chips

Grease and flour 8-inch square baking pan. In small bowl combine flour, sugar, cocoa, baking soda and salt. Add water, oil, vinegar and vanilla; beat with spoon or wire whisk until smooth. Pour batter into prepared pan. Sprinkle chocolate chips over top. Bake at 350° for 35 to 40 minutes or until wooden pick inserted in center comes out clean. Cool in pan.

6 to 8 servings

VARIATION
Chocolate Banana Snack Cake: Decrease water to ¹/₂ cup; stir in ¹/₂ cup mashed, ripe banana (1 medium banana) before pouring batter into pan.

Fudgey Pecan Cake

³/₄ cup butter or margarine,
   melted
1¹/₂ cups sugar
1¹/₂ teaspoons vanilla
3 egg yolks
¹/₂ cup plus 1 tablespoon
   HERSHEY'S Cocoa
¹/₂ cup unsifted all-purpose flour
3 tablespoons vegetable oil
3 tablespoons water
³/₄ cup finely chopped pecans
3 egg whites, at room
   temperature
¹/₈ teaspoon cream of tartar
¹/₈ teaspoon salt
   Royal Glaze (page 89)
   Pecan halves (optional)

Line bottom of 9-inch springform pan with aluminum foil; butter foil and side of pan. Set aside. Combine ³/₄ cup melted butter, the sugar and vanilla in large mixer bowl; beat well. Add egg yolks, one at a time, beating well after each addition. Blend in cocoa, flour, oil and water; beat well. Stir in chopped pecans. Beat egg whites, cream of tartar and salt in small mixer bowl until stiff peaks form. Carefully fold into chocolate mixture. Pour into prepared pan. Bake at 350° for 45 minutes or until top begins to crack slightly. (Cake will not test done in center.) Cool 1 hour. Cover; chill until firm. Remove side of pan.

Prepare Royal Glaze. Pour over cake, allowing glaze to run down side. With narrow metal spatula, spread glaze evenly on top and side. Allow to harden. Garnish with pecan halves.

10 to 12 servings

Fudgey Pecan Cake

Carrot Cake

1½ cups unsifted all-purpose
  flour
¾ cup sugar
½ cup packed light brown sugar
1¼ teaspoons baking soda
1 teaspoon cinnamon
½ teaspoon salt
3 eggs
¾ cup vegetable oil
1½ teaspoons vanilla
2 cups grated carrots
2 cups (12-ounce package)
  HERSHEY'S MINI CHIPS
  Semi-Sweet Chocolate
½ cup chopped walnuts
  Cream Cheese Frosting

Combine flour, sugar, brown sugar, baking soda, cinnamon and salt in large mixer bowl. Beat eggs, oil and vanilla in small mixer bowl; add to dry ingredients. Blend well. Stir in carrots, MINI CHIPS Chocolates and walnuts. Pour into greased and floured 13×9-inch pan. Bake at 350° for 35 to 40 minutes or until cake tester comes out clean. Cool completely; frost with Cream Cheese Frosting.

10 to 12 servings

CREAM CHEESE FROSTING

1 package (3 ounces) cream
  cheese, softened
¼ cup butter or margarine,
  softened
2 cups confectioners' sugar
1 teaspoon vanilla

Beat cream cheese and butter in small mixer bowl until smooth and well blended. Gradually add confectioners' sugar; stir in vanilla. Beat until smooth.

Ice-Itself Chocolate Layer Cake

1 cup flaked coconut
½ cup chopped pecans
⅓ cup packed light brown sugar
3 tablespoons butter or
  margarine, melted
3 tablespoons evaporated milk
2 tablespoons light corn syrup
½ cup butter or margarine,
  softened
1 cup plus 2 tablespoons sugar
1 egg
½ teaspoon vanilla
1¼ cups plus 2 tablespoons
  unsifted all-purpose flour
⅓ cup HERSHEY'S Cocoa
1 teaspoon baking soda
½ teaspoon salt
1 cup buttermilk or sour milk*

Line two 8-inch layer pans with foil; butter foil. Combine coconut, pecans, brown sugar, 3 tablespoons melted butter, the evaporated milk and corn syrup in small bowl. Divide mixture and spread evenly over bottom of each pan.

Cream ½ cup butter and the sugar in large mixer bowl until light and fluffy. Add egg and vanilla; blend well. Combine flour, cocoa, baking soda and salt; add alternately with buttermilk to creamed mixture. Carefully spread half the batter into each prepared pan; do not mix with coconut topping. Bake at 350° for 30 to 35 minutes or until cake springs back when touched lightly. Invert immediately onto wire rack; gently remove foil and discard. Cover layers loosely with foil to keep topping soft. Cool completely; place one layer on top of other. Keep well covered.

8 to 10 servings

*To sour milk: Use 1 tablespoon vinegar plus milk to equal 1 cup.

Pies & Pastries

Bavarian Chocolate Pie

9-inch baked pastry shell or
crumb crust
1 envelope unflavored gelatin
1²/₃ cups milk, divided
²/₃ cup sugar
¹/₃ cup HERSHEY'S Cocoa
2 tablespoons butter or
margarine
³/₄ teaspoon vanilla extract
¹/₂ cup chilled whipping cream
Spiced Cream

Prepare pastry shell; cool. In medium saucepan sprinkle gelatin over 1 cup milk; let stand 2 minutes to soften. Combine sugar and cocoa; add to gelatin mixture in saucepan. Cook over low heat, stirring constantly, until mixture boils. Remove from heat; add butter and stir until melted. Blend in remaining ²/₃ cup milk and vanilla. Cool; chill, stirring occasionally, until mixture begins to set. Beat cream until stiff; carefully fold into chocolate mixture. Pour into baked pastry shell; chill 2 to 3 hours or until set. Garnish with Spiced Cream.

8 servings

SPICED CREAM

¹/₂ cup chilled whipping cream
1 tablespoon confectioners'
sugar
¹/₄ teaspoon vanilla extract
¹/₄ teaspoon cinnamon
Dash ground nutmeg

In small mixer bowl combine all ingredients; beat until stiff.

About 1 cup topping

Left: Two-Tone Cream Pie
Right: Chocolate Chip Walnut Pie

Two-Tone Cream Pie

9-inch baked pastry shell
1 package (4³/4 ounces) vanilla
**   pudding and pie filling**
3¹/2 cups milk
1 cup REESE'S Peanut Butter
**   Chips**
1 cup HERSHEY'S Semi-Sweet
**   Chocolate Chips or MINI**
**   CHIPS**

Prepare pastry shell; cool. In medium saucepan combine pudding mix and milk. Cook over medium heat, stirring constantly, until mixture comes to full boil; remove from heat. Pour 2 cups hot pudding into small bowl and add peanut butter chips; stir until chips are melted and mixture is smooth. To remaining hot pudding, add chocolate chips; stir until chips are melted and mixture is smooth. Pour chocolate mixture into baked pastry shell. Gently pour and spread peanut butter mixture over top. Press plastic wrap directly onto surface. Chill several hours or overnight. Garnish as desired.

8 servings

Chocolate Chip Walnut Pie

9-inch baked pastry shell
³/4 cup packed light brown sugar
¹/2 cup all-purpose flour
¹/2 teaspoon baking powder
¹/4 teaspoon cinnamon
2 eggs, slightly beaten
1 cup HERSHEY'S Semi-Sweet
**   Chocolate Chips, MINI**
**   CHIPS or Milk Chocolate**
**   Chips**
1 cup coarsely chopped walnuts
**   Spiced Cream (see page 37)**

Prepare pastry shell; cool. In medium bowl combine brown sugar, flour, baking powder and cinnamon. Add eggs; stir until well blended. Add chocolate chips and walnuts. Pour into baked pastry shell. Bake at 350° for 25 to 30 minutes or until lightly browned and set. Serve slightly warm or at room temperature with Spiced Cream.

8 servings

Brandy Alexander Pie

Chocolate Petal Crust
30 large marshmallows
1/2 cup milk
1 cup HERSHEY'S Semi-Sweet
    Chocolate Chips
1 teaspoon vanilla
1 to 2 tablespoons brandy
1 to 2 tablespoons crème de
    cacao
2 cups heavy or whipping
    cream

Prepare Chocolate Petal Crust; set aside. Combine marshmallows and milk in medium saucepan; cook over low heat, stirring constantly, until marshmallows are melted and mixture is smooth. Pour half the marshmallow mixture into small bowl; set aside. Add chocolate chips to the remaining marshmallow mixture; return to low heat and stir until chips are melted. Remove from heat and stir in vanilla; cool to room temperature. Stir brandy and crème de cacao into reserved marshmallow mixture in small bowl; chill until mixture mounds slightly when dropped from a spoon.

Whip cream until stiff. Fold 2 cups of the whipped cream into cooled chocolate mixture; spoon into cooled crust. Blend remaining whipped cream into chilled brandy mixture; spread over chocolate mixture. Chill about 2 hours or until firm. Garnish as desired.

8 servings

CHOCOLATE PETAL CRUST

1/2 cup butter or margarine,
    softened
1 cup sugar
1 egg
1 teaspoon vanilla
1 1/4 cups unsifted all-purpose
    flour
1/2 cup HERSHEY'S Cocoa
3/4 teaspoon baking soda
1/4 teaspoon salt

Cream butter, sugar, egg and vanilla in large mixer bowl. Combine flour, cocoa, baking soda and salt; stir into creamed mixture. Shape soft dough into two rolls, 1 1/2 inches in diameter each. Wrap in plastic wrap; chill several hours. Cut one roll into 1/8-inch slices; arrange slices, edges touching, on bottom, up side and onto rim of greased 9-inch pie pan. (Small spaces in crust will not affect pie.) Bake at 375° for 8 to 10 minutes. Cool.

Enough dough for 2 crusts

Note: Remaining roll of dough may be frozen for later use. Or, bake as chocolate refrigerator cookies. Cut roll into 1/8-inch slices. Place on ungreased cookie sheet. Bake at 375° for 8 to 10 minutes or until almost set. Cool slightly. Remove from cookie sheet; cool completely on wire rack. Makes about 1 1/2 dozen cookies.

Vanilla Chip Fruit Tart

¾ cup butter or margarine, softened
½ cup confectioners' sugar
1½ cups all-purpose flour
1⅔ cups (10-ounce package) HERSHEY'S Vanilla Milk Chips
¼ cup whipping cream
1 package (8 ounces) cream cheese, softened
Fruit Topping

In small mixer bowl beat butter and confectioners' sugar until light and fluffy; blend in flour. Press mixture onto bottom and up side of 12-inch round pizza pan. Bake at 300° for 20 to 25 minutes or until lightly browned; cool completely. In micro-proof bowl microwave vanilla chips and cream at HIGH (100%) for 1 to 1½ minutes or until chips are melted and mixture is smooth when stirred vigorously. Beat in cream cheese; spread mixture over cooled crust. Cover; chill. Prepare Fruit Topping; arrange on top of vanilla mixture. Cover; refrigerate assembled tart until just before serving.

10 to 12 servings

FRUIT TOPPING

¼ cup sugar
1 tablespoon cornstarch
½ cup pineapple juice
½ teaspoon lemon juice
Assorted fresh fruit, sliced

In small saucepan combine sugar and cornstarch; stir in juices. Cook over medium heat, stirring constantly, until thickened; cool. Meanwhile, slice and arrange fruit on top of filling; carefully pour or brush juice mixture over fruit.

Fudge Brownie Pie

2 eggs
1 cup sugar
½ cup butter or margarine, melted
½ cup unsifted all-purpose flour
⅓ cup HERSHEY'S Cocoa
¼ teaspoon salt
1 teaspoon vanilla
½ cup chopped nuts (optional)
Ice cream
Hot Fudge Sauce

Beat eggs in small mixer bowl; blend in sugar and melted butter. Combine flour, cocoa and salt; add to butter mixture. Stir in vanilla and nuts.

Pour into lightly greased 8-inch pie pan. Bake at 350° for 25 to 30 minutes or until almost set (pie will not test done). Cool; cut into wedges. Serve wedges topped with scoop of ice cream and drizzled with Hot Fudge Sauce.

6 to 8 servings

HOT FUDGE SAUCE

¾ cup sugar
½ cup HERSHEY'S Cocoa
½ cup plus 2 tablespoons (5-ounce can) evaporated milk
⅓ cup light corn syrup
⅓ cup butter or margarine
1 teaspoon vanilla

Combine sugar and cocoa in small saucepan; blend in evaporated milk and corn syrup. Cook over medium heat, stirring constantly, until mixture boils; boil and stir 1 minute. Remove from heat; stir in butter and vanilla. Serve warm.

About 1¾ cups sauce

Chocolate Mousse Filled Tartlets

1/2 cup butter or margarine,
  softened
1 package (3 ounces) cream
  cheese, softened
1/4 cup confectioners' sugar
1 cup all-purpose flour
  Chocolate Mousse Filling
  Whipped cream, fresh
  strawberries, chopped nuts
  or chocolate curls

In small mixer bowl, cream butter and cream cheese. Add confectioners' sugar; beat until smooth and fluffy. Add flour; blend thoroughly. Cover; chill about 1 hour.

Shape chilled mixture into 2 dozen 1-inch balls; place each ball into ungreased 1³/₄-inch muffin cup. Press dough onto bottoms and sides of cups.

Bake at 350° for 15 minutes or until edges are brown. Cool on wire rack; remove from pans. Prepare Chocolate Mousse Filling. With star tip in pastry bag, pipe mousse into tart shells. (Or, spoon mousse into shells, if desired.) Garnish with whipped cream, strawberries, chopped nuts or chocolate curls. Chill about 1 hour.

24 tartlets

CHOCOLATE MOUSSE FILLING

1 teaspoon unflavored gelatin
1 tablespoon cold water
2 tablespoons boiling water
1/2 cup sugar
1/4 cup HERSHEY'S Cocoa
1 cup chilled whipping cream
1 teaspoon vanilla extract

In custard cup, sprinkle gelatin over cold water; let stand 1 minute to soften. Add boiling water; stir until gelatin is completely dissolved and mixture is clear. Cool slightly.

In small cold mixer bowl, combine sugar and cocoa. Add whipping cream and vanilla; beat on medium speed, scraping bottom of bowl occasionally, until stiff peaks form. Pour in gelatin mixture; beat until well blended.

About 2 cups filling

Peanut Butter Cream Pie

1 package (3¹/₂ ounces) instant
  vanilla pudding and pie
  filling
1 cup sour cream
1 cup milk
1¹/₂ cups REESE'S Peanut Butter
  Chips
2 tablespoons vegetable oil
  8-inch (6 ounces) packaged
  crumb crust
  Whipped topping

In small mixer bowl blend pudding mix, sour cream and milk; set aside. In top of double boiler over hot, not boiling, water melt peanut butter chips with oil, stirring constantly to blend. (OR in small micro-proof bowl place chips and oil. Microwave at HIGH (100%) for 45 seconds; stir. If necessary, microwave at HIGH additional 15 seconds or until melted and smooth when stirred.) Gradually add to pudding mixture, blending well. Pour into crust. Cover; chill several hours or overnight. Garnish with whipped topping.

6 to 8 servings

Top: Chocolate-Filled Cream Puffs
Middle: Chocolate-Almond Tarts
Bottom: Napoleons (see page 44)

Chocolate-Filled Cream Puffs

1 cup water
1/2 cup butter or margarine
1/4 teaspoon salt
1 cup unsifted all-purpose flour
4 eggs
Chocolate Cream Filling
Confectioners' sugar

Heat water, butter and salt to rolling boil in medium saucepan. Add flour all at once; stir vigorously over low heat about 1 minute or until mixture leaves side of pan and forms a ball. Remove from heat; add eggs, one at a time, beating well after each addition until smooth and velvety.

Drop by scant 1/4 cupfuls onto ungreased cookie sheet. Bake at 400° for 35 to 40 minutes or until puffed and golden brown. While puff is warm, horizontally slice off small portion of top; reserve tops. Remove any soft filaments of dough; cool puffs. Prepare Chocolate Cream Filling; fill puffs. Replace tops; dust with confectioners' sugar. Chill.

About 12 cream puffs

CHOCOLATE CREAM FILLING

1 1/4 cups sugar
1/3 cup HERSHEY'S Cocoa
1/3 cup cornstarch
1/4 teaspoon salt
3 cups milk
3 egg yolks, slightly beaten
2 tablespoons butter or margarine
1 1/2 teaspoons vanilla

Combine sugar, cocoa, cornstarch and salt in medium saucepan; stir in milk. Cook over medium heat, stirring constantly, until mixture boils; boil and stir 1 minute. Remove from heat. Gradually stir small amount of chocolate mixture into egg yolks; blend well. Return egg mixture to chocolate mixture in pan; stir and heat just until boiling. Remove from heat; blend in butter and vanilla. Pour into bowl; press plastic wrap directly onto surface. Cool.

VARIATION
Miniature Cream Puffs: Drop dough by level teaspoonfuls onto ungreased cookie sheet. Bake at 400° for about 15 minutes. Fill as directed above.

About 8 dozen miniature cream puffs

Chocolate-Almond Tarts

Chocolate Tart Shells
3/4 cup sugar
1/4 cup HERSHEY'S Cocoa
2 tablespoons cornstarch
2 tablespoons flour
1/4 teaspoon salt
2 cups milk
2 egg yolks, slightly beaten
2 tablespoons butter or margarine
1/4 teaspoon almond extract
Sliced almonds

Prepare Chocolate Tart Shells; set aside. Combine sugar, cocoa, cornstarch, flour and salt in medium saucepan; blend in milk and egg yolks. Cook over medium heat, stirring constantly, until mixture boils; boil and stir 1 minute. Remove from heat; blend in butter and almond extract.

Pour into cooled shells; press plastic wrap directly onto surface. Chill. Garnish tops with sliced almonds.

6 tarts

CHOCOLATE TART SHELLS

1 1/2 cups vanilla wafer crumbs (about 45 wafers)
1/3 cup confectioners' sugar
1/4 cup HERSHEY'S Cocoa
6 tablespoons butter or margarine, melted

Combine crumbs, confectioners' sugar, cocoa and melted butter in medium bowl; stir until completely blended. Divide mixture among six 4-ounce tart pans; press mixture firmly onto bottoms and up sides of pans. Bake at 350° for 5 minutes. Cool.

Napoleons

2 sheets (17¼-ounce package)
  frozen puff pastry
Chocolate Cream Filling
Vanilla Frosting
Chocolate Glaze

Thaw folded pastry sheets as directed; gently unfold. Roll each on floured surface to 15×12-inch rectangle. Place on ungreased cookie sheets; prick each sheet thoroughly with fork. Bake at 350° for 18 to 22 minutes or until puffed and lightly browned. Cool completely on cookie sheets. Prepare Chocolate Cream Filling.

Cut one rectangle lengthwise into three equal pieces. Place one piece on serving plate; spread with one-fourth of the Chocolate Cream Filling. Top with second piece of pastry; spread with one-fourth of the filling. Place remaining piece on top; set aside. Repeat procedure with remaining pastry and filling.

Prepare Vanilla Frosting; spread half the frosting on each rectangle. Prepare Chocolate Glaze; drizzle half the glaze in decorative design over frosting on each rectangle. Cover; chill at least 1 hour or until filling is firm. Cut each rectangle into six pieces.

12 servings

CHOCOLATE CREAM FILLING

½ cup sugar
3 tablespoons cornstarch
1½ cups milk
3 egg yolks, slightly beaten
¾ cup HERSHEY'S MINI
  CHIPS Semi-Sweet
  Chocolate
½ teaspoon vanilla

Combine sugar, cornstarch and milk in medium saucepan. Cook over medium heat, stirring constantly, until mixture just begins to boil. Remove from heat. Gradually stir small amount of mixture into egg yolks; blend well. Return egg mixture to mixture in pan. Cook over medium heat, stirring constantly, 1 minute. Remove from heat; add MINI CHIPS Chocolates and vanilla, stirring until chips are melted and mixture is smooth. Press plastic wrap directly onto surface. Cool; chill thoroughly.

VANILLA FROSTING

1½ cups confectioners' sugar
1 tablespoon light corn syrup
¼ teaspoon vanilla
1 to 2 tablespoons hot water

Combine confectioners' sugar, corn syrup, vanilla and hot water in small mixer bowl; beat to spreading consistency.

CHOCOLATE GLAZE

¼ cup butter or margarine
⅓ cup HERSHEY'S Cocoa

Melt butter in small saucepan. Remove from heat; stir in cocoa until smooth. Cool slightly.

Easy Chocolate Mousse Pie

Graham Cracker Crust (recipe
  follows)
1 package (8 ounces) cream
  cheese, softened
½ cup HERSHEY'S Cocoa
1 cup confectioners' sugar
1½ teaspoons vanilla
2 cups heavy or whipping
  cream

Prepare Graham Cracker Crust; set aside. Beat cream cheese and cocoa in large mixer bowl until fluffy and well blended. Gradually add confectioners' sugar; blend well. Stir in vanilla. Whip cream until stiff; fold into cheese mixture.

Pour into cooled crust; chill until firm. Garnish as desired.

8 servings

GRAHAM CRACKER CRUST

(Continued from page 44)

1½ cups graham cracker crumbs
⅓ cup butter or margarine, melted
3 tablespoons sugar

Combine graham cracker crumbs, butter and sugar in small bowl. Press mixture firmly onto bottom and up side of 9-inch pie pan. Bake at 350° for 10 minutes; cool.

Fudge Pecan Pie

½ cup sugar
⅓ cup HERSHEY'S Cocoa
⅓ cup unsifted all-purpose flour
¼ teaspoon salt
1¼ cups light corn syrup
3 eggs
3 tablespoons butter or margarine, melted
1½ teaspoons vanilla
½ cup chopped pecans
9-inch unbaked pastry shell
Pecan halves

Combine sugar, cocoa, flour, salt, corn syrup, eggs, melted butter and vanilla in large mixer bowl; beat 30 seconds on medium speed *(do not overbeat)*. Stir in chopped pecans.

Pour into unbaked pastry shell. Bake at 350° for 55 to 60 minutes; immediately arrange pecan halves on top. Cool. (For fullest flavor, cover and let stand one day before serving.)

8 servings

VARIATION
Fudge Walnut Pie: Substitute dark corn syrup for light corn syrup, 1 tablespoon imitation maple flavor for vanilla and chopped walnuts and walnut halves for chopped pecans and pecan halves. Prepare and bake as directed above.

Fudge Pecan Pie

Chocolate Banana Cream Pie

Chocolate Banana Cream Pie

9-inch pastry shell or crumb
  crust
1¼ cups sugar
⅓ cup HERSHEY'S Cocoa
⅓ cup cornstarch
¼ teaspoon salt
3 cups milk
3 tablespoons butter or
  margarine
1½ teaspoons vanilla
2 medium bananas, sliced
Sweetened whipped cream
Additional banana slices
  (optional)

Bake pastry shell; set aside. Combine sugar, cocoa, cornstarch and salt in medium saucepan; gradually add milk, stirring until smooth. Cook over medium heat, stirring constantly, until mixture boils; boil and stir 3 minutes. Remove from heat; blend in butter and vanilla. Pour into bowl; press plastic wrap directly onto surface. Cool to room temperature.

Cover bottom of cooled shell with small amount of filling. Arrange banana slices over filling; cover with remaining filling. Chill 3 to 4 hours or until firm. Garnish with sweetened whipped cream and banana slices.

8 servings

Cookies & Bar Cookies

Best Brownies

½ cup butter or margarine, melted
1 cup sugar
1 teaspoon vanilla
2 eggs
½ cup unsifted all-purpose flour
⅓ cup HERSHEY'S Cocoa
¼ teaspoon baking powder
¼ teaspoon salt
½ cup chopped nuts (optional)
Creamy Brownie Frosting

Blend butter, sugar and vanilla in large bowl. Add eggs; using a wooden spoon, beat well. Combine flour, cocoa, baking powder and salt; gradually blend into egg mixture. Stir in nuts.

Spread in greased 9-inch square pan. Bake at 350° for 20 to 25 minutes or until brownie begins to pull away from edges of pan. Cool; frost with Creamy Brownie Frosting. Cut into squares.

About 16 brownies

CREAMY BROWNIE FROSTING

3 tablespoons butter or margarine, softened
3 tablespoons HERSHEY'S Cocoa
1 tablespoon light corn syrup or honey
½ teaspoon vanilla
1 cup confectioners' sugar
1 to 2 tablespoons milk

Cream butter, cocoa, corn syrup and vanilla in small mixer bowl. Add confectioners' sugar and milk; beat to spreading consistency.

About 1 cup frosting

Scrumptious Chocolate Layer Bars ⤳⤳⤳⤳⤳⤳⤳⤳⤳⤳

2 cups (12-ounce package)
   HERSHEY'S Semi-Sweet
   Chocolate Chips
1 package (8 ounces) cream
   cheese
1/2 cup plus 2 tablespoons
   (5-ounce can) evaporated
   milk
1 cup chopped walnuts
1/4 cup sesame seeds (optional)
1/2 teaspoon almond extract
3 cups unsifted all-purpose
   flour
1 1/2 cups sugar
1 teaspoon baking powder
1/2 teaspoon salt
1 cup butter or margarine
2 eggs
1/2 teaspoon almond extract

Combine chocolate chips, cream cheese and evaporated milk in medium saucepan. Cook over low heat, stirring constantly, until chips are melted and mixture is smooth. Remove from heat; stir in walnuts, sesame seeds and 1/2 teaspoon almond extract. Blend well; set aside.

Combine remaining ingredients in large mixer bowl; blend well on low speed until mixture resembles coarse crumbs. Press half the mixture in greased 13×9-inch pan; spread with chocolate mixture. Sprinkle rest of crumbs over filling. (If mixture softens and forms a stiff dough, pinch off small pieces to use as topping.) Bake at 375° for 35 to 40 minutes or until golden brown. Cool; cut into bars.

About 3 dozen bars

Peanut Butter Paisley Brownies ⤳⤳⤳⤳⤳⤳⤳⤳⤳⤳

1/2 cup butter or margarine,
   softened
1/4 cup peanut butter
1 cup sugar
1 cup packed light brown sugar
3 eggs
1 teaspoon vanilla
2 cups unsifted all-purpose
   flour
2 teaspoons baking powder
1/4 teaspoon salt
1/2 cup (5.5-ounce can)
   HERSHEY'S Syrup

Blend butter and peanut butter in large mixer bowl. Add sugar and brown sugar; beat well. Add eggs, one at a time, beating well after each addition. Blend in vanilla. Combine flour, baking powder and salt; add to peanut butter mixture.

Spread half the batter in greased 13×9-inch pan. Spoon syrup over top. Carefully spread with remaining batter. Swirl with spatula or knife for marbled effect. Bake at 350° for 35 to 40 minutes or until lightly browned. Cool; cut into squares.

About 3 dozen brownies

Clockwise from top left: Scrumptious Chocolate Layer Bars,
Peanut Butter Paisley Brownies and Best Brownies (see page 47)

Reese's Cookies

1 cup shortening, *or* ³/₄ cup
   butter or margarine,
   softened
1 cup sugar
¹/₂ cup packed light brown sugar
1 teaspoon vanilla
2 eggs
2 cups unsifted all-purpose
   flour
1 teaspoon baking soda
1 cup REESE'S Peanut Butter
   Chips
1 cup HERSHEY'S Semi-Sweet
   Chocolate Chips

Cream shortening or butter, sugar, brown sugar and vanilla in large mixer bowl until light and fluffy. Add eggs; beat well. Combine flour and baking soda; add to creamed mixture. Stir in peanut butter chips and chocolate chips.

Drop by teaspoonfuls onto ungreased cookie sheet. Bake at 350° for 10 to 12 minutes or until lightly browned. Cool slightly. Remove from cookie sheet; cool completely on wire rack.

About 5 dozen cookies

Holiday Chocolate Cookies

¹/₂ cup butter or margarine,
   softened
³/₄ cup sugar
1 egg
1 teaspoon vanilla
1¹/₂ cups unsifted all-purpose
   flour
¹/₃ cup HERSHEY'S Cocoa
¹/₂ teaspoon baking powder
¹/₂ teaspoon baking soda
¹/₄ teaspoon salt
   Decorator's Frosting

Cream butter, sugar, egg and vanilla in large mixer bowl until light and fluffy. Combine remaining ingredients except Decorator's Frosting; add to creamed mixture, blending well.

Roll a small portion of dough at a time on lightly floured surface to ¹/₄-inch thickness. (If too soft, chill dough until firm enough to roll.) Cut with 2¹/₂-inch cutter; place on ungreased cookie sheet. Bake at 325° for 5 to 7 minutes or until only a slight indentation remains when touched lightly. Cool 1 minute. Remove from cookie sheet; cool completely on wire rack. Prepare Decorator's Frosting and decorate with holiday designs or messages.

About 3 dozen cookies

DECORATOR'S FROSTING

1¹/₂ cups confectioners' sugar
2 tablespoons shortening
2 tablespoons milk
¹/₂ teaspoon vanilla
   Red, green or yellow food
   color

Combine all ingredients except food color in small mixer bowl; beat until smooth and of spreading consistency. Tint with drops of food color, blending well.

Macaroon Kiss Cookies

Macaroon Kiss Cookies ∿∿∿∿∿∿∿∿∿∿∿∿∿∿∿∿∿∿∿∿

⅓ **cup butter or margarine,
    softened**
1 **package (3 ounces) cream
    cheese, softened**
¾ **cup sugar**
1 **egg yolk**
2 **teaspoons almond extract**
2 **teaspoons orange juice**
1¼ **cups unsifted all-purpose
    flour**
2 **teaspoons baking powder**
¼ **teaspoon salt**
5 **cups (14-ounce package)
    flaked coconut**
54 **HERSHEY'S KISSES
    Chocolates (9-ounce
    package), unwrapped**

Cream butter, cream cheese and sugar in large mixer bowl until
light and fluffy. Add egg yolk, almond extract and orange juice;
beat well. Combine flour, baking powder and salt; gradually add
to creamed mixture. Stir in 3 cups of the coconut. Cover tightly;
chill 1 hour or until firm enough to handle.

Shape dough into 1-inch balls; roll in remaining coconut. Place on
ungreased cookie sheet. Bake at 350° for 10 to 12 minutes or until
lightly browned. Remove from oven; immediately press unwrapped KISS on top of each cookie. Cool 1 minute. Carefully remove from cookie sheet; cool completely on wire rack.

About 4½ dozen cookies

Chocolate-Cherry Squares

Chocolate-Cherry Squares

1 cup unsifted all-purpose flour
1/3 cup butter or margarine
1/2 cup packed light brown sugar
1/2 cup chopped nuts
    Filling
    Red candied cherry halves

Combine flour, butter and brown sugar in large mixer bowl. Blend on low speed to form fine crumbs, about 2 to 3 minutes. Stir in nuts. Reserve 3/4 cup crumb mixture for topping; pat remaining crumbs into ungreased 9-inch square pan. Bake at 350° for 10 minutes or until lightly browned. Prepare Filling; spread over warm crust. Sprinkle with reserved crumb mixture and garnish with cherry halves. Bake at 350° for 25 minutes or until lightly browned. Cool; cut into squares. Store in refrigerator.

About 3 dozen squares

FILLING

1 package (8 ounces) cream
    cheese, softened
1/2 cup sugar
1/3 cup HERSHEY'S Cocoa
1/4 cup milk
1 egg
1/2 teaspoon vanilla
1/2 cup chopped red candied
    cherries

Combine cream cheese, sugar, cocoa, milk, egg and vanilla in small mixer bowl; beat until smooth. Fold in cherries.

Cocoa Kiss Cookies

1 cup butter or margarine,
  softened
$2/3$ cup sugar
1 teaspoon vanilla
$1^2/_3$ cups unsifted all-purpose
  flour
$1/_4$ cup HERSHEY'S Cocoa
1 cup finely chopped pecans
54 HERSHEY'S KISSES
  Chocolates (9-ounce
  package), unwrapped
Confectioners' sugar

Cream butter, sugar and vanilla in large mixer bowl until light and fluffy. Combine flour and cocoa; blend into creamed mixture. Add pecans; beat on low speed until well blended. Chill dough 1 hour or until firm enough to handle.

Shape scant tablespoon of dough around each unwrapped KISS, covering completely; shape into balls. Place on ungreased cookie sheet. Bake at 375° for 10 to 12 minutes or until almost set. Cool slightly. Remove from cookie sheet; cool completely on wire rack. Roll in confectioners' sugar.

About $4^1/_2$ dozen cookies

Chocolate Chip Whole Wheat Cookies

$3/_4$ cup shortening
$1^1/_2$ cups packed light brown
  sugar
1 egg
$1/_4$ cup water
1 teaspoon vanilla
1 cup unsifted whole wheat
  flour
$1/_2$ teaspoon baking soda
$1/_2$ teaspoon salt
2 cups quick-cooking oats
1 cup chopped dried apricots or
  raisins
1 cup HERSHEY'S MINI
  CHIPS Semi-Sweet
  Chocolate

Cream shortening and brown sugar in large mixer bowl until light and fluffy. Add egg, water and vanilla; beat well. Combine whole wheat flour, baking soda and salt; stir into creamed mixture. Stir in oats, dried apricots and MINI CHIPS Chocolates.

Drop by teaspoonfuls onto lightly greased cookie sheet; flatten slightly. Bake at 350° for 10 to 12 minutes or until golden brown. Remove from cookie sheet; cool completely on wire rack.

About 5 dozen cookies

Reese's Chewy Chocolate Cookies

$1^1/_4$ cups butter or margarine,
  softened
2 cups sugar
2 eggs
2 teaspoons vanilla
2 cups unsifted all-purpose
  flour
$3/_4$ cup HERSHEY'S Cocoa
1 teaspoon baking soda
$1/_2$ teaspoon salt
$1^2/_3$ cups (10-ounce package)
  REESE'S Peanut Butter
  Chips

Cream butter and sugar in large mixer bowl until light and fluffy. Add eggs and vanilla; beat well. Combine flour, cocoa, baking soda and salt; gradually blend into creamed mixture. Stir in peanut butter chips.

Drop by teaspoonfuls onto ungreased cookie sheet. Bake at 350° for 8 to 9 minutes. *Do not overbake.* (Cookies will be soft; they will puff during baking and flatten upon cooling.) Cool until set, about 1 minute. Remove from cookie sheet; cool completely on wire rack.

About $4^1/_2$ dozen cookies

Hershey's Great American Chocolate Chip Cookies

1 cup butter, softened
3/4 cup sugar
3/4 cup packed light brown sugar
1 teaspoon vanilla
2 eggs
2 1/4 cups unsifted all-purpose flour
1 teaspoon baking soda
1/2 teaspoon salt
2 cups (12-ounce package) HERSHEY'S Semi-Sweet Chocolate Chips
1 cup chopped nuts (optional)

Cream butter, sugar, brown sugar and vanilla in large mixer bowl until light and fluffy. Add eggs; beat well. Combine flour, baking soda and salt; gradually add to creamed mixture. Beat well. Stir in chocolate chips and nuts.

Drop by teaspoonfuls onto ungreased cookie sheet. Bake at 375° for 8 to 10 minutes or until lightly browned. Cool slightly. Remove from cookie sheet; cool completely on wire rack.

About 6 dozen cookies

VARIATION

Milk Chocolate Chip Cookies: Substitute 2 cups (11.5-ounce package) HERSHEY'S Milk Chocolate Chips for the semi-sweet chocolate chips.

Chocolate Cookie Sandwiches

1/2 cup shortening
1 cup sugar
1 egg
1 teaspoon vanilla
1 1/2 cups unsifted all-purpose flour
1/3 cup HERSHEY'S Cocoa
1/2 teaspoon baking soda
1/2 teaspoon salt
1/4 cup milk
Creme Filling

CREME FILLING

2 tablespoons butter or margarine, softened
2 tablespoons shortening
1/2 cup marshmallow creme
3/4 teaspoon vanilla
2/3 cup confectioners' sugar

Cream shortening, sugar, egg and vanilla in large mixer bowl until light and fluffy. Combine flour, cocoa, baking soda and salt; add alternately with milk to creamed mixture until ingredients are combined.

Drop by teaspoonfuls onto ungreased cookie sheet. Bake at 375° for 11 to 12 minutes or just until soft-set (*do not overbake*). Cool 1 minute. Remove from cookie sheet; cool completely on wire rack. Prepare Creme Filling. Spread bottom of one cookie with about 1 tablespoon filling; cover with another cookie. Repeat with remaining cookies and filling.

About 15 filled cookies

Cream butter and shortening in small mixer bowl; gradually beat in marshmallow creme. Blend in vanilla and confectioners' sugar; beat to spreading consistency.

Clockwise from top left:
Hershey's Great American Chocolate Chip Cookies
Reese's Chewy Chocolate Cookies (see page 53)
Chocolate Chip Whole Wheat Cookies (see page 53)
Chocolate Cookie Sandwiches

Puddings, Mousses & Souffles

Strawberry-Chocolate Bavarian Cream

1 package (10 ounces) frozen
    sliced strawberries, thawed*
2 envelopes unflavored gelatine
1/2 cup sugar
1 cup HERSHEY'S Semi-Sweet
    Chocolate Chips
2 1/4 cups milk
1 teaspoon vanilla
1 cup heavy or whipping cream
    Strawberry Cream

Drain strawberries; reserve syrup. Add water to syrup to equal 3/4 cup. Stir gelatine into liquid; set aside. Puree or mash berries to equal 1/2 cup. Reserve for use in Strawberry Cream.

Combine sugar, chocolate chips and 1/2 cup of the milk in medium saucepan. Cook over low heat, stirring constantly, until mixture is smooth and very hot. Add gelatine mixture, stirring until gelatine is completely dissolved. Remove from heat; add remaining 1 3/4 cups milk and the vanilla. Pour into bowl; chill, stirring occasionally, until mixture mounds when dropped from a spoon.

Whip cream until stiff; fold into chocolate mixture. Pour into oiled 5- or 6-cup mold; chill until firm. Unmold and garnish with Strawberry Cream.

8 to 10 servings

*You may substitute 1 cup sweetened sliced fresh strawberries for the frozen.

STRAWBERRY CREAM

1 cup heavy or whipping cream
1 teaspoon vanilla
1/2 cup strawberry puree
    (reserved from recipe above)
2 or 3 drops red food color

Whip cream and vanilla in small mixer bowl until stiff. Fold in strawberry puree and food color.

Top: Strawberry-Chocolate Bavarian Cream
Bottom: Double Chocolate Mousse (see page 58)

Two Great Tastes Pudding Parfaits

1 package (4³/₄ ounces) vanilla
    pudding and pie filling
3¹/₂ cups milk
1 cup REESE'S Peanut Butter
    Chips
1 cup HERSHEY'S Semi-Sweet
    Chocolate Chips
    Whipped topping (optional)

In large, heavy saucepan combine pudding mix and 3¹/₂ cups milk (rather than amount listed in package directions). Cook over medium heat, stirring constantly, until mixture comes to full boil. Remove from heat; divide hot mixture between 2 heatproof medium bowls. Immediately stir peanut butter chips into mixture in one bowl and chocolate chips into mixture in second bowl. Stir both mixtures until melted and smooth. Cool slightly, stirring occasionally. Alternately spoon peanut butter and chocolate mixtures into parfait glasses, champagne glasses or dessert dishes. Place plastic wrap directly onto surface of each dessert; refrigerate several hours or overnight. Garnish with whipped topping, if desired.

4 to 6 servings

Chocolate Cream Pudding

1 cup sugar
¹/₄ cup HERSHEY'S Cocoa
¹/₃ cup cornstarch
¹/₄ teaspoon salt
3 cups milk
3 egg yolks, slightly beaten
2 tablespoons butter or
    margarine
1¹/₂ teaspoons vanilla

Combine sugar, cocoa, cornstarch and salt in heavy saucepan; add milk and egg yolks. Cook over medium heat, stirring constantly, until mixture boils; boil and stir 1 minute. Remove from heat; blend in butter and vanilla. Pour into bowl or individual dessert dishes; press plastic wrap directly onto surface. Cool; chill until set.

6 to 8 servings

Individual Fudge Souffles

¹/₂ cup butter or margarine,
    softened
1¹/₄ cups sugar
1 teaspoon vanilla
4 eggs
²/₃ cup milk
¹/₂ teaspoon instant coffee
    granules
²/₃ cup unsifted all-purpose flour
²/₃ cup HERSHEY'S Cocoa
1¹/₂ teaspoons baking powder
1 cup heavy or whipping cream
2 tablespoons confectioners'
    sugar

Grease and sugar eight 5- or 6-ounce custard cups or ramekins; set aside. Cream butter, sugar and vanilla in large mixer bowl until light and fluffy. Add eggs, one at a time, beating well after each addition. Scald milk; remove from heat and add coffee granules, stirring until dissolved. Combine flour, cocoa and baking powder; add alternately with milk-coffee mixture to creamed mixture. Beat 1 minute on medium speed.

Divide batter evenly among prepared custard cups. Place in two 8-inch square pans; place pans in oven. Pour hot water into pans to depth of ¹/₈ inch. Bake at 325° for 40 to 45 minutes for custard cups (50 to 55 minutes for ramekins), adding more water if necessary, until cake tester inserted halfway between edge and center comes out clean. Remove pans from oven and allow custard cups to stand in water 5 minutes. Remove custard cups from water; cool slightly. Serve in custard cups or invert onto dessert dishes. Beat cream with confectioners' sugar until stiff; spoon onto warm souffles.

8 servings

Cocoa Bavarian Cream

2 envelopes unflavored gelatine
1½ cups cold milk
1¼ cups sugar
¾ cup HERSHEY'S Cocoa
1 tablespoon light corn syrup
3 tablespoons butter or
    margarine
1¾ cups milk
1½ teaspoons vanilla
10 to 12 ladyfingers, split
1 cup heavy or whipping cream

Sprinkle gelatine onto 1½ cups milk in medium saucepan; let stand 3 to 4 minutes to soften. Combine sugar and cocoa; add to gelatine mixture in saucepan. Add corn syrup. Cook over medium heat, stirring constantly, until mixture boils. Remove from heat; stir in butter until melted. Blend in 1¾ cups milk and the vanilla; pour into large mixer bowl. Cool; chill until almost set.

Meanwhile, line bottom and side of 1½-quart mold with ladyfingers, rounded sides against mold. Whip cream until stiff. Beat chilled chocolate mixture until smooth. Add whipped cream to chocolate on low speed just until blended. Pour into ladyfinger-lined mold; chill until set. Unmold before serving.

12 servings

Chocolate-Berry Parfaits

Chocolate Cream Pudding
    (page 58)
1 package (10 ounces) frozen
    sliced strawberries, thawed,
    or 1 cup sweetened sliced
    fresh strawberries
1 cup heavy or whipping
    cream*
¼ cup confectioners' sugar*
    Fresh strawberries (optional)

Prepare Chocolate Cream Pudding; cool completely. Drain strawberries; puree in blender or sieve to equal ½ to ¾ cup. Beat cream and confectioners' sugar until stiff; fold in strawberry puree. Alternately layer chocolate pudding and strawberry cream in parfait glasses. Chill until set. Garnish with strawberries.

8 to 10 servings

*You may substitute 2 cups frozen non-dairy whipped topping, thawed, for the cream and confectioners' sugar.

Chocolate-Berry Parfaits

Brownie Fudge Dessert

½ cup HERSHEY'S Cocoa
1 cup butter or margarine
3 tablespoons vegetable oil
1 cup sugar
4 eggs, slightly beaten
2 teaspoons vanilla
½ cup unsifted all-purpose flour
30 pecan halves
   Ice cream or sweetened
     whipped cream

Combine cocoa, butter and oil in top of double boiler over hot, not boiling, water; stir over low heat until butter is melted. Remove from heat; stir in sugar. Add eggs and vanilla just until well combined. Stir flour into mixture just until blended.

Pour batter into ungreased 9-inch square pan and arrange pecan halves evenly on top. Place pan with batter in 13×9-inch pan; place both in oven. Pour hot water to depth of 1 inch into 13×9-inch pan. Bake at 350° for 40 to 45 minutes or until knife inserted ½ inch from edge comes out clean and brownie-like crust has formed; *do not overbake*. Remove from water bath; let cool on wire rack until warm. Scoop onto serving plates and top with your favorite ice cream. Or chill, cut into squares and serve with sweetened whipped cream.

9 servings

Chocolate-Orange Pudding Cake

1 cup all-purpose flour
¾ cup granulated sugar
3 tablespoons plus ¼ cup
    HERSHEY'S Cocoa, divided
2 teaspoons baking powder
½ teaspoon salt
½ cup milk
2 tablespoons vegetable oil
1 teaspoon vanilla extract
½ cup chopped nuts, divided
¾ cup packed light brown sugar
1¼ cups boiling water
¼ to ½ teaspoon grated orange
    peel
   Vanilla ice cream (optional)

In large bowl combine flour, granulated sugar, 3 tablespoons cocoa, baking powder and salt. Stir in milk, oil, vanilla and ¼ cup nuts. Spread batter in 2- or 2½-quart micro-proof casserole. In small bowl combine brown sugar, remaining ¼ cup cocoa, remaining ¼ cup nuts, water and orange peel. Carefully pour liquid mixture over batter in casserole; *do not mix*. Microwave at HIGH (100%) for 7 to 9 minutes, rotating ¼ turn halfway through cooking time, or until cake rises to the surface and sauce forms on bottom. Let stand 10 minutes. Serve warm. Spoon into dessert dishes, spooning sauce from bottom of casserole over each serving. Top with scoop of ice cream, if desired.

6 to 8 servings

Chocolate-Banana Sherbet

2 medium-size ripe bananas
1 cup apricot nectar, peach or
    pineapple juice, divided
1/2 cup HERSHEY'S Semi-Sweet
    Chocolate Chips
2 tablespoons sugar
1 cup milk

Slice bananas into blender container or food processor. Add 3/4 cup fruit juice; blend until smooth. In small micro-proof bowl place chocolate chips, remaining 1/4 cup fruit juice and sugar. Microwave at HIGH (100%) for 45 seconds or until chips are melted and mixture is smooth when stirred. Add to mixture in blender; blend until thoroughly combined. Add milk; blend until smooth. Pour into 9-inch square pan or 2 ice cube trays. Cover; freeze until hard around edges. Into large mixer bowl or food processor spoon partially frozen mixture; beat or process until smooth. Cover; freeze until firm; stirring several times before mixture freezes. Allow to soften at room temperature 5 minutes before serving; scoop into dessert dishes.

About 8 servings

Chocolate Tortoni

1 cup chilled whipping cream
1/2 cup chilled HERSHEY'S
    Syrup
1/4 cup almond macaroon crumbs
    or vanilla wafer crumbs
1/4 cup plus 2 tablespoons
    chopped, toasted almonds,
    divided*
1/4 cup chopped maraschino
    cherries, drained
1 1/2 tablespoons rum or 1/2
    teaspoon rum extract
    Maraschino cherries (optional)

In small mixer bowl beat whipping cream until stiff; gently fold in chocolate syrup. Stir in macaroon crumbs, 1/4 cup chopped almonds, chopped maraschino cherries and rum. Divide mixture among 4 dessert dishes; cover and freeze until firm, about 4 hours. Just before serving, sprinkle with remaining 2 tablespoons chopped almonds. Garnish with maraschino cherries, if desired.

4 servings

*To toast almonds: Spread almonds on cookie sheet. Bake at 350°, stirring occasionally, until lightly browned, 8 to 10 minutes; cool.

Lite Chocolate Mint Parfaits

2/3 cup sugar
1/4 cup HERSHEY'S Cocoa
3 tablespoons cornstarch
    Dash salt
2 1/2 cups cold skim milk, divided
1 tablespoon margarine
1 1/2 teaspoons vanilla extract,
    divided
1 envelope whipped topping
    mix (to make 2 cups
    whipped topping)
1/4 teaspoon mint extract
3 to 4 drops green food color
    (optional)

In medium saucepan combine sugar, cocoa, cornstarch and salt; gradually stir in 2 cups milk. Cook over medium heat, stirring constantly, until mixture boils; boil and stir 1 minute. Remove from heat; blend in margarine and 1 teaspoon vanilla. Pour into medium bowl. Press plastic wrap directly onto surface of pudding; refrigerate. In small bowl combine topping mix, remaining 1/2 cup milk and 1/2 teaspoon vanilla; prepare according to package directions. Fold 1/2 cup topping into pudding. Blend mint extract and green food color into remaining topping. Alternately spoon chocolate pudding and mint whipped topping into parfait glasses. Refrigerate until thoroughly chilled.

7 servings

Hot Chocolate Souffle 〜〜〜〜〜〜〜〜〜〜〜〜〜

3/4 cup HERSHEY'S Cocoa
3/4 cup sugar
1/2 cup unsifted all-purpose flour
1/4 teaspoon salt
  2 cups milk
  6 egg yolks, well beaten
  2 tablespoons butter
  1 teaspoon vanilla
  8 egg whites, at room
      temperature
1/4 teaspoon cream of tartar
1/4 cup sugar
    Sweetened whipped cream
      (optional)

Lightly butter 2½-quart souffle dish; sprinkle with sugar. Measure length of heavy-duty aluminum foil to fit around souffle dish; fold in thirds lengthwise. Lightly oil one side of collar; tape securely to outside of dish (oiled side in), allowing collar to extend at least 2 inches above rim. Set aside.

Combine cocoa, 3/4 cup sugar, the flour and salt in medium saucepan; gradually blend in milk. Cook over medium heat, stirring constantly with wire whisk, until mixture boils; remove from heat. Gradually stir small amount of chocolate mixture into beaten egg yolks; blend well. Return egg mixture to chocolate mixture in pan. Add butter and vanilla, stirring until combined. Set aside; cool to lukewarm.

Beat egg whites with cream of tartar in large mixer bowl until soft peaks form. Add 1/4 cup sugar, 2 tablespoons at a time, beating until stiff peaks form. Gently fold one-third of the chocolate mixture into beaten egg whites. Fold in remaining chocolate mixture, half at a time, just until combined.

Gently pour mixture, without stirring, into prepared dish; smooth top with spatula. Place dish in larger pan; place in oven on bottom rack. Pour hot water into pan to depth of 1 inch (be sure bottom of foil collar does not touch water bath). Bake at 350° for 1 hour and 10 minutes or until cake tester inserted halfway between edge and center comes out clean. Carefully remove foil. Serve immediately with sweetened whipped cream.

8 to 10 servings

Mocha Fudge Pudding Cake 〜〜〜〜〜〜〜〜〜〜〜

3/4 cup sugar
  1 cup unsifted all-purpose flour
  2 teaspoons baking powder
1/4 teaspoon salt
1/2 cup butter or margarine
  1 bar (1 ounce) HERSHEY'S
      Unsweetened Baking
      Chocolate
1/2 cup milk
  1 teaspoon vanilla
1/2 cup sugar
1/2 cup packed light brown sugar
1/4 cup HERSHEY'S Cocoa
  1 cup hot strong coffee
    Ice cream

Combine 3/4 cup sugar, the flour, baking powder and salt in medium bowl. Melt butter with baking chocolate in small saucepan over low heat; add to dry ingredients with milk and vanilla. Beat until smooth. Pour into 8- or 9-inch square pan.

Combine 1/2 cup sugar, the brown sugar and cocoa in small bowl; sprinkle evenly over batter. Pour coffee over top; *do not stir.* Bake at 350° for 40 minutes or until center is almost set. Serve warm with ice cream.

8 to 10 servings

Hot Chocolate Souffle

Chocolate Tapioca

3/4 cup sugar
1/3 cup HERSHEY'S Cocoa
3 tablespoons quick-cooking
   tapioca
1/8 teaspoon salt
2 3/4 cups milk
1 egg, slightly beaten
1 teaspoon vanilla

Combine sugar, cocoa, tapioca and salt in medium saucepan; blend in milk and egg. Let stand 5 minutes. Cook over medium heat, stirring constantly, until mixture boils. Remove from heat; stir in vanilla. Pour into bowl or individual dessert dishes; press plastic wrap directly onto surface. Cool; chill until set.

4 to 6 servings

St. Patrick's Day Parfaits

3 cups miniature or 30 large
   marshmallows
1/2 cup milk
2 tablespoons green crème de
   menthe
1 cup HERSHEY'S Semi-Sweet
   Chocolate Chips
1/4 cup confectioners' sugar
1 1/2 cups heavy or whipping
   cream

Combine marshmallows and milk in medium saucepan; cook over low heat, stirring constantly, until marshmallows are melted and mixture is smooth. Measure 1 cup marshmallow mixture into small bowl. Blend in crème de menthe; set aside. Add chocolate chips and confectioners' sugar to marshmallow mixture remaining in saucepan; return to low heat and stir until chips are melted. Remove from heat; cool to room temperature.

Whip cream just until soft peaks form; fold 1 1/2 cups into marshmallow-mint mixture. Fold remaining whipped cream into chocolate mixture. Alternately spoon chocolate and mint mixtures into parfait glasses. Chill thoroughly or freeze. Garnish as desired.

6 servings

St. Patrick's Day Parfaits

Chocolate-Amaretto Ice

3/4 cup sugar
1/2 cup HERSHEY'S Cocoa
2 cups light cream or half-and-half
2 tablespoons almond flavored liqueur
Sliced almonds (optional)

In small saucepan combine sugar and cocoa; gradually stir in light cream. Cook over low heat, stirring constantly, until sugar dissolves and mixture is smooth and hot; *do not boil*. Remove from heat; stir in liqueur. Pour into 8-inch square pan. Cover; freeze until firm, stirring several times before mixture freezes. Scoop into dessert dishes. Garnish with sliced almonds, if desired.

4 servings

Banana Fudge Pops

1 ripe, medium banana
1 1/2 cups orange-banana juice
1/2 cup sugar
1/4 cup HERSHEY'S Cocoa
1 can (5 ounces) evaporated milk
6 paper cold drink cups (5 ounces each)
6 wooden popsicle sticks

Slice banana into blender container; add juice. Cover; blend until smooth. Add sugar and cocoa; cover and blend well. Add evaporated milk; cover and blend. Pour mixture into cups. Freeze about 1 hour; insert popsicle sticks into fudge pops. Cover; freeze until firm. Peel off cups to serve.

6 pops

Frozen Coco-Berry Yogurt Supreme

1 envelope unflavored gelatin
2 tablespoons cold water
2 tablespoons boiling water
1 cup strawberry yogurt
1 package (10 ounces) frozen strawberries, thawed and pureed
1/2 cup chilled whipping cream
1/3 cup sugar
3 tablespoons HERSHEY'S Cocoa
1 teaspoon vanilla extract
1/4 cup slivered almonds
1/4 cup granola-type cereal

In small bowl sprinkle gelatin over cold water; let stand 1 minute to soften. Add boiling water; stir until gelatin is completely dissolved and mixture is clear. In medium bowl combine yogurt, strawberries, whipping cream, sugar, cocoa and vanilla. Add gelatin mixture; blend thoroughly. Pour mixture into 8-inch square pan; freeze until thickened. Remove mixture from pan to small mixer bowl; beat until ice crystals are broken. Fold in almonds and granola. Return mixture to pan; cover and freeze until firm. Allow to soften at room temperature 5 minutes before serving.

About 6 servings

Candies

Rich Cocoa Fudge

3 cups sugar
²/₃ cup HERSHEY'S Cocoa
¹/₈ teaspoon salt
1¹/₂ cups milk
¹/₄ cup butter or margarine
1 teaspoon vanilla

Butter 8- or 9-inch square pan; set aside. Combine sugar, cocoa and salt in heavy 4-quart saucepan; stir in milk. Cook over medium heat, stirring constantly, until mixture comes to full rolling boil. Boil, without stirring, to soft-ball stage, 234°F on a candy thermometer (or until syrup, when dropped into very cold water, forms a soft ball that flattens when removed from water). Bulb of candy thermometer should not rest on bottom of saucepan.

Remove from heat. Add butter and vanilla; *do not stir*. Cool at room temperature to 110°F (lukewarm). Beat until fudge thickens and loses some of its gloss. Quickly spread in prepared pan; cool. Cut into 1- to 1¹/₂-inch squares.

About 3 dozen candies

VARIATIONS
Marshmallow-Nut Cocoa Fudge: Increase cocoa to ³/₄ cup. Cook fudge as directed. Add 1 cup marshmallow creme with butter and vanilla; *do not stir*. Cool to 110°F (lukewarm). Beat 10 minutes; stir in 1 cup broken nuts and pour into prepared pan. (Fudge does not set until poured into pan).

Nutty Rich Cocoa Fudge: Beat cooked fudge as directed. *Immediately* stir in 1 cup broken almonds, pecans or walnuts and quickly spread in prepared pan.

Double-Decker Fudge

1 cup REESE'S Peanut Butter
  Chips
1 cup HERSHEY'S Semi-Sweet
  Chocolate Chips
2¼ cups sugar
1¾ cups (7-ounce jar)
  marshmallow creme
¾ cup evaporated milk
¼ cup butter or margarine
1 teaspoon vanilla

Measure peanut butter chips into one bowl and chocolate chips into another; set aside. Butter 8-inch square pan; set aside. Combine sugar, marshmallow creme, evaporated milk and butter in heavy 3-quart saucepan. Cook over medium heat, stirring constantly, until mixture boils; continue cooking and stirring for 5 minutes.

Remove from heat; stir in vanilla. Immediately stir half the hot mixture into peanut butter chips until completely melted. Quickly pour into prepared pan. Stir remaining hot mixture into chocolate chips until completely melted. Quickly spread over top of peanut butter layer; cool. Cut into 1-inch squares.

About 4 dozen candies

Chocolate-Almond Fudge

4 cups sugar
1¾ cups (7-ounce jar)
  marshmallow creme
1½ cups (12-ounce can)
  evaporated milk
1 tablespoon butter or
  margarine
2 cups (12-ounce package)
  HERSHEY'S MINI CHIPS
  Semi-Sweet Chocolate
1 HERSHEY'S Milk Chocolate
  Bar with Almonds
  (8 ounces), chopped
1 teaspoon vanilla
¾ cup chopped slivered almonds

Butter 9-inch square pan; set aside. Combine sugar, marshmallow creme, evaporated milk and butter in heavy 4-quart saucepan. Cook over medium heat, stirring constantly, until mixture comes to a full rolling boil; boil and stir 7 minutes. Remove from heat; *immediately* add MINI CHIPS Chocolates and chocolate bar pieces, stirring until completely melted. Blend in vanilla; stir in almonds. Pour into prepared pan; cool completely. Cut into 1-inch squares.

About 5 dozen candies

Center: Chocolate-Almond Fudge
Upper right: Double-Decker Fudge
Below: Nutty Rich Cocoa Fudge

Homemade Chocolate-Coated Candies

Did you ever look at a display of elegant, glossy—and expensive—chocolate-coated candies and wish that you could make them yourself? While that might seem a fantasy best left to the professionals, you need no longer be intimidated. The process is not difficult, but it does take time and patience. And remember, practice makes perfect—coating with chocolate becomes easier each time you do it. Before starting, review the important information that follows about making chocolate-coated candies.

Making the centers. Select the recipes for the centers you wish to coat and prepare them at least a day ahead. For variety, try different shapes—balls, cubes, rectangles, triangles, even hearts.

Choosing the right day. Make the coating only on a dry, clear day. Don't even *think* about dipping candies on a humid day! Humidity, steam or wet equipment causes chocolate to thicken, tighten and become grainy. Even a few drops of water can cause problems!

Ingredients. Select the kind of chocolate you wish to use for the coating. In addition, you need solid vegetable shortening. *Never substitute butter, margarine or oil!* These contain moisture, which will cause the chocolate to tighten and become grainy.

Assembling the equipment. Before you begin the coating process, assemble the equipment you need:
- Tape and wax paper
- A special candy thermometer that registers as low as 80°F is useful, but not necessary (most ordinary candy thermometers do not register below 100°F)
- A rubber spatula
- A glass bowl or glass measuring cup to hold the chocolate and shortening
- A larger glass bowl or a pan to hold the warm water
- A fondue fork or table fork to dip the centers into the coating

If you carefully and patiently follow our instructions, you'll be rewarded with your own homemade "dream" candies.

In advance, prepare an assortment of centers. Refrigerate until ready to coat with chocolate.

Combine chocolate and shortening in completely dry bowl. Don't let even one drop of water into mixture!

Chocolate-shortening mixture must be stirred and scraped down constantly with rubber spatula.

Chocolate mixture should be completely fluid and very smooth before starting to coat centers.

When coating is ready, rest a center on fork; carefully and completely dip into chocolate mixture. Tap fork on side of bowl to remove excess coating.

Invert center onto prepared cookie sheet. Using tip of fork, decorate top of candy with small amount of melted chocolate.

"Simply Stirred" Chocolate Coating

2 HERSHEY'S Milk Chocolate
   Bars (8 ounces each),
   broken into pieces
¹/₄ cup shortening*
            OR
2 cups (12-ounce package)
   HERSHEY'S Semi-Sweet
   Chocolate Chips
2 tablespoons plus 2 teaspoons
   shortening*
            OR
2 cups (11.5-ounce package)
   HERSHEY'S Milk
   Chocolate Chips
2 tablespoons shortening*

Before starting, review basic information on opposite page. Be sure that centers (pages 70-71) are chilled. Cover cookie sheet or tray with wax paper; fasten with tape.

Place chocolate and shortening in 4-cup glass measuring cup or 1¹/₂-quart glass bowl. Place measuring cup or bowl in larger glass bowl or pan of very warm—not hot—water (100°–110°F) that reaches *halfway* up cup or bowl. Don't let even one drop of water mix with chocolate!

Stir mixture *constantly* with rubber spatula until chocolate is completely melted and mixture is smooth. *Don't rush!* It will take about 20 minutes to melt the chocolate. If water begins to cool, pour out and add more warm water. (Chocolate mixture should be between 84°F and 88°F for coating.)

Remove measuring cup or bowl from water. Set one chilled center on tines of fondue fork or table fork. Completely dip center into coating. Gently tap fork on side of cup to remove excess coating. Invert candy onto prepared cookie sheet. Decorate top of coated center with small amount of melted chocolate, using tip of fork. Repeat with remaining centers. Store candies, loosely covered, in a cool, dry place.

Enough coating for about 5 dozen centers

*Do not use butter, margarine or oil.

Note: If chocolate becomes too thick while coating, return cup or bowl containing chocolate to larger glass bowl or pan with 1 inch of very warm tap water (100°–110°F). Stir mixture constantly until of desired consistency. *Be careful not to get any water into mixture.* When coating reaches desired consistency, remove from water; continue dipping centers.

An assortment of homemade chocolate-coated candies. In foil cups: leftover "Simply Stirred" Chocolate Coating (see page 69) combined with chopped or sliced nuts.

Easy Buttercream Centers

1 package (3 ounces) cream
    cheese, softened
1/2 cup butter or margarine,
    softened
4 cups confectioners' sugar
1 1/2 teaspoons vanilla

Beat cream cheese and butter in large mixer bowl until smooth. Gradually blend in confectioners' sugar and vanilla. (If necessary, chill about 1 hour or until mixture is firm enough to handle.) Shape into 1-inch balls; place on wax paper-covered tray or cookie sheet. Cover loosely; chill 3 to 4 hours or overnight. Centers should feel dry to touch before coating. Coat centers as directed (pages 68–69).

About 5 dozen centers

VARIATIONS
Chocolate Buttercream Centers: Blend 1/3 cup HERSHEY'S Cocoa with confectioners' sugar and vanilla into mixture. Add 1 to 2 teaspoons milk until mixture holds together.

Flavored Buttercream Centers: Divide buttercream mixture into three parts. Add any one of the following to each part:
1/2 teaspoon almond extract
1/2 teaspoon brandy extract
2/3 cup flaked coconut
1/4 teaspoon mint extract plus
    3 drops green food color

1/4 teaspoon orange extract
1/4 teaspoon rum extract
1/2 teaspoon strawberry extract
    plus 3 drops red food
    color

Easy Cherry Cordial Centers

¹/₄ cup butter or margarine,
  softened
2¹/₄ cups confectioners' sugar
1 tablespoon milk
¹/₂ teaspoon vanilla
¹/₈ teaspoon almond extract
  About 48 maraschino cherries
  with stems, drained

Cover cookie sheet or tray with wax paper; set aside. Thoroughly cream butter with confectioners' sugar and milk in small mixer bowl; blend in vanilla and almond extract. (If mixture is too soft, add extra confectioners' sugar.) Mold just enough mixture around each cherry to completely cover cherry. Place on prepared cookie sheet. Cover loosely; chill 3 to 4 hours or overnight.

Remove a third of the centers from refrigerator just before dipping; keep remaining centers chilled. Coat centers as directed (pages 68–69). Store coated cordials, uncovered, at room temperature for about 1 week or until centers liquefy.

About 4 dozen centers

Chocolate Centers

¹/₃ cup butter or margarine,
  softened
¹/₄ cup heavy or whipping cream
1¹/₂ teaspoons vanilla
3 cups confectioners' sugar
¹/₂ cup HERSHEY'S Semi-Sweet
  Chocolate Chips, melted

Combine butter, cream, vanilla and 1 cup of the confectioners' sugar in small mixer bowl; beat until smooth. Gradually blend in remaining 2 cups confectioners' sugar and the melted chocolate. Chill about 1 hour or until mixture is firm enough to handle.

Shape into 1-inch balls; place on wax paper-covered tray or cookie sheet. Cover loosely; chill 3 to 4 hours or overnight. Centers should feel dry to touch before coating. Coat centers as directed (pages 68–69).

About 5 dozen centers

Chocolate Truffles

¹/₂ cup unsalted butter, softened
2¹/₂ cups confectioners' sugar
¹/₂ cup HERSHEY'S Cocoa
¹/₄ cup heavy or whipping cream
1¹/₂ teaspoons vanilla
  Centers: Pecan or walnut
    halves, whole almonds,
    candied cherries, after-
    dinner mints
  Coatings: Confectioners'
    sugar, flaked coconut,
    chopped nuts

Cream butter in large mixer bowl. Combine 2¹/₂ cups confectioners' sugar and the cocoa; add alternately with cream and vanilla to butter. Blend well. Chill until firm. Shape small amount of mixture around desired center; roll into 1-inch balls. Drop into desired coating and turn until well covered. Chill until firm.

About 3 dozen truffles

VARIATION
Chocolate Rum Truffles: Decrease vanilla to 1 teaspoon and add ¹/₂ teaspoon rum extract.

Cocoa Divinity

3 tablespoons shortening
1/2 cup HERSHEY'S Cocoa
2 1/2 cups sugar
1/4 teaspoon salt
1/2 cup light corn syrup
1/3 cup water
2 egg whites, at room temperature
1 teaspoon vanilla
3/4 cup chopped walnuts (optional)

Melt shortening in top of double boiler over hot, not boiling, water; add cocoa and stir until smooth. Set aside over warm water. Combine sugar, salt, corn syrup and water in heavy 2-quart saucepan. Cook over medium heat, stirring constantly, until sugar dissolves and mixture boils. Continue to boil without stirring. When syrup reaches 246°F on a candy thermometer, start beating egg whites in large mixer bowl until stiff peaks form. (Bulb of candy thermometer should not rest on bottom of saucepan.)

Continue cooking syrup mixture, without stirring, to hard-ball stage, 260°F (or until syrup, when dropped into very cold water, forms a firm ball that is hard enough to hold its shape, yet plastic). Immediately pour hot syrup in thin stream over beaten egg whites, beating constantly on high speed. Add vanilla; beat until candy starts to become firm. Quickly blend in reserved cocoa mixture with wooden spoon. Stir in nuts. Drop by teaspoonfuls onto wax paper-covered cookie sheet; cool. Store in airtight container.

About 3 1/2 dozen candies

Butter Almond Crunch

1 1/2 cups HERSHEY'S MINI CHIPS Semi-Sweet Chocolate
1 3/4 cups chopped almonds
1 1/2 cups butter or margarine
1 3/4 cups sugar
3 tablespoons light corn syrup
3 tablespoons water

Spread 1 cup of the MINI CHIPS Chocolates in buttered 13×9-inch pan; set aside. Spread almonds in shallow pan; toast at 350° for about 7 minutes or until golden brown. Set aside.

Melt butter in heavy 3-quart saucepan; blend in sugar, corn syrup and water. Cook over medium heat, stirring constantly, to hard-crack stage, 300°F on a candy thermometer (or until syrup, when dropped into very cold water, separates into threads that are hard and brittle). Bulb of candy thermometer should not rest on bottom of saucepan. Remove saucepan from heat; stir in 1 1/2 cups of the toasted almonds.

Immediately spread mixture evenly over MINI CHIPS Chocolates in prepared pan, being careful not to disturb chips. Sprinkle with remaining 1/4 cup toasted almonds and 1/2 cup MINI CHIPS Chocolates; score into 1 1/2-inch squares. Cool completely; remove from pan. Break into pieces. Store in tightly covered container.

About 2 pounds candy

Top: Chocolate Chip Nougat Log (see page 74). Bottom: Butter Almond Crunch. Center: Assortment includes Cocoa Divinity and Creamy Cocoa Taffy (see page 74)

Chocolate Chip Nougat Log ∽∽∽∽∽∽∽∽∽∽∽∽∽∽∽∽∽

1 cup sugar
²/₃ cup light corn syrup
2 tablespoons water
¹/₄ cup egg whites (about 2), at
    room temperature
2 cups sugar
1¹/₄ cups light corn syrup
¹/₄ cup butter or margarine,
    melted
2 teaspoons vanilla
2 cups chopped walnuts
4 or 5 drops red food color
    (optional)
1 cup HERSHEY'S MINI
    CHIPS Semi-Sweet
    Chocolate

Line 15¹/₂×10¹/₂×1-inch jelly roll pan with aluminum foil; butter foil. Set aside. Combine 1 cup sugar, ²/₃ cup corn syrup and the water in small heavy saucepan. Cook over medium heat, stirring constantly, until sugar dissolves. Continue cooking without stirring. When syrup reaches 230°F on a candy thermometer, start beating egg whites in large mixer bowl; beat until stiff, but not dry. (Bulb of candy thermometer should not rest on bottom of saucepan.)

When syrup reaches soft-ball stage, 238°F (or until syrup, when dropped into very cold water, forms a soft ball that flattens when removed from water), remove from heat. Pour hot syrup in thin stream over beaten egg whites, beating constantly on high speed. Continue beating 4 to 5 minutes or until mixture becomes very thick. Cover and set aside.

Combine 2 cups sugar and 1¹/₄ cups corn syrup in heavy 2-quart saucepan. Cook over medium heat, stirring constantly, until sugar dissolves. Cook, without stirring, to soft-crack stage, 275°F (or until syrup, when dropped into very cold water, separates into threads that are hard but not brittle).

Pour hot syrup all at once over reserved egg white mixture in bowl; blend with wooden spoon. Stir in melted butter and vanilla; add nuts and mix thoroughly. Add food color. Pour into prepared pan. Sprinkle evenly with MINI CHIPS Chocolates. Let cool overnight.

To form logs, invert pan and remove foil. Cut in half crosswise; roll from cut end, jelly-roll style. Cut into ¹/₄-inch slices. Store, well covered, in cool, dry place.

About 7 dozen candies

Note: If desired, nougat can be cut into 1-inch squares rather than rolled.

Creamy Cocoa Taffy ∽∽∽∽∽∽∽∽∽∽∽∽∽∽∽∽∽

1¹/₄ cups sugar
³/₄ cup light corn syrup
¹/₃ cup HERSHEY'S Cocoa
¹/₈ teaspoon salt
2 teaspoons white vinegar
¹/₄ cup evaporated milk
1 tablespoon butter or
    margarine

Butter 9-inch square pan; set aside. Combine sugar, corn syrup, cocoa, salt and vinegar in heavy 2-quart saucepan. Cook over medium heat, stirring constantly, until mixture boils; add evaporated milk and butter. Continue to cook, stirring occasionally, to firm-ball stage, 248°F on a candy thermometer (or until syrup, when dropped into very cold water, forms a firm ball that does not flatten when removed from water). Bulb of candy thermometer should not rest on bottom of saucepan.

Pour mixture into prepared pan. Let stand until taffy is cool enough to handle. Butter hands; stretch taffy, folding and pulling until light in color and hard to pull. Place taffy on table; pull into ¹/₂-inch-wide strips (twist two strips together, if desired). Cut into 1-inch pieces with buttered scissors. Wrap individually in plastic wrap.

About 1¹/₄ pounds candy

Breads & Coffeecakes

Chocolate Streusel Coffeecake

Chocolate Streusel
1/2 cup butter or margarine, softened
1 cup sugar
3 eggs
1 cup sour cream
1 teaspoon vanilla
2 cups unsifted all-purpose flour
1 teaspoon baking powder
1 teaspoon baking soda
1/4 teaspoon salt

Prepare Chocolate Streusel; set aside. Cream butter and sugar in large mixer bowl until light and fluffy. Add eggs; blend well on low speed. Stir in sour cream and vanilla. Combine flour, baking powder, baking soda and salt; add to batter. Blend well.

Sprinkle 1 cup of the Chocolate Streusel into greased and floured 12-cup Bundt pan. Spread one-third of the batter (about 1 1/3 cups) in pan; sprinkle with half the remaining streusel (about 1 cup). Repeat layers, ending with batter on top. Bake at 350° for 50 to 55 minutes or until cake tester comes out clean. Cool 10 minutes; invert onto serving plate. Cool completely.

12 to 16 servings

CHOCOLATE STREUSEL

3/4 cup packed light brown sugar
1/4 cup unsifted all-purpose flour
1/4 cup butter or margarine, softened
3/4 cup chopped nuts
3/4 cup HERSHEY'S MINI CHIPS Semi-Sweet Chocolate

Combine brown sugar, flour and butter in medium bowl until crumbly. Stir in nuts and MINI CHIPS Chocolates.

*Clockwise from top: Chocolate Chip Muffins, Chocolate Tea Bread
and Chocolate Chip Banana Bread*

Chocolate Chip Muffins

1½ cups unsifted all-purpose
    flour
½ cup sugar
2 teaspoons baking powder
½ teaspoon salt
½ cup milk
¼ cup vegetable oil
1 egg, beaten
½ cup HERSHEY'S MINI
    CHIPS Semi-Sweet
    Chocolate
½ cup chopped nuts
¼ cup chopped maraschino
    cherries, well drained
2 teaspoons grated orange peel

Combine flour, sugar, baking powder and salt in medium bowl. Add milk, oil and egg; stir just until blended. Stir in MINI CHIPS Chocolates, nuts, cherries and orange peel.

Fill greased or paper-lined muffin cups (2½ inches in diameter) two-thirds full with batter. Bake at 400° for 25 to 30 minutes or until golden brown. Remove from pan; cool completely.

About 12 muffins

Chocolate Tea Bread

¼ cup butter or margarine,
    softened
⅔ cup sugar
1 egg
1½ cups unsifted all-purpose
    flour
⅓ cup HERSHEY'S Cocoa
1 teaspoon baking soda
¼ teaspoon salt
1 cup buttermilk or sour milk*
¾ cup chopped walnuts
¾ cup raisins (optional)

Cream butter, sugar and egg in large mixer bowl until light and fluffy. Combine flour, cocoa, baking soda and salt; add alternately with buttermilk to creamed mixture. Beat on low speed just until blended; stir in nuts and raisins.

Pour into greased 8½×4½×2½-inch loaf pan. Bake at 350° for 55 to 60 minutes or until cake tester comes out clean. Remove from pan; cool completely on wire rack.

1 loaf

*To sour milk: Use 1 tablespoon vinegar plus milk to equal 1 cup.

Chocolate Chip Banana Bread

2 cups unsifted all-purpose
    flour
1 cup sugar
1 teaspoon baking powder
1 teaspoon salt
½ teaspoon baking soda
1 cup mashed ripe bananas
    (about 3 small)
½ cup shortening
2 eggs
1 cup HERSHEY'S MINI
    CHIPS Semi-Sweet
    Chocolate
½ cup chopped walnuts

Grease bottom only of 9×5×3-inch loaf pan; set aside. Combine all ingredients except MINI CHIPS Chocolates and walnuts in large mixer bowl; blend well on medium speed. Stir in MINI CHIPS Chocolates and walnuts.

Pour into prepared pan. Bake at 350° for 60 to 70 minutes or until cake tester comes out clean. Cool 10 minutes; remove from pan. Cool completely on wire rack.

1 loaf

Cocoa Brunch Rings ∞∞∞∞∞∞∞∞∞∞∞∞∞∞∞∞∞∞∞∞∞∞

1/2 cup milk
1/2 cup sugar
1 teaspoon salt
1/2 cup butter or margarine
2 packages active dry yeast
1/2 cup warm water
2 eggs, slightly beaten
3 1/2 to 3 3/4 cups unsifted
    all-purpose flour
3/4 cup HERSHEY'S Cocoa
    Orange Filling

Scald milk in small saucepan; stir in sugar, salt and butter. Set aside; cool to lukewarm. Dissolve yeast in warm water (105° to 115°F) in large mixer bowl; add milk mixture, eggs and 2 cups of the flour. Beat 2 minutes on medium speed until smooth. Combine 1 1/2 cups of the flour and the cocoa; stir into yeast mixture.

Turn dough out onto well-floured board; knead in more flour until dough is smooth enough to handle. Knead about 5 minutes or until smooth and elastic. Place in greased bowl; turn to grease top. Cover; let rise in warm place until doubled, about 1 to 1 1/2 hours. Punch down dough; turn over. Cover; let rise 30 minutes longer.

Prepare Orange Filling; set aside. Divide dough in half. On lightly floured board, roll out each half to a 13×9-inch rectangle. Spread one-fourth of the Orange Filling on each rectangle to within 1/2 inch of edges; reserve remaining filling for frosting. Roll up dough from long side as for jelly roll; pinch edge to seal. Cut rolls into 1-inch slices. Place slices, sealed edges down, in two greased 4- to 6-cup ring molds. Tilt slices slightly, overlapping so filling shows. Cover; let rise in warm place until doubled, about 45 minutes. Bake at 350° for 20 to 25 minutes or until filling is lightly browned. Immediately remove from molds and place on serving plates. Frost with remaining Orange Filling or, if a glaze is preferred, stir in a few drops orange juice until of desired consistency; spoon over rings. Serve warm.

2 rings

ORANGE FILLING

3 cups confectioners' sugar
6 tablespoons butter or
    margarine, softened
1/4 cup orange juice
4 teaspoons grated orange peel

Combine confectioners' sugar, butter, orange juice and orange peel in small mixer bowl; beat on low speed until smooth.

Chocolate Waffles ∞∞∞∞∞∞∞∞∞∞∞∞∞∞∞∞∞∞∞∞∞∞

1 cup unsifted all-purpose flour
3/4 cup sugar
1/2 cup HERSHEY'S Cocoa
1/2 teaspoon baking powder
1/2 teaspoon baking soda
1/4 teaspoon salt
1 cup buttermilk or sour milk*
2 eggs
1/4 cup butter or margarine,
    melted

Combine flour, sugar, cocoa, baking powder, baking soda and salt in medium bowl. Add buttermilk and eggs; beat with wooden spoon just until blended. Gradually add melted butter, beating until smooth. Bake in waffle iron according to manufacturer's directions. Serve warm with pancake syrup or, for dessert, with ice cream, fruit-flavored syrups and sweetened whipped cream.

10 to 12 four-inch waffles

*To sour milk: Use 1 tablespoon vinegar plus milk to equal 1 cup.

Top: Cocoa Brunch Ring
Bottom: Chocolate-Filled Braid (see page 80)

Chocolate-Filled Braid

Chocolate Filling
2½ to 2¾ cups unsifted
 all-purpose flour
2 tablespoons sugar
½ teaspoon salt
1 package active dry yeast
½ cup milk
¼ cup water
½ cup butter or margarine
1 egg, at room temperature
 Melted butter (optional)
 Confectioners' Sugar Glaze
 (optional)

Prepare Chocolate Filling; set aside. Combine 1 cup of the flour, the sugar, salt and yeast in large mixer bowl; set aside. Combine milk, water and ½ cup butter in small saucepan; cook over low heat until liquids are very warm (120° to 130°F)—butter does not need to melt. Gradually add to dry ingredients; beat 2 minutes on medium speed. Add egg and ½ cup of the flour; beat 2 minutes on high speed. Stir in enough additional flour to make a stiff dough. Cover; allow to rest 20 minutes.

Turn dough out onto well-floured board; roll into 18×10-inch rectangle. Spread Chocolate Filling lengthwise down center third of dough. Cut 1-inch-wide strips diagonally along both sides of filling to within ¾ inch of filling. Alternately fold opposite strips of dough at an angle across filling. Carefully transfer to greased cookie sheet. Shape into ring, stretching slightly; pinch ends together. Cover loosely with wax paper brushed with vegetable oil; top with plastic wrap. Chill at least 2 hours or overnight.

Remove braid from refrigerator just before baking. Uncover dough; let stand at room temperature 10 minutes. Bake at 375° for 30 to 35 minutes or until lightly browned. Remove from cookie sheet; cool completely on wire rack. Brush with melted butter or drizzle with Confectioners' Sugar Glaze.

10 to 12 servings

CHOCOLATE FILLING

¾ cup HERSHEY'S Semi-Sweet
 Chocolate Chips
2 tablespoons sugar
⅓ cup evaporated milk
½ cup finely chopped nuts
1 teaspoon vanilla
¼ teaspoon cinnamon

Combine chocolate chips, sugar and evaporated milk in small saucepan. Cook over low heat, stirring constantly, until chips melt and mixture is smooth. Stir in nuts, vanilla and cinnamon. Cool.

CONFECTIONERS' SUGAR GLAZE

1 cup confectioners' sugar
1 tablespoon butter or
 margarine, softened
½ teaspoon vanilla
1 to 2 tablespoons milk

Beat confectioners' sugar, butter, vanilla and milk in small mixer bowl until glaze is smooth and of desired consistency.

Chocolate Chip Pancakes

2 cups buttermilk baking mix
1 cup milk
2 eggs
½ cup HERSHEY'S MINI
 CHIPS Semi-Sweet
 Chocolate

Combine buttermilk baking mix, milk and eggs in medium bowl; beat with wooden spoon until smooth. Stir in MINI CHIPS Chocolates. For each pancake, pour 2 tablespoons batter onto hot, lightly greased griddle; cook until bubbles appear. Turn; cook other side until lightly browned. (For thinner pancakes, add 1 tablespoon milk to batter; pancakes should be at least ¼ inch thick.) Serve warm with butter or margarine; sprinkle with confectioners' sugar or top with syrup.

About 18 pancakes

Microwave Specialties

Cocoa Applesauce Muffins

Crunch Topping
1/4 cup HERSHEY'S Cocoa
1/4 cup vegetable oil
3/4 cup applesauce
1 egg, beaten
1 1/4 cups unsifted all-purpose
   flour
3/4 cup sugar
3/4 teaspoon baking soda
1/4 teaspoon salt
1/4 teaspoon cinnamon
1/2 cup chopped nuts

Prepare Crunch Topping; set aside. Combine cocoa and oil in small bowl; stir until smooth. Add applesauce and egg; blend well. Combine flour, sugar, baking soda, salt and cinnamon in medium bowl; stir in applesauce mixture and nuts just until dry ingredients are moistened.

Place 6 paper muffin cups (2 1/2 inches in diameter) in microwave cupcake or muffin maker or in 6-ounce micro-proof custard cups. Fill each cup half full with batter. Sprinkle about 2 teaspoons Crunch Topping on top of each muffin. Microwave at HIGH (100%) for 2 1/2 to 3 1/2 minutes, turning 1/4 turn at end of each minute, or until cake tester comes out clean. (Tops may still appear moist.) Let stand several minutes. (Moist spots will disappear upon standing.) Repeat cooking procedure with remaining batter. Serve warm.

12 to 14 muffins

CRUNCH TOPPING

1 tablespoon butter or
   margarine
2 tablespoons HERSHEY'S
   Cocoa
1/4 cup packed light brown sugar
1/4 cup chopped nuts
2 tablespoons flour
1/4 teaspoon cinnamon

Microwave butter in small micro-proof bowl at HIGH (100%) for 15 seconds or until melted; add cocoa and blend until smooth. Stir in brown sugar, nuts, flour and cinnamon.

Top: Chocolate Chip Bran Muffins
Bottom: Cocoa Applesauce Muffins (see page 81)

Chocolate Chip Bran Muffins

1¹/₂ cups bran flakes cereal
¹/₂ cup boiling water
 1 cup buttermilk or sour milk*
¹/₄ cup vegetable oil
 1 egg, slightly beaten
1¹/₄ cups unsifted all-purpose
   flour
¹/₂ cup sugar
 1 teaspoon baking soda
¹/₄ teaspoon salt
¹/₂ cup HERSHEY'S MINI
   CHIPS Semi-Sweet
   Chocolate
¹/₄ cup finely chopped dried
   apricots
   Bran flakes cereal

Combine 1¹/₂ cups bran flakes cereal and boiling water in medium bowl; blend well. Cool. Add buttermilk, oil and egg; blend well. Combine flour, sugar, baking soda and salt in medium bowl; stir in cereal mixture, MINI CHIPS Chocolates and apricots just until dry ingredients are moistened.

Place 6 paper muffin cups (2¹/₂ inches in diameter) in microwave cupcake or muffin maker or in 6-ounce micro-proof custard cups. Fill each cup half full with batter. Sprinkle 2 teaspoons bran flakes cereal on top of each muffin. Microwave at HIGH (100%) for 2¹/₂ to 3¹/₂ minutes, turning ¹/₄ turn at end of each minute, or until cake tester comes out clean. (Tops may still appear moist.) Let stand several minutes. (Moist spots will disappear upon standing.) Repeat cooking procedure with remaining batter. Serve warm.

About 1¹/₂ dozen muffins

*To sour milk: Use 1 tablespoon vinegar plus milk to equal 1 cup.

Easiest-Ever Cocoa Fudge

3²/₃ cups (1-pound package)
   confectioners' sugar, sifted
¹/₂ cup HERSHEY'S Cocoa
¹/₂ cup butter or margarine, cut
   into pieces
¹/₄ cup milk
¹/₂ cup chopped nuts (optional)
 1 tablespoon vanilla

Combine confectioners' sugar, cocoa, butter and milk in medium micro-proof bowl. Microwave at HIGH (100%) for 2 to 3 minutes or until butter is melted. Stir until mixture is smooth. Stir in nuts and vanilla; blend well. Spread evenly in buttered 8-inch square pan; cool. Cut into 1-inch squares.

About 5 dozen candies

Microwave Hot Cocoa

5 tablespoons sugar
3 tablespoons HERSHEY'S
    Cocoa
Dash salt
3 tablespoons hot water
2 cups milk
1/4 teaspoon vanilla

Combine sugar, cocoa, salt and hot water in 1-quart micro-proof measuring cup. Microwave at HIGH (100%) for 1 to 1½ minutes or until boiling. Add milk; stir and microwave an additional 1½ to 2 minutes or until hot. Stir in vanilla; blend well.

4 servings

One serving: Place 2 heaping teaspoons sugar, 1 heaping teaspoon HERSHEY'S Cocoa and dash salt in micro-proof cup. Add 2 teaspoons cold milk; stir until smooth. Fill cup with milk; microwave at HIGH (100%) for 1 to 1½ minutes or until hot. Stir to blend.

Peanutty Chocolate Snack Squares

5 graham crackers, broken into
    squares
1/2 cup sugar
1 cup light corn syrup
1 cup HERSHEY'S Semi-Sweet
    Chocolate Chips
1 cup peanut butter
1 cup dry roasted peanuts

Line bottom of 8-inch square pan with graham cracker squares, cutting to fit as necessary. Combine sugar and corn syrup in 2-quart micro-proof bowl. Microwave at HIGH (100%), stirring every 2 minutes, until mixture boils; boil 3 minutes. Stir in chocolate chips, peanut butter and peanuts. Pour over crackers; spread carefully. Cover; refrigerate until firm. Cut into 2-inch squares.

16 squares

Pear Slices au Chocolat

1 cup HERSHEY'S Semi-Sweet
    Chocolate Chips
1 teaspoon shortening
2 large fresh pears
1 maraschino cherry, drained

In small micro-proof bowl, place chocolate chips and shortening. Microwave at HIGH (100%) for 1 to 1½ minutes or just until chips are melted and smooth when stirred. Wash pears; pat dry. Slice each pear vertically into 8 slices; core slices. Dip 2/3 of each slice into chocolate mixture; place on wax-paper-covered tray. Refrigerate about 30 minutes. Arrange on serving platter in flower-like spiral design, with maraschino cherry as center.

About 16 slices

A Note About Microwave Ovens

Because microwave ovens vary in wattage and power output, cooking times given for microwave recipes may need to be adjusted. It is best to rely on the desired result ("until mixture boils," for example) as well as the recommended cooking time to determine doneness. Results were found to be most consistent if food was stirred or rotated several times during microwave cooking, even if cooked in a turntable-type microwave oven. All recipes were tested in several different brands/models of microwave ovens.

Microwave Hershey Bar Pie

Chocolate Crumb Crust or
Graham Cracker Crust
(page 45)
1 HERSHEY'S Milk Chocolate
Bar (7 ounces), broken into
pieces
1/3 cup milk
1 1/2 cups miniature marshmallows
1 cup heavy or whipping cream
Sweetened whipped cream

Bake crumb crust; set aside. Combine chocolate bar pieces, milk and miniature marshmallows in medium micro-proof bowl. Microwave at HIGH (100%) for 1 1/2 to 2 1/2 minutes or until chocolate is softened and mixture is melted and smooth when stirred. Cool completely.

Whip cream until stiff; fold into chocolate mixture. Spoon into crust. Cover; chill several hours or until firm. Garnish with sweetened whipped cream. Serve with cherry pie filling, if desired.

8 servings

CHOCOLATE CRUMB CRUST

1/2 cup butter or margarine
1 1/2 cups graham cracker crumbs
6 tablespoons HERSHEY'S
Cocoa
1/3 cup confectioners' sugar

Grease micro-proof 9-inch pie plate. In small micro-proof bowl, microwave butter at HIGH (100%) for 1 minute or until melted. Stir in graham cracker crumbs, cocoa and confectioners' sugar until well blended. Press on bottom and up side of prepared pie plate. Microwave an additional 1 to 1 1/2 minutes until bubbly. (Do not overcook.) Cool completely before filling.

Creamy Chocolate Tarts

2/3 cup HERSHEY'S Semi-Sweet
Chocolate Chips
1/4 cup milk
1 tablespoon sugar
1/2 teaspoon vanilla extract
1/2 cup chilled whipping cream
6 (4-ounce package) single-serve
graham crusts
Cherry pie filling, chilled
(optional)
Sweetened whipped cream or
whipped topping (optional)

In small micro-proof bowl place chocolate chips, milk and sugar; microwave at HIGH (100%) for 1 minute or until milk is hot and chips are melted when stirred. With wire whisk or rotary beater beat until mixture is smooth; stir in vanilla. Cool to room temperature. In cold small mixer bowl beat whipping cream until stiff; carefully fold chocolate mixture into whipped cream until blended. Spoon into crusts. Cover; refrigerate until set. Garnish as desired or top with cherry pie filling and sweetened whipped cream.

6 servings

Easy Hot Fudge Sauce

1/2 cup HERSHEY'S Cocoa
1 1/3 cups (14-ounce can) sweetened
condensed milk*
3 tablespoons milk
1 tablespoon butter or
margarine
1 teaspoon vanilla

Combine cocoa, sweetened condensed milk and milk in medium micro-proof bowl. Microwave at HIGH (100%) for 1 minute; stir. Microwave an additional 1 to 1 1/2 minutes, stirring occasionally with wire whisk, or until mixture is smooth and hot. Stir in butter and vanilla. Serve warm.

About 1 1/2 cups sauce

*Do not use evaporated milk.

Fudgey Microwave Brownies

½ cup vegetable oil
1¼ cups granulated sugar
2 eggs
2 tablespoons light corn syrup
2 teaspoons vanilla extract
1 cup all-purpose flour
½ cup HERSHEY'S Cocoa
¼ teaspoon baking powder
¼ teaspoon salt
   Confectioners' sugar
   (optional)

Grease 8-inch square micro-proof pan. In large bowl combine oil, granulated sugar, eggs, corn syrup and vanilla. Combine flour, cocoa, baking powder and salt; add to egg mixture, beating until smooth. Pour batter into prepared pan. Microwave at MEDIUM-HIGH (70%) for 3 minutes. Rotate ½ turn; microwave at MEDIUM-HIGH additional 3 minutes. Check for doneness: Brownies begin to pull away from sides of pan and surface has no wet spots. (If brownies are not done, rotate ¼ turn; continue to microwave at MEDIUM-HIGH, checking every 30 seconds for doneness. *Do not overcook*.) Place on heatproof surface; allow to stand 20 minutes. Sprinkle confectioners' sugar over top, if desired. Cut into squares.

16 brownies

Microwave S'Mores

4 graham crackers
1 bar (1.55 ounces) HERSHEY'S Milk Chocolate Bar
4 large marshmallows

Break graham crackers in half. Break chocolate bar into 4 sections. Center one section on each of 4 graham cracker halves. Top each with marshmallow. Place on paper towel. Microwave at HIGH (100%) for 10 to 15 seconds or until marshmallow puffs. Top each with another graham cracker half; press gently. Let stand 1 minute to soften chocolate. Serve immediately.

4 snacks

VARIATION
Peanutty S'Mores: Spread thin layer of peanut butter on graham cracker or substitute 1.75-ounce bar MR. GOODBAR Chocolate Bar for milk chocolate bar. Proceed as directed.

Individual Cocoa Cheesecakes

⅓ cup graham cracker crumbs
⅓ cup plus 1 tablespoon sugar, divided
1 tablespoon butter or margarine, melted
1 package (8 ounces) cream cheese, softened
3 tablespoons HERSHEY'S Cocoa
1 teaspoon vanilla extract
1 tablespoon milk
1 egg

In small bowl combine graham cracker crumbs, 1 tablespoon sugar and butter. Press about 1 tablespoon crumb mixture onto bottom of 6 micro-proof ramekins (2½ to 3 inches in diameter). In small mixer bowl beat cream cheese, remaining ⅓ cup sugar, cocoa and vanilla. Add milk and egg, beating just until smooth and well blended. Divide cream cheese mixture evenly among ramekins, filling each to ¼ inch from top. Microwave at MEDIUM-HIGH (70%) for 2 minutes, rotating dishes after 1 minute. Microwave at HIGH (100%) for 30 to 40 seconds or until puffed in center. Cool; chill before serving. Garnish as desired.

6 cheesecakes

Note: Substitute paper-lined microwave-safe muffin cups (2½ inches in diameter) for ramekins, if desired.

Microwave Classic Chocolate Sauce

2 bars (2 ounces) HERSHEY'S
    Unsweetened Baking
    Chocolate
2 tablespoons butter or
    margarine
1 cup sugar
1/4 teaspoon salt
3/4 cup evaporated milk
1/2 teaspoon vanilla

Place baking chocolate and butter in small micro-proof bowl. Microwave at HIGH (100%) for 1 minute or until chocolate is softened and mixture is melted and smooth when stirred. Add sugar, salt and evaporated milk; blend well. Microwave an additional 2 to 3 minutes, stirring with wire whisk after each minute, or until mixture is smooth and hot. Stir in vanilla. Serve warm.

About 1 1/2 cups sauce

Easy Rocky Road

2 cups (12-ounce package)
    HERSHEY'S Semi-Sweet
    Chocolate Chips
1/4 cup butter or margarine
2 tablespoons shortening
6 cups (10 1/2-ounce bag)
    miniature marshmallows
1/2 cup chopped nuts

Place chocolate chips, butter and shortening in large micro-proof bowl. Microwave at MEDIUM (50%) for 5 to 7 minutes or until chips are softened and mixture is melted and smooth when stirred. Add marshmallows and nuts; blend well. Spread evenly in buttered 8-inch square pan. Cover; chill until firm. Cut into 2-inch squares.

16 squares

Melting Chocolate in a Microwave Oven

It's neat, easy and quicker than quick. Note that in the microwave oven, chocolate squares and chips will keep their shape even when they are softened. Stir to determine whether chocolate is fluid and melted. For best results, follow these procedures.

Unsweetened Baking Chocolate and Semi-Sweet Baking Chocolate: Unwrap, break bars in half and place desired amount in micro-proof measuring cup or bowl. Microwave at HIGH (100%) for half the minimum time listed below; stir. Continue to microwave until chocolate is softened; stir. Allow to stand several minutes to finish melting; stir again. (If unmelted chocolate still remains, return to microwave for an additional 30 seconds; stir until fluid.)

1 bar (1 ounce)	1 to 1 1/2 minutes
2 bars (2 ounces)	1 1/2 to 2 minutes
3 bars (3 ounces)	2 to 2 1/2 minutes
4 bars (4 ounces)	2 1/2 to 3 minutes

Chips (Semi-Sweet, Milk, MINI CHIPS Chocolates or Peanut Butter): Place 1 cup (about 6 ounces) chips in 2-cup micro-proof measuring cup or bowl. Microwave at HIGH (100%) for 1 to 1 1/2 minutes or until softened; stir. Allow to stand for several minutes to finish melting; stir until smooth.

Clockwise from top: Easy Rocky Road, Fast Chocolate-Pecan Fudge and Chocolate Crackles

Chocolate Crackles

10 tablespoons butter or
      margarine
 6 tablespoons HERSHEY'S
      Cocoa
 1 cup sugar
 2 teaspoons baking powder
¹/₂ teaspoon salt
 2 eggs
 1 teaspoon vanilla
 2 cups unsifted all-purpose
      flour
¹/₂ cup chopped nuts
      Confectioners' sugar

Microwave butter in medium micro-proof bowl at HIGH (100%) for 45 to 60 seconds or until melted. Add cocoa; blend well. Beat in sugar, baking powder, salt, eggs and vanilla. Stir in flour and nuts. Refrigerate at least 8 hours or until firm.

Shape dough into 1-inch balls; roll in confectioners' sugar. Cover micro-proof plate with wax paper. Place 8 balls 2 inches apart in circular shape on wax paper. Microwave at MEDIUM (50%) for 1¹/₂ to 2 minutes or until surface is dry but cookies are soft when touched. Cool on wax paper on countertop. Repeat cooking procedure with remaining dough. Before serving, sprinkle with additional confectioners' sugar.

About 4 dozen cookies

Fast Chocolate-Pecan Fudge

¹/₂ cup butter or margarine
³/₄ cup HERSHEY'S Cocoa
 4 cups confectioners' sugar
 1 teaspoon vanilla
¹/₂ cup evaporated milk
 1 cup pecan pieces
      Pecan halves (optional)

Microwave butter in 2-quart micro-proof bowl at HIGH (100%) for 1 to 1¹/₂ minutes or until melted. Add cocoa; stir until smooth. Stir in confectioners' sugar and vanilla; blend well (mixture will be dry and crumbly). Stir in evaporated milk. Microwave at HIGH (100%) for 1 minute; stir. Microwave an additional 1 minute or until mixture is hot. Stir mixture until smooth; add pecans. Pour into aluminum-foil-lined 8- or 9-inch square pan. Garnish with pecan halves. Cover; chill until firm, about 2 hours. Cut into 1-inch squares. Store, covered, in refrigerator.

About 4 dozen candies

Sauces & Frostings

Chocolate-Coconut Frosting

⅓ cup sugar
1 tablespoon cornstarch
¾ cup evaporated milk
3 HERSHEY'S Milk Chocolate Bars (1.55 ounces each), broken into pieces
1 tablespoon butter or margarine
1 cup flaked coconut
½ cup chopped nuts

Combine sugar and cornstarch in small saucepan; blend in evaporated milk. Cook over medium heat, stirring constantly, until mixture boils; remove from heat. Add chocolate bar pieces and butter; stir until chocolate is melted and mixture is smooth. Stir in coconut and nuts. Immediately spread on cake.

About 2 cups frosting

Hershey® Icing

½ cup butter or margarine, softened
3⅔ cups (1-pound package) confectioners' sugar
½ cup (5.5-ounce can) HERSHEY'S Syrup
3 HERSHEY'S Milk Chocolate Bars (1.55 ounces each), broken into pieces
2 to 3 tablespoons milk

Cream butter and confectioners' sugar in small mixer bowl; blend in syrup. Melt chocolate bar pieces in top of double boiler over hot, not boiling, water; add to syrup mixture. Add milk; beat to spreading consistency.

About 2½ cups frosting

Royal Glaze

8 bars (8 ounces) HERSHEY'S
   Semi-Sweet Baking
   Chocolate, broken into
   pieces*
1/2 cup heavy or whipping cream

Combine chocolate and cream in small saucepan. Cook over very low heat, stirring constantly, until chocolate is melted and mixture is smooth; *do not boil.* Remove from heat; cool, stirring occasionally, until mixture begins to thicken, about 10 to 15 minutes.

About 1 cup

*You may substitute 1 1/3 cups HERSHEY'S Semi-Sweet Chocolate Chips for the baking chocolate.

Mt. Gretna Chocolate Fondue

4 bars (4 ounces) HERSHEY'S
   Unsweetened Baking
   Chocolate
1 cup light cream
1 cup sugar
1/4 cup creamy peanut butter
1 1/2 teaspoons vanilla
   Fondue Dippers

Combine chocolate and cream in medium saucepan. Cook over low heat, stirring constantly, until chocolate is melted and mixture is smooth. Add sugar and peanut butter; continue cooking until slightly thickened. Remove from heat; stir in vanilla. Pour into fondue pot or chafing dish; serve warm with Fondue Dippers.

About 2 cups fondue

FONDUE DIPPERS
In advance, prepare a selection of the following: marshmallows; angel food, sponge or pound cake pieces; strawberries; grapes; pineapple chunks; mandarin orange segments; cherries; fresh fruit slices. (Drain fruit well. Brush fresh fruit with lemon juice to prevent fruit from turning brown.)

Mt. Gretna Chocolate Fondue

Chocolate Nut Sauce

$^1/_3$ cup butter or margarine
$^2/_3$ cup coarsely chopped pecans
    or almonds
$1^1/_3$ cups sugar
$^1/_2$ cup HERSHEY'S Cocoa
$^1/_4$ teaspoon salt
1 cup light cream
$^3/_4$ teaspoon vanilla

Melt butter in medium saucepan over low heat; sauté chopped nuts in melted butter until lightly browned. Remove from heat; stir in sugar, cocoa and salt. Add cream; blend well. Cook over low heat, stirring constantly, until mixture just begins to boil. Remove from heat; add vanilla. Serve warm.

About 2 cups sauce

Chocolate-Peppermint Topping

1 cup frozen non-dairy whipped
    topping, thawed
3 tablespoons HERSHEY'S
    Syrup
4 drops peppermint extract

Combine whipped topping, syrup and peppermint extract in small bowl; blend well. A particularly good topping for angel food cake.

About 1 cup topping

Hot Fudge Sauce

$^3/_4$ cup sugar
$^1/_2$ cup HERSHEY'S Cocoa
$^2/_3$ cup evaporated milk
$^1/_3$ cup light corn syrup
$^1/_3$ cup butter or margarine
1 teaspoon vanilla

Combine sugar and cocoa in medium saucepan; blend in evaporated milk and corn syrup. Cook over low heat, stirring constantly, until mixture boils; boil and stir 1 minute. Remove from heat; stir in butter and vanilla. Serve warm.

About 2 cups sauce

Note: This sauce can be refrigerated for later use. Reheat in saucepan over very low heat, stirring constantly.

Quick Chocolate Frosting

4 bars (4 ounces) HERSHEY'S
    Unsweetened Baking
    Chocolate
$^1/_4$ cup butter or margarine
3 cups confectioners' sugar
1 teaspoon vanilla
$^1/_8$ teaspoon salt
$^1/_3$ cup milk

Melt baking chocolate and butter in small saucepan over very low heat, stirring constantly, until chocolate is melted and mixture is smooth. Pour into small mixer bowl; add confectioners' sugar, vanilla and salt. Blend in milk; beat to spreading consistency. (If frosting is too thick, add additional milk, 1 teaspoonful at a time, until frosting is desired consistency.)

About 2 cups frosting

Top right: Chocolate Nut Sauce
Center left: Chocolate-Peppermint Topping
Bottom: Hot Fudge Sauce

Chocolate Fudge Frosting

	1 cup frosting	2 cups frosting
Butter or margarine	3 tablespoons	¹/₃ cup
HERSHEY'S Cocoa		
For light flavor	2 tablespoons	3 tablespoons
For medium flavor	¹/₄ cup	¹/₃ cup
For dark flavor	¹/₂ cup	²/₃ cup
Confectioners' sugar	1¹/₃ cups	2²/₃ cups
Milk	2 to 3 tablespoons	¹/₃ cup
Vanilla	¹/₂ teaspoon	1 teaspoon

Melt butter in small saucepan over medium heat. Add amount of cocoa for flavor you prefer. Cook over medium heat, stirring constantly, until mixture just begins to boil. Remove from heat. Pour into small mixer bowl; cool completely. Add confectioners' sugar alternately with milk, beating to spreading consistency. Blend in vanilla.

Classic Chocolate Sauce

2 bars (2 ounces) HERSHEY'S
Unsweetened Baking
Chocolate
2 tablespoons butter or
margarine
1 cup sugar
¹/₄ teaspoon salt
³/₄ cup evaporated milk
¹/₂ teaspoon vanilla

Melt baking chocolate and butter in saucepan over very low heat, stirring occasionally, until chocolate is melted and mixture is smooth. Stir in sugar and salt. Add evaporated milk and blend well. Cook, stirring constantly, until mixture just begins to boil. Remove from heat; add vanilla. Serve warm.

About 2 cups sauce

Quick & Easy Chocolate Frosting

3 bars (3 ounces) HERSHEY'S
Unsweetened Baking
Chocolate
3 tablespoons butter or
margarine
3 cups confectioners' sugar
¹/₄ teaspoon salt
¹/₂ cup milk
1 teaspoon vanilla

Melt baking chocolate and butter in small saucepan over very low heat, stirring constantly, until chocolate is melted and mixture is smooth. Pour into small mixer bowl. Add confectioners' sugar, salt, milk and vanilla; beat until well blended. Chill 10 to 15 minutes or until spreading consistency.

About 2 cups frosting

Chocolate Buttercream Frosting

	1 cup frosting	2 cups frosting
Confectioners' sugar	1 cup	$2^2/_3$ cups
HERSHEY'S Cocoa		
For light flavor	2 tablespoons	$1/_4$ cup
For medium flavor	$1/_4$ cup	$1/_2$ cup
For dark flavor	$1/_3$ cup	$3/_4$ cup
Butter or margarine, softened	3 tablespoons	6 tablespoons
Milk	2 tablespoons	4 to 5 tablespoons
Vanilla	$1/_2$ teaspoon	1 teaspoon

In small bowl, combine confectioners' sugar with amount of cocoa for flavor you prefer. Cream butter and $1/_2$ cup cocoa mixture in small mixer bowl. Add remaining cocoa mixture, milk and vanilla; beat to spreading consistency. For a glossier texture, add 1 tablespoon light corn syrup to the mixture.

Sweetened Whipped Cream

1 cup heavy or whipping cream
1 to 2 tablespoons
    confectioners' sugar
$1/_2$ teaspoon vanilla

Beat cream, confectioners' sugar and vanilla in small mixer bowl until stiff peaks form.

About 2 cups topping

Chocolate Satin Glaze

2 tablespoons sugar
2 tablespoons water
$1/_2$ cup HERSHEY'S MINI
    CHIPS Semi-Sweet
    Chocolate

Combine sugar and water in small saucepan; cook over medium heat, stirring constantly, until mixture boils and sugar is dissolved. Remove from heat; immediately add MINI CHIPS Chocolates, stirring until melted. Continue stirring until glaze is desired consistency.

About $1/_2$ cup glaze

Chocolate Cream Cheese Frosting

3 packages (3 ounces each)
    cream cheese, softened
$1/_3$ cup butter or margarine,
    softened
5 cups confectioners' sugar
1 cup HERSHEY'S Cocoa
5 to 7 tablespoons light cream

Blend cream cheese and butter in large mixer bowl. Combine confectioners' sugar and cocoa; add alternately with cream to cream cheese mixture. Beat to spreading consistency.

About 3 cups frosting

Index

Chocolate

LOVER'S

Cookies & Brownies

Chocolate
L O V E R ' S
Cookies & Brownies

PUBLICATIONS INTERNATIONAL, LTD.

Recipe Development: Beatrice Ojakangas
Photography and Food Styling: Burke/Triolo Studio
Pewter tray on page 60 courtesy of Princess Table, Los Angeles.

Manufactured in the U.S.A.

h g f e d c b a

ISBN 0-88176-682-8

Library of Congress Catalog Card Number 90-60062

Pictured on front cover:

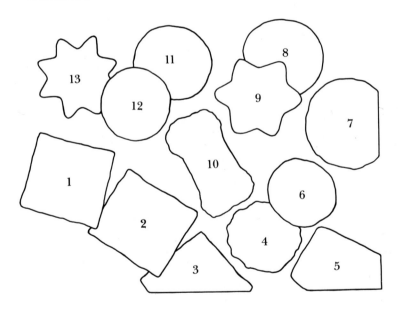

1 White Chocolate & Almond Brownies *(page 38)*
2 Pecan Caramel Brownies *(page 35)*
3 Chocolate-Mint Brownies *(page 53)*
4 Whole Grain Chippers *(page 69)*
5 Orange & Chocolate Ribbon Cookies *(page 77)*
6 Chocolate-Mint Sandwiches *(page 78)*
7 Peanutty Double Chip Cookies *(page 63)*
8 Mocha Pecan Pinwheels *(page 72)*
9 Cinnamon-Chocolate Cutouts *(page 79)*
10 Chocolate Pistachio Fingers *(page 84)*
11 Mrs. J's Chip Cookies *(page 63)*
12 Chocolate Cherry Cookies *(page 73)*
13 Chocolate Spritz *(page 88)*

Chocolate
L O V E R ' S
Cookies & Brownies

Chocolate Cookie Basics

One reason cookies and brownies have enjoyed such enduring popularity is that making them is as much fun as eating them. The following information on chocolate and on baking and storing cookies will enhance your chocolate-cookie-making fun.

TYPES OF CHOCOLATE

Unsweetened Chocolate: Also called bitter or baking chocolate, this is pure chocolate with no sugar or flavorings added. It is used only in baking and is commonly packaged in individually wrapped 1-ounce squares.

Bittersweet Chocolate: This is pure chocolate with some sugar added. Specialty food shops carry bittersweet chocolate in 1-ounce squares or in bars. If unavailable, substitute half unsweetened chocolate and half semisweet chocolate.

Semisweet Chocolate: Pure chocolate is combined with sugar and extra cocoa butter. It is sold in a variety of forms, including 1-ounce squares, bars, chips and chunks.

Milk Chocolate: This is pure chocolate with sugar, extra cocoa butter and milk solids added. It is available in various shapes—bars, chips, stars, etc.

White Chocolate: Also known as confectioners' or compound chocolate, this is not considered real chocolate since most or all of the cocoa butter has been removed and replaced by another vegetable fat. White chocolate is available in bars, blocks, disks, chips and chunks.

Unsweetened Cocoa: This is formed by extracting most of the cocoa butter from pure chocolate and grinding the remaining chocolate solids into a powder. It contains no additives.

MELTING CHOCOLATE

Make sure the utensils you use for melting are completely dry. Moisture makes the chocolate become stiff and grainy. If this happens, add ½ teaspoon shortening (not butter) for each ounce of chocolate and stir until smooth. Chocolate scorches easily, and once scorched it cannot be used. Follow one of these three methods for successful melting.

Double Boiler: This is the safest method because it prevents scorching. Simply place the chocolate in the top of a double boiler or in a bowl over hot, not boiling, water; stir until smooth.

Direct Heat: Place the chocolate in a heavy saucepan over very low heat. Stir constantly and remove from the heat as soon as it melts to prevent scorching.

Microwave Oven: Place an unwrapped 1-ounce chocolate square or 1 cup of chips in a small microwavable bowl. Microwave on High 1 to 1½ minutes, stirring after 1 minute. Be sure to stir microwaved chocolate since it holds its shape when melted. Times may differ with various oven wattages.

COOKIE-MAKING TIPS

• Read through the recipe and check the ingredients, pan sizes and any special requirements, such as chilling the dough. Be sure to measure all the ingredients accurately and always preheat the oven before baking.

• To easily shape drop cookies, use an ice cream scoop with a release bar. The bar usually has a number on it indicating the number of scoops that can be made from one quart of ice cream. The handiest size is a #80 to #90 scoop. This will yield about one rounded teaspoonful of dough for each cookie.

• When a recipe calls for greasing the cookie sheets, use shortening or a nonstick cooking spray for best results. Or, use parchment paper instead of greasing. It eliminates clean-up, bakes the cookies more evenly and allows them to cool right on the paper instead of on wire racks.

• For even baking and browning, bake cookies in the center of the oven. If heat distribution in your oven is uneven, turn the cookie sheet halfway through the baking time.

• Most cookies bake quickly and should be watched carefully to avoid overbaking. It is generally better to slightly underbake, rather than to overbake cookies.

STORING COOKIES

• Unbaked dough can be refrigerated for up to two weeks or frozen for up to six weeks. Rolls of dough should be sealed tightly in plastic wrap; other doughs should be stored in airtight containers. Label dough with baking information for convenience.

• Store soft and crisp cookies separately at room temperature. Use airtight containers for soft cookies and place an apple or bread slice in the container for a day if they begin to dry out. Store crisp cookies in containers with loose-fitting lids to prevent moisture buildup. If they become soggy, heat undecorated cookies in a 300°F oven for about 3 minutes to restore crispness.

• Store cookies with sticky glazes or fragile decorations in single layers. If dipped or edged with chocolate, they should be layered between sheets of waxed paper.

• Freeze baked cookies in airtight containers or freezer bags for up to 6 months. Unwrap cookies when thawing them. If soggy, crisp undecorated cookies in a 300°F oven for about 3 minutes. Meringue-based cookies do not freeze well and chocolate-dipped cookies will discolor if frozen.

Extra-Easy Cookies

Chocolate Sugar Drops (page 10), Chocolate-Coconut Cookies (page 10),
Chocolate & Peanut-Butter Tweed Cookies (page 11)

CHOCO-COCO PECAN CRISPS

½ cup butter or margarine, softened
1 cup packed light brown sugar
1 egg
1 teaspoon vanilla
1½ cups all-purpose flour
⅓ cup unsweetened cocoa
½ teaspoon baking soda
1 cup chopped pecans
1 cup flaked coconut

Cream butter and sugar in large bowl until blended. Beat in egg and vanilla. Combine flour, cocoa, baking soda and pecans in small bowl until well blended. Add to creamed mixture, blending until stiff dough is formed. Sprinkle coconut on work surface. Divide dough into 4 parts. Shape each part into a roll, about 1½ inches in diameter; roll in coconut until thickly coated. Wrap in plastic wrap; refrigerate until firm, at least 1 hour or up to 2 weeks. (For longer storage, freeze up to 6 weeks.) Preheat oven to 350°F. Line cookie sheets with parchment paper or leave ungreased. Cut rolls into ⅛-inch-thick slices; place 2 inches apart on ungreased cookie sheets. Bake 10 to 13 minutes or until firm, but not overly browned. Remove to wire racks to cool.

Makes about 6 dozen cookies

HOLIDAY FRUIT DROPS

½ cup butter, softened
¾ cup packed brown sugar
1 egg
1¼ cups all-purpose flour
1 teaspoon vanilla
½ teaspoon baking soda
½ teaspoon cinnamon
  Pinch salt
1 cup (8 ounces) diced candied pineapple
1 cup (8 ounces) red and green candied cherries
8 ounces chopped pitted dates
1 cup (6 ounces) semisweet chocolate chips
½ cup whole hazelnuts
½ cup pecan halves
½ cup coarsely chopped walnuts

Preheat oven to 325°F. Lightly grease cookie sheets or line with parchment paper. Cream butter and sugar in large bowl. Beat in egg until light. Mix in flour, vanilla, baking soda, cinnamon and salt. Stir in pineapple, cherries, dates, chocolate chips, hazelnuts, pecans and walnuts. Drop dough by rounded teaspoonfuls 2 inches apart onto prepared cookie sheets. Bake 15 to 20 minutes or until firm and lightly browned around edges. Remove to wire racks to cool.

Makes about 8 dozen cookies

Note: The hazelnuts, pecans and cherries are not chopped, but left whole.

Choco-Coco Pecan Crisps (left), Holiday Fruit Drops (right)

CHOCOLATE-COCONUT COOKIES

For a festive touch, top these easy-to-make cookies with red candied cherries and add them to your holiday cookie tray.

2 squares (1 ounce each) unsweetened chocolate
½ cup butter or margarine, softened
1 cup packed light brown sugar
1 egg
1¼ cups all-purpose flour
¼ teaspoon baking powder
⅛ teaspoon baking soda
Dash salt
½ cup chopped walnuts or pecans
½ cup flaked coconut
Pecan halves or halved red candied cherries

Preheat oven to 350°F. Lightly grease cookie sheets or line with parchment paper. Melt chocolate in top of double boiler over hot, not boiling, water. Remove from heat; cool. Cream butter and sugar in large bowl until blended. Add egg and melted chocolate; beat until light. Combine flour, baking powder, baking soda and salt in small bowl. Stir into creamed mixture until blended. Mix in nuts and coconut. Drop dough by teaspoonfuls 2 inches apart onto prepared cookie sheets. Press a pecan or cherry half into center of each cookie. Bake 10 to 12 minutes or until firm. Remove to wire racks to cool.

Makes 4 dozen cookies

CHOCOLATE SUGAR DROPS

Sugar cookies have never been easier! The dough is rolled into balls and flattened with the bottom of a glass dipped into sugar. Be sure to dip the glass into sugar before flattening each cookie.

½ cup butter or margarine, softened
½ cup vegetable oil
½ cup powdered sugar
½ cup granulated sugar
1 egg
2 cups all-purpose flour
¼ cup unsweetened cocoa
½ teaspoon baking soda
½ teaspoon cream of tartar
¼ teaspoon salt
1 teaspoon vanilla
Granulated sugar

Cream butter, oil, powdered sugar, ½ cup granulated sugar and the egg in large bowl until light and fluffy. Combine the flour, cocoa, baking soda, cream of tartar and salt in small bowl. Add to creamed mixture with vanilla, stirring until dough is smooth. Cover; refrigerate 30 minutes or overnight, if desired.

Preheat oven to 350°F. Lightly grease cookie sheets or line with parchment paper. Shape dough into balls the size of marbles. Place 2 inches apart on prepared cookie sheets. Flatten each cookie to about ⅓-inch thickness with bottom of glass dipped into granulated sugar. Bake 10 minutes or until firm. Do not overbake. Remove to wire racks to cool.

Makes about 5 dozen cookies

CHOCOLATE & PEANUT-BUTTER TWEED COOKIES

The chopped chocolate and peanut butter chips in these cookies give them a tweedy texture and appearance.

1 cup butter or margarine, softened
½ cup packed light brown sugar
¼ cup granulated sugar
1 egg
¼ teaspoon baking soda
2½ cups all-purpose flour
½ cup *each* semisweet chocolate chips and peanut butter chips, chopped*

Cream butter and sugars in large bowl until smooth. Add egg and baking soda; beat until light. Stir in flour until dough is smooth. Blend in chopped chips. Divide dough into 4 parts. Shape each part into a roll, about 1½ inches in diameter. Wrap in plastic wrap; refrigerate until firm, at least 1 hour or up to 2 weeks. (For longer storage, freeze up to 6 weeks.)

Preheat oven to 375°F. Lightly grease cookie sheets or line with parchment paper. Cut rolls into ⅛-inch-thick slices; place 2 inches apart on prepared cookie sheets. Bake 10 to 12 minutes or until lightly browned. Remove to wire racks to cool.

Makes about 6 dozen cookies

*Chips can be chopped in a food processor.

HONEY-GINGER BOURBON BALLS

1 cup gingersnap cookie crumbs
1¼ cups powdered sugar, divided
1 cup finely chopped pecans or walnuts
1 square (1 ounce) unsweetened chocolate
1½ tablespoons honey
¼ cup bourbon

Combine crumbs, 1 cup of the sugar and the nuts in large bowl. Combine chocolate and honey in small bowl over hot water; stir until chocolate is melted. Blend in bourbon. Stir bourbon mixture into crumb mixture until well blended. Shape into 1-inch balls. Sprinkle remaining ¼ cup powdered sugar over balls. Refrigerate until firm.

Makes about 4 dozen balls

Note: These improve with aging. Store them in an airtight container in the refrigerator. They will keep several weeks, but are best after two to three days.

CHOCOLATE-FROSTED LEBKUCHEN

Lebkuchen are holiday favorites in Germany. The dough is traditionally baked on wafers called oblaten. You can find oblaten in some specialty food stores.

4 eggs
1 cup sugar
1½ cups all-purpose flour
1 cup (6 ounces) pulverized
  almonds*
⅓ cup candied lemon peel,
  finely chopped
⅓ cup candied orange peel,
  finely chopped
1½ teaspoons ground
  cinnamon
1 teaspoon grated lemon
  rind
½ teaspoon ground
  cardamom
½ teaspoon ground nutmeg
¼ teaspoon ground cloves
  Bittersweet Glaze (recipe
  follows)

In large bowl of electric mixer, combine eggs and sugar. Beat at high speed for 10 minutes. Meanwhile, in separate bowl, combine flour, almonds, lemon and orange peels, cinnamon, lemon rind, cardamom, nutmeg and cloves. Blend in egg mixture, stirring until evenly mixed. Cover; refrigerate 12 hours or overnight.

Preheat oven to 350°F. Grease cookie sheets and dust with flour or line with parchment paper. Drop dough by rounded teaspoonfuls 2 inches apart onto prepared cookie sheets. Bake 8 to 10 minutes or until just barely browned. Do not overbake. Remove to wire racks. While cookies bake, prepare Bittersweet Glaze. Spread over tops of warm cookies using pastry brush. Cool until glaze is set. Store in airtight container.

Makes about 5 dozen cookies

*To pulverize almonds, place in food processor or blender. Process until thoroughly ground with a dry, not pasty, texture.

BITTERSWEET GLAZE
3 squares (1 ounce each)
  bittersweet or semisweet
  chocolate, chopped
1 tablespoon butter or
  margarine

Melt chocolate and butter in small bowl over hot water. Stir until smooth.

Chocolate-Frosted Lebkuchen, Honey-Ginger Bourbon Balls (page 11)

COCOA SNICKERDOODLES

Snickerdoodle is a nineteenth-century nonsense word for a quick-to-make confection. The dough is dropped into a mixture of cocoa, cinnamon and sugar, making the cookies crinkle when baked.

1 cup butter or margarine, softened
¾ cup packed brown sugar
¾ cup plus 2 tablespoons granulated sugar
2 eggs
2 cups uncooked rolled oats
1½ cups all-purpose flour
¼ cup plus 2 tablespoons unsweetened cocoa
1 teaspoon baking soda
2 tablespoons ground cinnamon

Preheat oven to 375°F. Lightly grease cookie sheets or line with parchment paper. Beat butter, brown sugar and the ¾ cup granulated sugar in large bowl until light and fluffy. Add eggs; mix well. Combine oats, flour, the ¼ cup cocoa and the baking soda in medium bowl. Stir into butter mixture until blended. Mix the 2 tablespoons granulated sugar, the cinnamon and the 2 tablespoons cocoa in small bowl. Drop dough by rounded teaspoonfuls into cinnamon mixture; toss to coat. Place 2 inches apart on prepared cookie sheets. Bake 8 to 10 minutes or until firm in center. Do not overbake. Remove to wire racks to cool.

Makes about 4½ dozen cookies

CHOCOLATE-PEANUT COOKIES

1 cup butter or margarine, softened
¾ cup granulated sugar
¾ cup packed light brown sugar
2 eggs
1 teaspoon vanilla
1 teaspoon baking soda
¼ teaspoon salt
2¼ cups all-purpose flour
2 cups chocolate-covered peanuts

Preheat oven to 375°F. Line cookie sheets with parchment paper or leave ungreased. Cream butter with sugars, eggs and vanilla in large bowl until light. Beat in baking soda and salt. Stir in flour to make stiff dough. Blend in chocolate-covered peanuts. Drop by rounded teaspoonfuls 2 inches apart onto cookie sheets. Bake 9 to 11 minutes or until just barely golden. Do not overbake. Remove to wire racks to cool.

Makes about 5 dozen cookies

Cocoa Snickerdoodles, Chocolate-Peanut Cookies

COWBOY COOKIES

Loaded with raisins, nuts and chocolate chips, these are a cookie-jar favorite that kids love!

½ cup butter or margarine, softened
½ cup packed light brown sugar
¼ cup granulated sugar
1 egg
1 teaspoon vanilla
1 cup all-purpose flour
2 tablespoons unsweetened cocoa
½ teaspoon baking powder
¼ teaspoon baking soda
1 cup uncooked rolled oats
1 cup (6 ounces) semisweet chocolate chips
½ cup raisins
½ cup chopped nuts

Preheat oven to 375°F. Lightly grease cookie sheets or line with parchment paper. Cream butter with sugars in large bowl until blended. Add egg and vanilla; beat until fluffy. Combine flour, cocoa, baking powder and baking soda in small bowl; stir into creamed mixture with oats, chocolate chips, raisins and nuts. Drop dough by teaspoonfuls 2 inches apart onto prepared cookie sheets. Bake 10 to 12 minutes or until lightly browned around edges. Remove to wire racks to cool.

Makes about 4 dozen cookies

BETH'S CHOCOLATE OATMEAL COOKIES

All butter or margarine may be used in place of the shortening in this recipe. The shortening, however, gives the cookies a more tender texture.

3 squares (1 ounce each) unsweetened chocolate
½ cup butter or margarine, softened
½ cup shortening
1½ cups sugar
2 eggs
2 teaspoons vanilla
1½ cups all-purpose flour
2 teaspoons baking powder
½ teaspoon salt
3 cups uncooked rolled oats
1 cup chopped walnuts

Preheat oven to 350°F. Lightly grease cookie sheets or line with parchment paper. Melt chocolate in top of double boiler over hot, not boiling, water. Remove from heat; cool. Cream butter, shortening and sugar in large bowl. Add eggs, beating well. Blend in melted chocolate and vanilla. Combine flour, baking powder and salt in small bowl. Add to creamed mixture; blend well. Mix in oats and nuts. Drop dough by rounded teaspoonfuls 2 inches apart onto prepared cookie sheets. Bake 10 to 12 minutes or until lightly browned. Remove to wire racks to cool.

Makes about 8 dozen cookies

Cowboy Cookies

ORIENTAL CHEWS

1 package (6 ounces) chow
    mein noodles
1 cup flaked coconut
1 cup (6 ounces) semisweet
    chocolate chips
1 cup (6 ounces)
    butterscotch-flavored
    chips
1 package (3 ounces)
    slivered almonds

Preheat oven to 350°F. Place noodles and coconut on cookie sheet in single layer. Bake 10 minutes or until crisp. Melt chocolate and butterscotch chips in top of double boiler over hot, not boiling, water. Remove from heat; stir in almonds, coconut and noodles. Drop mixture by teaspoonfuls onto waxed paper. Cool until set.

Makes about 5 dozen chews

MOCHA-WALNUT RUM BALLS

1 package (8½ ounces)
    chocolate cookie wafers
2 cups powdered sugar,
    divided
1¼ cups finely chopped
    toasted walnuts
2 tablespoons instant coffee
    granules
⅓ to ½ cup rum
2 tablespoons light corn
    syrup
½ teaspoon instant espresso
    coffee powder

Pulverize cookie wafers in food processor or blender to form powdery crumbs. Combine crumbs, 1½ cups of the sugar and the walnuts in large bowl. Dissolve coffee granules in ⅓ cup rum; stir in corn syrup. Blend into crumb mixture until crumbs are moistened enough to hold together. Add 2 to 3 tablespoons more rum, if necessary. Shape into 1-inch balls. Mix the remaining ½ cup sugar with the espresso coffee powder. Roll balls in sugar mixture to coat. Store loosely packed between sheets of waxed paper or foil in airtight container up to 2 weeks.

Makes about 100 balls

PEOPLE CHOW

Serve a generous bowlful of this chow to the nibblers in your crowd!

1 cup butter or margarine
1 package (12 ounces)
    semisweet chocolate
    chips
18 cups dry cereal (mixture of
    bite-sized wheat, corn
    and rice cereal squares
    or toasted oat cereal)
2 cups nuts (cashews,
    peanuts, mixed nuts,
    pecans or walnuts)
6 cups powdered sugar

Melt butter and chocolate chips in medium-sized heavy saucepan over low heat; stir to blend. Place cereal and nuts in large bowl. Pour chocolate mixture over; mix until cereal and nuts are thoroughly coated. Turn chocolate mixture into very large bowl or dishpan. Sprinkle sugar over, 2 cups at a time, carefully folding and mixing until thoroughly coated.

Makes about 24 cups

DATE FUDGE COOKIES

The dates in these cookies keep them fresh and moist for a long time.

1 cup (6 ounces) semisweet chocolate chips
½ cup butter or margarine, softened
1 cup granulated sugar
2 eggs
1½ cups all-purpose flour
Dash salt
1 package (8 ounces) chopped pitted dates
½ cup coarsely chopped pecans or walnuts
Brown-Sugar Icing (recipe follows)

Preheat oven to 375°F. Lightly grease cookie sheets or line with parchment paper. Melt chocolate chips in top of double boiler over hot, not boiling, water. Remove from heat; cool. Cream butter, granulated sugar and eggs in large bowl until smooth. Beat in melted chocolate. Gradually add flour and salt, mixing until smooth. Stir in dates and nuts. Drop dough by rounded teaspoonfuls 2 inches apart onto prepared cookie sheets. Bake 10 to 12 minutes or until slightly firm. Cool 5 minutes on cookie sheets, then remove to wire racks. While cookies bake, prepare Brown-Sugar Icing. Spread over cookies while still warm. Cool until icing is set.

Makes about 5 dozen cookies

BROWN-SUGAR ICING
½ cup packed dark brown sugar
¼ cup water
2 squares (1 ounce each) unsweetened chocolate
2 cups powdered sugar
¼ cup butter or margarine
1 teaspoon vanilla

Combine brown sugar, water and chocolate in small heavy saucepan. Stir over medium heat until chocolate is melted and mixture boils. Boil 1 minute. Remove from heat, beat in powdered sugar, butter and vanilla. Continue beating until mixture has cooled slightly and thickened. Spread over cookies while icing is still warm.

CRISPY CHOCOLATE LOGS

1 cup (6 ounces) semisweet chocolate chips
½ cup butter or margarine
1 package (10 ounces) marshmallows
6 cups crispy rice cereal

Lightly oil a 13×9-inch baking pan. Melt chocolate chips and butter in large bowl over hot water, stirring constantly. Add marshmallows; stir until melted. Add cereal; stir until evenly coated with chocolate mixture. Press into prepared pan; cool until mixture is firm. Cut into 2×1½-inch logs using a sharp, thin knife.

Makes 36 logs

NUTTY CLUSTERS

2 squares (1 ounce each) unsweetened chocolate
½ cup butter or margarine, softened
1 cup granulated sugar
1 egg
⅓ cup buttermilk
1 teaspoon vanilla
1¾ cups all-purpose flour
½ teaspoon baking soda
1 cup mixed salted nuts, coarsely chopped
Chocolate Icing (recipe follows)

Preheat oven to 400°F. Line cookie sheets with parchment paper or leave ungreased. Melt chocolate in top of double boiler over hot, not boiling, water. Remove from heat; cool. Cream butter and granulated sugar in large bowl until smooth. Beat in egg, melted chocolate, buttermilk and vanilla until light. Stir in flour, baking soda and nuts. Drop dough by teaspoonfuls 2 inches apart onto cookie sheets. Bake 8 to 10 minutes or until almost no imprint remains when touched. Immediately remove cookies from cookie sheet to wire rack. While cookies bake, prepare Chocolate Icing. Frost cookies while still warm.

Makes about 4 dozen cookies

CHOCOLATE ICING
2 squares (1 ounce each) unsweetened chocolate
2 tablespoons butter or margarine
2 cups powdered sugar
2 to 3 tablespoons water

Melt chocolate and butter in small heavy saucepan over low heat, stirring until completely melted. Add powdered sugar and water, mixing until smooth.

OAT & DRIED-FRUIT BALLS

3 cups uncooked rolled oats
1 cup flaked coconut
1 cup chopped dried mixed fruit
¼ cup sunflower seeds or chopped walnuts
1 cup sugar
½ cup milk
½ cup butter or margarine
6 tablespoons unsweetened cocoa
¼ teaspoon salt
1 teaspoon vanilla

Combine oats, coconut, fruit and sunflower seeds in large bowl; set aside. Combine sugar, milk, butter, cocoa and salt in 2-quart saucepan until blended. Heat to boiling. Boil 3 minutes, stirring constantly; remove from heat. Stir in vanilla. Pour hot sugar syrup into oat mixture; stir until well blended. When cool enough to handle, shape rounded tablespoonfuls into balls; place on waxed paper until completely cooled and firm.

Makes about 5 dozen balls

PEANUT-BUTTER CHOCOLATE STARS

1 cup peanut butter
1 cup packed light brown
    sugar
1 egg
48 milk chocolate candy stars
    or other solid milk
    chocolate candy

Preheat oven to 350°F. Line cookie sheets with parchment paper or leave ungreased. Combine peanut butter, sugar and egg in medium bowl until blended and smooth. Shape into 48 balls about 1½ inches in diameter. Place 2 inches apart on cookie sheets. Press a chocolate star onto the top of each cookie. Bake 10 to 12 minutes or until set. Remove to wire racks to cool.

Makes 4 dozen cookies

FUDGE COOKIES

Satisfying and rich with chocolate, these fudgy cookies are gilded with a good fudge frosting, too.

1 cup (6 ounces) semisweet
    chocolate chips
½ cup butter or margarine,
    softened
1 cup granulated sugar
2 eggs
1½ cups all-purpose flour
    Dash salt
1½ cups coarsely chopped
    pecans or walnuts
    Fudge Frosting (recipe
    follows)

Preheat oven to 375°F. Lightly grease cookie sheets or line with parchment paper. Melt chocolate chips in top of double boiler over hot, not boiling, water. Remove from heat; cool. Cream butter, granulated sugar and eggs in large bowl until smooth. Beat in melted chocolate. Gradually add flour and salt, mixing until smooth. Stir in nuts. Drop dough by rounded teaspoonfuls 2 inches apart onto prepared cookie sheets. Bake 10 to 12 minutes or until slightly firm. Cool 5 minutes on cookie sheet, then remove to wire racks. While cookies bake, prepare Fudge Frosting. Frost cookies while still warm. Cool until frosting is set.

Makes about 5 dozen cookies

FUDGE FROSTING
1 square (1 ounce)
    semisweet chocolate
3 tablespoons heavy cream
1 cup powdered sugar
1 teaspoon vanilla

Melt chocolate with cream in small heavy saucepan over medium heat, stirring until chocolate melts completely. Remove from heat; beat in powdered sugar and vanilla. Spread over cookies while frosting is still warm.

Fudge Cookies, Oat & Dried-Fruit Balls (page 20), Peanut-Butter Chocolate Stars

ICE CREAM COOKIES

These cookies are simple, buttery and chocolatey—perfect to serve alongside ice cream or to make into ice cream sandwiches.

2 squares (1 ounce each)
    unsweetened chocolate
1 cup butter, softened
1 cup powdered sugar
4 egg yolks
1 teaspoon vanilla
3 cups all-purpose flour
    Powdered sugar

Melt chocolate in top of double boiler over hot, not boiling, water. Remove from heat; cool. Cream butter and 1 cup sugar in large bowl until blended. Add egg yolks, vanilla and melted chocolate; beat until light. Blend in flour to make stiff dough. Divide dough into 4 parts. Shape each part into a roll, about 1½ inches in diameter. Wrap in plastic wrap; refrigerate until firm, at least 30 minutes or up to 2 weeks. (For longer storage, freeze up to 6 weeks.)

Preheat oven to 350°F. Line cookie sheets with parchment paper or leave ungreased. Cut rolls into ⅛-inch-thick slices; place 2 inches apart on ungreased cookie sheets. Bake 8 to 10 minutes or just until set, but not browned. Remove to wire racks to cool. Dust with powdered sugar.

Makes about 8 dozen cookies

Ice Cream Cookie Sandwiches: Prepare and bake cookies as directed; cool completely. Spread desired amount of softened ice cream on bottoms of half the cookies. Top with remaining cookies, bottom sides down, forming sandwiches. Dust tops with powdered sugar; serve immediately. Makes about 4 dozen sandwich cookies.

Ice Cream Cookie Sandwiches

Monster Cookies

Top left: White Chocolate Biggies (page 28), bottom left: Peanut Butter Jumbos (page 29)

WHITE CHOCOLATE BIGGIES

These huge chocolate cookies are studded with white chocolate chips, pecans and raisins. They bake to about four inches in diameter.

1½ cups butter or margarine, softened
1 cup granulated sugar
¾ cup packed light brown sugar
2 teaspoons vanilla
2 eggs
2½ cups all-purpose flour
⅔ cup unsweetened cocoa
1 teaspoon baking soda
½ teaspoon salt
1 package (10 ounces) large white chocolate chips
¾ cup pecan halves, coarsely chopped
½ cup golden raisins

Preheat oven to 350°F. Lightly grease cookie sheets or line with parchment paper. Cream butter, sugars, vanilla and eggs in large bowl until light. Combine flour, cocoa, baking soda and salt in medium bowl; blend into creamed mixture until smooth. Stir in white chocolate chips, pecans and raisins. Scoop out about ⅓ cupful of dough for each cookie. Place on prepared cookie sheets, spacing about 4 inches apart. Press each cookie to flatten slightly. Bake 12 to 14 minutes or until firm in center. Cool 5 minutes on cookie sheet, then remove to wire racks to cool completely.

Makes about 2 dozen cookies

CHOCOLATE PLATTER COOKIES

1 cup unsalted butter, softened
1 cup packed light brown sugar
½ cup granulated sugar
2 eggs
2⅓ cups all-purpose flour
1 teaspoon baking soda
½ teaspoon salt
1 package (12 ounces) semisweet chocolate chunks
2 cups chopped pecans

Preheat oven to 375°F. Lightly grease cookie sheets or line with parchment paper. Cream butter with sugars until smooth. Add eggs; beat until fluffy. Combine flour, baking soda and salt in small bowl. Add to creamed mixture, mixing until dough is stiff. Stir in chocolate chunks and pecans. Scoop out about ⅓ cupful of dough for each cookie. Place on prepared cookie sheets, spacing 4 inches apart. Using back of fork, flatten each cookie to about ½ inch thick. Bake 15 minutes or until light golden. Remove to wire racks to cool.

Makes about 16 cookies

PEANUT BUTTER JUMBOS

½ cup butter or margarine,
  softened
1 cup packed brown sugar
1 cup granulated sugar
1½ cups peanut butter
3 eggs
2 teaspoons baking soda
1 teaspoon vanilla
4½ cups uncooked rolled oats
1 cup (6 ounces) semisweet
  chocolate chips
1 cup candy-coated
  chocolate pieces

Preheat oven to 350°F. Lightly grease cookie sheets or line with parchment paper. Cream butter, sugars, peanut butter and eggs in large bowl until light. Blend in baking soda, vanilla and oats until well mixed. Stir in chocolate chips and candy pieces. Scoop out about ⅓ cupful of dough for each cookie. Place on prepared cookie sheets, spacing about 4 inches apart. Press each cookie to flatten slightly. Bake 15 to 20 minutes or until firm in center. Remove to wire racks to cool.

Makes about 1½ dozen cookies

GIANT RAISIN-CHIP FRISBEES

Decorate frisbees with candles for a birthday party—kids love them!

1 cup butter or margarine,
  softened
1 cup packed brown sugar
½ cup granulated sugar
2 eggs
1 teaspoon vanilla
1½ cups all-purpose flour
¼ cup unsweetened cocoa
1 teaspoon baking soda
1 cup (6 ounces) semisweet
  chocolate chips
¾ cup raisins
¾ cup chopped walnuts

Preheat oven to 350°F. Line cookie sheets with parchment paper or lightly grease and dust with flour. Cream butter with sugars in large bowl. Add eggs and vanilla; beat until light. Combine flour, cocoa and baking soda in small bowl. Add to creamed mixture with chocolate chips, raisins and walnuts; stir until well blended. Scoop out about ½ cupful of dough for each cookie. Place on prepared cookie sheets, spacing about 5 inches apart. Using knife dipped in water, smooth balls of dough out to 3½ inches in diameter. Bake 10 to 12 minutes or until golden. Remove to wire racks to cool.

Makes about 16 cookies

TRACY'S PIZZA-PAN COOKIES

Cream cheese adds flavor and a chewy texture to these pizza-sized cookies.

1 cup butter or margarine, softened
¾ cup granulated sugar
¾ cup packed brown sugar
1 package (8 ounces) cream cheese, softened
1 teaspoon vanilla
2 eggs
2¼ cups all-purpose flour
1 teaspoon baking soda
¼ teaspoon salt
1 package (12 ounces) semisweet chocolate chips
1 cup chopped walnuts or pecans

Preheat oven to 375°F. Lightly grease two 12-inch pizza pans. Cream butter, sugars, cream cheese and vanilla in large bowl. Add eggs; beat until light. Combine flour, baking soda and salt in small bowl. Add to creamed mixture; blend well. Stir in chocolate chips and nuts. Divide dough in half; press each half evenly into a prepared pan. Bake 20 to 25 minutes or until lightly browned around edges. Cool completely in pans on wire racks. To serve, cut into slim wedges or break into pieces.

Makes two 12-inch cookies

SUPER-DUPER CHOCOLATE PECAN COOKIES

½ cup butter or margarine, softened
⅓ cup peanut butter
⅓ cup granulated sugar
⅓ cup packed light brown sugar
1 egg
1 teaspoon vanilla
1¼ cups all-purpose flour
½ teaspoon baking soda
1 package (12 ounces) semisweet chocolate chunks *or* 4 semisweet chocolate bars (3 ounces each), cut into squares
1 cup pecan halves, cut into pieces

Preheat oven to 350°F. Lightly grease two cookie sheets or line with parchment paper. Cream butter, peanut butter, sugars, egg and vanilla in large bowl until light. Blend in flour and baking soda. Scoop out about ⅓ cupfuls of dough to form 12 balls. Place on prepared cookie sheets, spacing about 4 inches apart. Press each cookie to flatten slightly. Press chocolate chunks and pecan pieces into cookies, dividing them equally. Bake 15 to 17 minutes or until firm in center. Remove to wire racks to cool.

Makes 1 dozen cookies

Brownies & Bars

Left: Pecan Caramel Brownies (page 35), right: Chocolate Peanut Bars (page 34)

CHOCOLATE PEANUT BARS

½ cup butter or margarine,
   softened
¼ cup granulated sugar
1 cup packed brown sugar,
   divided
2 eggs, separated
1 teaspoon vanilla
2 cups all-purpose flour
2 teaspoons baking powder
½ teaspoon baking soda
¼ teaspoon salt
2 to 4 tablespoons milk
1 cup (6 ounces) semisweet
   chocolate chips
¾ cup salted peanuts,
   coarsely chopped

Preheat oven to 350°F. Lightly grease a 13×9-inch pan. Cream butter, granulated sugar and ¼ cup of the brown sugar in large bowl. Beat in egg yolks and vanilla. Combine flour, baking powder, baking soda and salt in small bowl. Blend into creamed mixture. Stir in enough milk to make a smooth, light dough. Press on bottom of prepared pan. Sprinkle chocolate chips over the top; press them down lightly into dough. In clean, dry bowl, beat egg whites until stiff, but not dry. Gradually beat in remaining ¾ cup brown sugar. Spread mixture evenly over dough in pan; top with peanuts. Bake 25 to 30 minutes or until top is puffed, lightly browned and feels dry. Cut into 2×1-inch bars while still warm.

Makes about 5 dozen bars

PEANUT-BUTTER-CHIP BROWNIES

½ cup butter or margarine
4 squares (1 ounce each)
   semisweet chocolate
½ cup sugar
2 eggs
1 teaspoon vanilla
½ cup all-purpose flour
1 package (12 ounces)
   peanut butter chips
1 cup (6 ounces) milk
   chocolate chips

Preheat oven to 350°F. Butter an 8-inch square pan. Melt butter and semisweet chocolate in small heavy saucepan over low heat, stirring just until chocolate melts completely. Remove from heat; cool. Beat sugar and eggs in large bowl until light. Blend in vanilla and chocolate mixture. Stir in flour until blended; fold in peanut butter chips. Spread batter evenly in prepared pan. Bake 25 to 30 minutes or just until firm and dry in center. Remove from oven; sprinkle milk chocolate chips over the top. Place pan on wire rack. When chocolate chips have melted, spread them over brownies. Refrigerate until chocolate topping is set. Cut into 2-inch squares.

Makes 16 brownies

PECAN CARAMEL BROWNIES

Pecans, caramel and chocolate make an irresistible combination.

50 caramel candy cubes
2 tablespoons milk
1½ cups granulated sugar
1 cup butter or margarine, melted
4 eggs
2 teaspoons vanilla
1 cup all-purpose flour
⅔ cup unsweetened cocoa
½ teaspoon baking powder
¼ teaspoon salt
1 cup (6 ounces) semisweet chocolate chips
⅓ cup pecan halves
Cocoa Glaze (recipe follows)

Preheat oven to 350°F. Butter a 13×9-inch pan. Unwrap caramels; melt with milk in small heavy saucepan over medium to low heat, stirring until caramels melt completely. Keep warm. Combine granulated sugar, butter, eggs, vanilla, flour, cocoa, baking powder and salt in large bowl. Beat with mixer at medium speed until smooth. Spread half of the batter in prepared pan. Bake 15 minutes. Carefully remove from oven; sprinkle with chocolate chips. Drizzle melted caramel mixture over the top, covering evenly. Spoon remaining batter over all. Return to oven; bake 20 minutes longer. Do not overbake. Meanwhile, toast pecan halves in another pan in same oven 3 to 5 minutes. Prepare Cocoa Glaze. Pour over warm brownies; arrange toasted pecans on top. Cool completely in pan on wire rack. Cut into 2-inch squares.

Makes about 2 dozen brownies

COCOA GLAZE
2 tablespoons butter or margarine
2 tablespoons unsweetened cocoa
2 tablespoons milk
Dash salt
1 cup powdered sugar
1 teaspoon vanilla

Combine butter, cocoa, milk and salt in small heavy saucepan. Bring to a boil over medium heat, stirring constantly. Remove from heat; add powdered sugar and beat until smooth. Stir in vanilla.

BROWNIE FUDGE

This recipe makes a huge batch of fudge-topped brownies—ideal to serve a crowd.

4 squares (1 ounce each)
  unsweetened chocolate
1 cup butter or margarine
2 cups sugar
4 eggs
1 cup all-purpose flour
1 cup chopped walnuts
2 teaspoons vanilla
  Fudge Topping (recipe
  follows)

Preheat oven to 350°F. Butter a 13×9-inch pan. Melt chocolate and butter in small heavy saucepan over low heat, stirring until completely melted; cool. Beat sugar and eggs in large bowl until light and fluffy. Gradually whisk chocolate mixture into egg mixture. Stir in flour, walnuts and vanilla. Spread batter evenly in prepared pan. Bake 25 to 35 minutes or just until set. Do not overbake. Meanwhile, prepare Fudge Topping. Remove brownies from oven. Immediately pour topping evenly over hot brownies. Cool in pan on wire rack. Place in freezer until firm. Cut into 1-inch squares.

Makes about 9 dozen brownies

FUDGE TOPPING
4½ cups sugar
  ⅓ cup butter or margarine
1 can (12 ounces) evaporated
  milk
1 jar (7 ounces) marshmallow
  creme
1 package (12 ounces)
  semisweet chocolate
  chips
1 package (12 ounces) milk
  chocolate chips
2 teaspoons vanilla
2 cups walnuts, coarsely
  chopped

Combine sugar, butter and milk in large saucepan. Bring to a boil over medium heat; boil 5 minutes, stirring constantly. Remove from heat; add remaining ingredients *except* walnuts. Beat until smooth. Stir in walnuts.

Left: White Chocolate & Almond Brownies (page 38), right: Brownie Fudge

WHITE CHOCOLATE & ALMOND BROWNIES

Use a high-quality white chocolate when you make these brownies. The white chocolate sweetens them so sugar is not needed in the recipe.

12 ounces white chocolate,
    broken into pieces
1 cup unsalted butter
3 eggs
¾ cup all-purpose flour
1 teaspoon vanilla
½ cup slivered almonds

Preheat oven to 325°F. Grease and flour 9-inch square pan. Melt chocolate and butter in large saucepan over low heat, stirring constantly. (Do not be concerned if the white chocolate separates.) Remove from heat when chocolate is just melted. With electric mixer, beat in eggs until mixture is smooth. Beat in flour and vanilla. Spread batter evenly in prepared pan. Sprinkle almonds evenly over the top. Bake 30 to 35 minutes or just until set in center. Cool completely in pan on wire rack. Cut into 2-inch squares.

Makes about 16 brownies

FUDGY FUDGE BROWNIES

Rich, moist and chewy, these brownies are for real chocolate lovers!

½ cup butter or margarine
2 squares (1 ounce each)
    unsweetened chocolate
2 eggs
1 cup granulated sugar
½ cup all-purpose flour
1 teaspoon vanilla
    Fudgy Frosting, optional
    (recipe follows)

Preheat oven to 325°F. Grease and flour an 8-inch square pan. Melt butter and chocolate in small heavy saucepan over low heat. Remove from heat; cool. Beat eggs in medium bowl until light and fluffy. Add granulated sugar, beating well. Blend in chocolate mixture. Stir in flour and vanilla. Spread batter evenly in prepared pan. Bake 30 minutes or until firm in center. Cool in pan on wire rack. Frost with Fudgy Frosting, if desired. Cut into 2-inch squares.

Makes 16 brownies

FUDGY FROSTING
2 squares (1 ounce each)
    unsweetened chocolate
½ cup heavy cream
1 cup granulated sugar
    Dash salt
1 teaspoon vanilla
½ to ¾ cup powdered sugar

Melt chocolate with cream in small heavy saucepan over low heat, stirring until chocolate melts completely. Stir in granulated sugar and salt. Bring to a boil. Boil 1 minute. Remove from heat; stir in vanilla. Beat until smooth. Add enough powdered sugar to make frosting a soft spreading consistency. Beat until slightly cooled; spread over brownies.

HEAVENLY HASH BROWNIES

This version of heavenly hash uses a combination of chocolate, nuts and marshmallows. For best results, be sure to use fresh marshmallows.

1 cup butter or margarine
¼ cup unsweetened cocoa
4 eggs
1¼ cups granulated sugar
1½ cups all-purpose flour
2 cups chopped walnuts or pecans
2 teaspoons vanilla
  Creamy Cocoa Icing (recipe follows)
1 package (10 ounces) miniature marshmallows

Preheat oven to 350°F. Grease a 13×9-inch pan. Melt butter in 2-quart saucepan; stir in cocoa. Remove from heat; beat in eggs and granulated sugar. Blend in flour, nuts and vanilla. Spread batter evenly in prepared pan. Bake 20 to 25 minutes or until center feels dry. Do not overbake. Meanwhile, prepare Creamy Cocoa Icing. Remove brownies from oven. Immediately sprinkle marshmallows over hot brownies. Pour hot icing evenly over marshmallows. Cool in pan on wire rack. Cut into 2-inch squares.

Makes about 2 dozen brownies

CREAMY COCOA ICING
6 tablespoons butter or margarine
¾ cup undiluted evaporated milk
6 cups powdered sugar
¾ cup unsweetened cocoa

Combine butter, milk, powdered sugar and cocoa in 2-quart saucepan. Stir over low heat until smooth and creamy.

COCONUT-ALMOND MOUND BARS

2 cups graham cracker crumbs
½ cup butter or margarine, softened
¼ cup powdered sugar
2 cups flaked coconut
1 can (14 ounces) sweetened condensed milk
½ cup whole blanched almonds
1 cup (6 ounces) milk chocolate chips

Preheat oven to 350°F. Lightly grease a 13×9-inch pan. Combine crumbs, butter and powdered sugar in large bowl until blended and smooth. Press on bottom of prepared pan. Bake 10 to 12 minutes or just until golden. Combine coconut and milk in small bowl; spread evenly over baked crust. Arrange almonds evenly over coconut mixture. Bake 15 to 18 minutes or until almonds are toasted. Remove from oven; sprinkle chocolate chips over the top. Let stand a few minutes until chips melt, then spread evenly over bars. Cool completely in pan on wire rack. Cut into 2×1½-inch bars.

Makes about 3 dozen bars

RASPBERRY FUDGE BROWNIES

½ cup butter or margarine
3 squares (1 ounce each)
    bittersweet chocolate*
2 eggs
1 cup sugar
1 teaspoon vanilla
¾ cup all-purpose flour
¼ teaspoon baking powder
    Dash salt
½ cup sliced or slivered
    almonds
½ cup raspberry preserves
1 cup (6 ounces) milk
    chocolate chips

Preheat oven to 350°F. Butter and flour an 8-inch square pan. Melt butter and bittersweet chocolate in small heavy saucepan over low heat. Remove from heat; cool. Beat the eggs, sugar and vanilla in large bowl until light. Beat in chocolate mixture. Stir in flour, baking powder and salt until just blended. Spread ¾ of the batter in prepared pan; sprinkle almonds over the top. Bake 10 minutes. Remove from oven; spread preserves over almonds. Carefully spoon remaining batter over preserves, smoothing top. Bake 25 to 30 minutes or just until top feels firm. Remove from oven; sprinkle chocolate chips over the top. Let stand a few minutes until chips melt, then spread evenly over brownies. Cool completely in pan on wire rack. When chocolate is set, cut into 2-inch squares.

Makes 16 brownies

*Bittersweet chocolate is available in specialty food stores. One square unsweetened chocolate plus 2 squares semisweet chocolate may be substituted.

HONEY BROWNIES

The rich chocolate taste of these cake-like brownies is enhanced by golden honey.

1 cup (6 ounces) semisweet
    chocolate chips
6 tablespoons butter or
    margarine
2 eggs
⅓ cup honey
1 teaspoon vanilla
½ cup all-purpose flour
½ teaspoon baking powder
    Dash salt
1 cup chopped walnuts

Preheat oven to 350°F. Butter an 8-inch square pan. Melt chocolate and butter in medium-sized heavy saucepan over low heat. Remove from heat; cool slightly. Stir in eggs, honey and vanilla. Combine flour, baking powder and salt in small bowl. Stir into chocolate mixture with walnuts. Spread batter evenly in prepared pan. Bake 20 to 25 minutes or just until center feels springy. Cool in pan on wire rack. Cut into 2-inch squares.

Makes 16 brownies

Raspberry Fudge Brownies

DECADENT BROWNIES

Designed after the popular dessert called chocolate decadence, these brownies are sinfully rich, smooth and chocolatey.

½ cup dark corn syrup
½ cup butter or margarine
6 squares (1 ounce each) semisweet chocolate
¾ cup sugar
3 eggs
1 cup all-purpose flour
1 cup chopped walnuts
1 teaspoon vanilla
  Fudge Glaze (recipe follows)

FUDGE GLAZE
3 squares (1 ounce each) semisweet chocolate
2 tablespoons dark corn syrup
1 tablespoon butter or margarine
1 teaspoon light cream or milk

Preheat oven to 350°F. Grease an 8-inch square pan. Combine corn syrup, butter and chocolate in large heavy saucepan. Place over low heat; stir until chocolate is melted and ingredients are blended. Remove from heat; blend in sugar. Stir in eggs, flour, chopped walnuts and vanilla. Spread batter evenly in prepared pan. Bake 20 to 25 minutes or just until center is set. Do not overbake. Meanwhile, prepare Fudge Glaze. Remove brownies from oven. Immediately spread glaze evenly over hot brownies. Cool in pan on wire rack. Cut into 2-inch squares.

Makes 16 brownies

Combine chocolate, corn syrup and butter in small heavy saucepan. Stir over low heat until chocolate is melted; mix in cream.

CINNAMON-WHEAT BROWNIES

2 squares (1 ounce each) unsweetened chocolate
½ cup butter or margarine, softened
1 cup packed dark brown sugar
2 eggs
1 teaspoon ground cinnamon
1 teaspoon vanilla
¼ teaspoon baking powder
¼ teaspoon ground ginger
⅛ teaspoon ground cloves
½ cup whole wheat flour
1 cup coarsely chopped walnuts

Preheat oven to 350°F. Butter an 8-inch square pan. Melt chocolate in top of double boiler over hot, not boiling, water. Remove from heat; cool. Cream butter, sugar, eggs and melted chocolate in large bowl until light and smooth. Blend in cinnamon, vanilla, baking powder, ginger and cloves. Stir in flour and walnuts until well blended. Spread batter evenly in prepared pan. Bake 25 to 30 minutes or until top feels firm and dry. Do not overbake. Cool in pan on wire rack. Cut into 2-inch squares.

Makes 16 brownies

MISSISSIPPI MUD BARS

½ cup butter or margarine, softened
¾ cup packed brown sugar
1 teaspoon vanilla
1 egg
½ teaspoon baking soda
¼ teaspoon salt
1 cup plus 2 tablespoons all-purpose flour
1 cup (6 ounces) semisweet chocolate chips, divided
1 cup (6 ounces) white chocolate chips, divided
½ cup chopped walnuts or pecans

Preheat oven to 375°F. Line a 9-inch square pan with foil; grease the foil. Cream butter and sugar in large bowl until blended and smooth. Beat in vanilla and egg until light. Blend in baking soda and salt. Add flour, mixing until well blended. Stir in ¾ cup *each* of the semisweet and white chocolate chips and the nuts. Spread dough in prepared pan. Bake 23 to 25 minutes or until center feels firm. Do not overbake. Remove from oven; sprinkle remaining ¼ cup *each* semisweet and white chocolate chips over the top. Let stand a few minutes until chips melt, then spread evenly over bars. Cool in pan on wire rack until chocolate is set. Cut into 2×1-inch bars.

Makes about 3 dozen bars

APPLESAUCE FUDGE BARS

Applesauce and a double dose of chocolate make these moist and fudgy.

3 squares (1 ounce each) semisweet chocolate
½ cup butter or margarine
⅔ cup unsweetened applesauce
2 eggs, beaten
1 cup packed light brown sugar
1 teaspoon vanilla
1 cup all-purpose flour
½ teaspoon baking powder
¼ teaspoon baking soda
½ cup walnuts, chopped
1 cup (6 ounces) milk chocolate chips

Preheat oven to 350°F. Grease a 9-inch square pan. Melt semisweet chocolate and butter in small heavy saucepan over low heat. Remove from heat; cool. Combine applesauce, eggs, sugar and vanilla in large bowl. Combine flour, baking powder and baking soda in small bowl. Mix dry ingredients into applesauce mixture; blend in chocolate mixture. Spread batter evenly in prepared pan. Sprinkle nuts over the top. Bake 25 to 30 minutes or just until set. Remove from oven; sprinkle chocolate chips over the top. Let stand a few minutes until chips melt, then spread evenly over bars. Cool in pan on wire rack. Cut into 2×1-inch bars.

Makes about 3 dozen bars

ROCKY ROAD BROWNIES

½ cup butter or margarine
½ cup unsweetened cocoa
1 cup sugar
1 egg
½ cup all-purpose flour
¼ cup buttermilk
1 teaspoon vanilla
1 cup miniature
   marshmallows
1 cup coarsely chopped
   walnuts
1 cup (6 ounces) semisweet
   chocolate chips

Preheat oven to 350°F. Lightly grease an 8-inch square pan. Combine butter and cocoa in medium-sized heavy saucepan over low heat, stirring constantly until smooth. Remove from heat; stir in sugar, egg, flour, buttermilk and vanilla. Mix until smooth. Spread batter evenly in prepared pan. Bake 25 minutes or until center feels dry. (Do not overbake or brownies will be dry.) Remove from oven; sprinkle marshmallows, walnuts and chocolate chips over the top. Return to oven for 3 to 5 minutes or just until topping is warmed enough to meld together. Cool in pan on wire rack. Cut into 2-inch squares.

Makes 16 brownies

CHUNKY OATMEAL BARS

Large chocolate chunks are scattered throughout these buttery oatmeal bars. If you can't find chocolate chunks, cut chocolate candy bars into chunks.

¾ cup butter or margarine,
   softened
1 cup packed light brown
   sugar
2 teaspoons vanilla
1 cup all-purpose flour
2 tablespoons unsweetened
   cocoa
1½ teaspoons baking powder
¼ teaspoon salt
¼ cup water
2 cups uncooked rolled oats
1 package (12 ounces)
   semisweet chocolate
   chunks

Preheat oven to 375°F. Lightly grease a 9-inch square pan. Cream butter with sugar until smooth. Add vanilla, beating until light. Combine flour, cocoa, baking powder and salt in small bowl. Blend into creamed mixture with water. Stir in oats and chocolate chunks. Spread dough evenly in prepared pan. Bake 25 to 30 minutes or just until center feels firm. Cool in pan on wire rack. Cut into 2×1-inch bars.

Makes about 3 dozen bars

Rocky Road Brownies

BROWNIES & BARS   45

DOUBLE CHOCOLATE
CRISPY BARS

Both sides of these crispy bars are painted with chocolate—dark chocolate on one side, white chocolate on the other.

6 cups crispy rice cereal
½ cup peanut butter
⅓ cup butter or margarine
2 squares (1 ounce each) unsweetened chocolate
1 package (8 ounces) marshmallows
1 cup (6 ounces) semisweet chocolate chips *or* 6 ounces bittersweet chocolate, chopped
6 ounces white chocolate, chopped
2 teaspoons shortening, divided

Preheat oven to 350°F. Line a 13×9-inch pan with waxed paper. Spread cereal on cookie sheet; toast in oven 10 minutes or until crispy. Place in large bowl. Meanwhile, combine peanut butter, butter and unsweetened chocolate in large heavy saucepan. Stir over low heat until chocolate is melted. Add marshmallows; stir until melted and smooth. Pour chocolate mixture over cereal; mix until evenly coated. Press firmly into prepared pan. Place semisweet and white chocolates into separate bowls. Add 1 teaspoon shortening to each bowl. Place bowls over very warm water; stir until chocolates are melted. Spread top of bars with melted semisweet chocolate; cool until chocolate is set. Turn bars out of pan onto a sheet of waxed paper, chocolate side down. Remove waxed paper from bottom of bars; spread white chocolate over surface. Cool until chocolate is set. Cut into 2×1½-inch bars using a sharp, thin knife.

Makes about 3 dozen bars

Clockwise from top left: Double Chocolate Crispy Bars, Chocolate Macadamia Bars (page 48), Naomi's Revel Bars (page 48)

CHOCOLATE MACADAMIA BARS

12 squares (1 ounce each)
  bittersweet chocolate *or*
  1 package (12 ounces)
  semisweet chocolate
  chips
1 package (8 ounces) cream
  cheese, softened
⅔ cup whipping cream or
  undiluted evaporated
  milk
1 cup chopped macadamia
  nuts or almonds
1 teaspoon vanilla, divided
1 cup butter or margarine,
  softened
1½ cups sugar
1 egg
3 cups all-purpose flour
1 teaspoon baking powder
¼ teaspoon salt

Preheat oven to 375°F. Lightly grease a 13×9-inch pan. Combine chocolate, cream cheese and cream in large heavy saucepan. Stir over low heat until chocolate is melted and mixture is smooth. Remove from heat; stir in nuts and ½ teaspoon of the vanilla. Cream butter and sugar in large bowl. Beat in egg and remaining ½ teaspoon vanilla. Add flour, baking powder and salt, blending well. Press half of the butter mixture on bottom of prepared pan. Spread chocolate mixture evenly over the top. Sprinkle remaining butter mixture over chocolate. Bake 35 to 40 minutes or until golden brown. Cool in pan on wire rack. Cut into 2×1½-inch bars.

Makes about 3 dozen bars

NAOMI'S REVEL BARS

1 cup plus 2 tablespoons
  butter or margarine,
  softened
2 cups packed brown sugar
2 eggs
2 teaspoons vanilla
2½ cups all-purpose flour
1 teaspoon baking soda
3 cups uncooked rolled oats
1 package (12 ounces)
  semisweet chocolate
  chips
1 can (14 ounces) sweetened
  condensed milk

Preheat oven to 325°F. Lightly grease a 13×9-inch pan. Cream the 1 cup butter and the sugar in large bowl. Add eggs; beat until light. Blend in vanilla. Combine flour and baking soda; stir into creamed mixture. Blend in oats. Spread ¾ of the oat mixture evenly in prepared pan. Combine chocolate chips, milk and the 2 tablespoons butter in small heavy saucepan. Stir over low heat until chocolate is melted. Pour chocolate mixture evenly over mixture in pan. Dot with remaining oat mixture. Bake 20 to 25 minutes or until edges are browned and center feels firm. Cool in pan on wire rack. Cut into 2×1½-inch bars.

Makes about 3 dozen bars

NORMA D's COCOA BROWNIES

This large pan of cake-like brownies is perfect for a potluck supper or club meeting.

2 cups all-purpose flour
2 cups granulated sugar
1 cup butter or margarine
1 cup hot coffee
¼ cup unsweetened cocoa
½ cup buttermilk
2 eggs, slightly beaten
1 teaspoon baking soda
1 teaspoon vanilla
   Cocoa Frosting (recipe
    follows)

COCOA FROSTING
  ½ cup butter or margarine
  2 tablespoons unsweetened
    cocoa
  ¼ cup milk
3½ cups powdered sugar
  1 teaspoon vanilla

Preheat oven to 400°F. Butter a 17½ × 11-inch jelly-roll pan. Combine flour and granulated sugar in large bowl. Combine butter, coffee and cocoa in small heavy saucepan. Bring to a boil over medium heat, stirring constantly. Combine buttermilk, eggs, baking soda and vanilla in small bowl. Stir cocoa mixture into flour mixture until smooth. Stir in buttermilk mixture until well blended. Pour batter into prepared pan. Bake 20 minutes or until center springs back when touched. Meanwhile, prepare Cocoa Frosting. Remove brownies from oven. Immediately pour warm frosting over hot brownies, spreading evenly. Cool in pan on wire rack. Cut into 2½-inch squares.

Makes about 30 brownies

Combine butter, cocoa and milk in large saucepan. Bring to a boil over medium heat. Remove from heat. Stir in powdered sugar and vanilla; beat until smooth.

CHOCOLATE CHIP & SOUR CREAM BROWNIES

½ cup butter or margarine,
   softened
1 cup packed light brown
   sugar
1 egg
1 cup sour cream
1 teaspoon vanilla
½ cup unsweetened cocoa
½ teaspoon baking soda
¼ teaspoon salt
2 cups all-purpose flour
1 cup (6 ounces) semisweet
   chocolate chips
  Powdered sugar

Preheat oven to 350°F. Butter a 13 × 9-inch pan. Cream butter and brown sugar in large bowl until blended. Add egg, sour cream and vanilla; beat until light. Add cocoa, baking soda and salt; beat until smooth. Blend in flour until well mixed. Stir in chocolate chips; spread batter evenly in prepared pan. Bake 25 to 30 minutes or until center springs back when touched. Cool in pan on wire rack. Sift powdered sugar over the top. Cut into 2½ × 1½-inch bars.

Makes about 30 brownies

ALMOND CHEESECAKE BROWNIES

4 squares (1 ounce each)
    semisweet chocolate
5 tablespoons butter or
    margarine, divided
1 package (3 ounces) cream
    cheese, softened
1 cup granulated sugar,
    divided
3 eggs, divided
½ cup plus 1 tablespoon
    all-purpose flour
1½ teaspoons vanilla, divided
½ teaspoon baking powder
¼ teaspoon salt
½ teaspoon almond extract
½ cup chopped or slivered
    almonds
    Almond Icing (recipe
    follows)

ALMOND ICING
½ cup semisweet chocolate
    chips
2 tablespoons butter or
    margarine
3 tablespoons milk
¼ teaspoon almond extract
1 cup powdered sugar

Preheat oven to 350°F. Butter an 8-inch square pan. Melt chocolate and 3 tablespoons of the butter in small heavy saucepan over low heat; set aside. Mix cream cheese with remaining 2 tablespoons butter in small bowl. Slowly add ¼ cup of the granulated sugar, blending well. Add 1 egg, the 1 tablespoon flour and ½ teaspoon of the vanilla; set aside. Beat remaining 2 eggs and ¾ cup granulated sugar in large bowl until light. Add the baking powder, salt and ½ cup flour. Blend in chocolate mixture, remaining 1 teaspoon vanilla and the almond extract. Stir in almonds. Spread half of the chocolate mixture in prepared pan. Cover with cream cheese mixture, then spoon remaining chocolate mixture over the top. Swirl with knife or spatula to create a marbled effect. Bake 30 to 35 minutes or until set in center. Do not overbake. Meanwhile, prepare Almond Icing. Cool brownies 5 minutes, then spread icing evenly over the top. Cool completely in pan on wire rack. Cut into 2-inch squares.

Makes 16 brownies

Combine chocolate chips, butter, milk and almond extract in small heavy saucepan. Stir over low heat until chocolate is melted. Add powdered sugar; beat until glossy and easy to spread.

Clockwise from left: Almond Cheesecake Brownies, Chocolate Dream Bars (page 52), Chocolate-Mint Brownies (page 53)

CHOCOLATE DREAM BARS

½ cup butter or margarine, softened
1½ cups packed light brown sugar, divided
1 egg yolk
1 cup plus 2 tablespoons all-purpose flour
2 eggs
1 cup (6 ounces) semisweet chocolate chips
½ cup chopped toasted walnuts

Preheat oven to 375°F. Grease a 13×9-inch pan. Cream butter with ½ cup of the sugar and the egg yolk in large bowl until light and well blended. (There should be no brown sugar lumps.) Stir in the 1 cup flour until well blended. Press dough on bottom of prepared pan. Bake 12 to 15 minutes or until golden. Meanwhile, beat remaining 1 cup sugar, the 2 tablespoons flour and eggs in same bowl until light and frothy. Spread mixture over hot baked crust. Return to oven; bake about 15 minutes or until topping is set. Remove from oven; sprinkle chocolate chips over the top. Let stand a few minutes until chips melt, then spread evenly over bars. Sprinkle walnuts over chocolate. Cool in pan on wire rack. Cut into 2×1-inch bars.

Makes about 5 dozen bars

TEX-MEX BROWNIES

Ground red pepper gives these south-of-the-border brownies a slightly hot bite that goes well with chocolate.

½ cup butter or margarine
2 squares (1 ounce each) unsweetened chocolate
½ to 1 teaspoon ground red pepper
2 eggs
1 cup sugar
½ cup all-purpose flour
1 teaspoon vanilla
1 cup (6 ounces) semisweet chocolate chips

Preheat oven to 325°F. Grease and flour an 8-inch square pan. Melt butter and unsweetened chocolate in small heavy saucepan over low heat. Remove from heat. Stir in pepper; cool. Beat eggs in medium bowl until light. Add sugar, beating well. Blend in chocolate mixture. Stir in flour and vanilla. Spread batter evenly in prepared pan. Bake 30 minutes or until firm in center. Remove from oven; sprinkle chocolate chips over the top. Let stand until chocolate is melted, then spread evenly over brownies. Cool completely in pan on wire rack. Cut into 2-inch squares.

Makes 16 brownies

CHOCOLATE-MINT BROWNIES

½ cup butter or margarine
2 squares (1 ounce each)
   unsweetened chocolate
2 eggs
1 cup packed light brown
   sugar
½ cup all-purpose flour
1 teaspoon vanilla
   Mint Frosting (recipe
   follows)
   Chocolate Glaze (recipe
   follows)

Preheat oven to 350°F. Grease and flour an 8-inch square pan. Melt butter and chocolate in small heavy saucepan over low heat; stir to blend. Remove from heat; cool. Beat eggs in medium bowl until light. Add brown sugar, beating well. Blend in chocolate mixture. Stir in flour and vanilla. Spread batter evenly in prepared pan. Bake 30 minutes or until firm in center. Cool in pan on wire rack. Prepare Mint Frosting. Spread over the top; refrigerate until firm. Prepare Chocolate Glaze. Drizzle over frosting; refrigerate until firm. Cut into 2-inch squares.

Makes 16 brownies

MINT FROSTING
1½ cups powdered sugar
2 to 3 tablespoons light
   cream or milk
1 tablespoon butter or
   margarine, softened
½ teaspoon peppermint
   extract
1 to 2 drops green food
   coloring

Blend powdered sugar, 2 tablespoons cream and the butter in small bowl until smooth. Add more cream, if necessary, to make spreading consistency. Blend in peppermint extract and enough green food coloring to make a pale mint-green color.

CHOCOLATE GLAZE
½ cup semisweet chocolate
   chips
2 tablespoons butter or
   margarine

Place chocolate chips and butter in small bowl over hot water. Stir until melted and smooth.

MARBLED PEANUT-BUTTER BROWNIES

Swirls of peanut butter and chocolate form an unbeatable flavor combination.

½ cup butter or margarine, softened
¼ cup peanut butter
1 cup packed light brown sugar
½ cup granulated sugar
3 eggs
1 teaspoon vanilla
2 cups all-purpose flour
2 teaspoons baking powder
⅛ teaspoon salt
1 cup chocolate-flavored syrup
½ cup coarsely chopped salted mixed nuts

Preheat oven to 350°F. Lightly grease a 13×9-inch pan. Cream butter and peanut butter in large bowl until blended; stir in sugars. Beat in eggs, one at a time, until batter is light. Blend in vanilla. Combine flour, baking powder and salt in small bowl. Stir into creamed mixture. Spread half of the batter evenly in prepared pan. Spread syrup over the top. Spoon remaining batter over syrup. Swirl with knife or spatula to create a marbled effect. Sprinkle chopped nuts over the top. Bake 35 to 40 minutes or until lightly browned. Cool in pan on wire rack. Cut into 2-inch squares.

Makes about 2 dozen brownies

WEST HAVEN DATE BARS

1 cup boiling water
1 cup chopped pitted dates
½ cup butter or margarine, softened
1 cup sugar
2 eggs
1 teaspoon vanilla
1½ cups all-purpose flour
2 tablespoons unsweetened cocoa
1 teaspoon baking soda
1 cup (6 ounces) semisweet chocolate chips
½ cup chopped walnuts or pecans

Preheat oven to 350°F. Lightly grease a 13×9-inch pan. Pour boiling water over dates in small bowl; let stand until cooled. Cream butter with sugar in large bowl. Add eggs and vanilla; beat until light. Blend in flour, cocoa and baking soda to make a smooth dough. Stir in date mixture. Spread batter evenly in prepared pan. Sprinkle chocolate chips and nuts over the top. Bake 25 to 30 minutes or just until center feels firm. Cut into 2×1½-inch bars while still warm.

Makes about 3 dozen bars

Marbled Peanut-Butter Brownies

MOCHA FUDGE BROWNIES

3 squares (1 ounce each) semisweet chocolate
½ cup butter or margarine, softened
¾ cup sugar
2 eggs
2 teaspoons instant espresso coffee powder
1 teaspoon vanilla
½ cup all-purpose flour
½ cup chopped toasted almonds
1 cup (6 ounces) milk chocolate chips, divided

Preheat oven to 350°F. Butter an 8-inch square pan. Melt semisweet chocolate in top of double boiler over hot, not boiling, water. Remove from heat; cool. Cream butter and sugar in medium bowl. Beat in eggs until light and fluffy. Add melted chocolate, coffee powder and vanilla. Blend in flour, almonds and ½ cup of the chocolate chips. Spread batter evenly in prepared pan. Bake 25 minutes or just until firm in center. Remove from oven; sprinkle remaining ½ cup chocolate chips over the top. Let stand a few minutes until chips melt, then spread evenly over brownies. Cool completely in pan on wire rack. Cut into 2-inch squares.

Makes 16 brownies

CHOCOLATE CARAMEL BARS

2 cups all-purpose flour
1½ cups packed brown sugar, divided
1¼ cups butter or margarine, softened, divided
1 cup chopped pecans
1 cup (6 ounces) milk chocolate chips

Preheat oven to 350°F. Blend flour with 1 cup of the sugar and ½ cup of the butter in large bowl until crumbly. Press firmly on bottom of a 13×9-inch pan; sprinkle pecans evenly over the top. Combine remaining ½ cup sugar and ¾ cup butter in small saucepan. Cook over medium heat, stirring constantly, until mixture comes to a boil. Boil 1 minute, stirring constantly, until butter and sugar blend into a caramel sauce. Pour sauce evenly over pecans in pan. Bake 18 to 20 minutes or until caramel layer bubbles evenly all over. Remove from oven; sprinkle chocolate chips over the top. Let stand a few minutes until chips melt, then spread evenly over bars. Cool until chocolate is set, then cut into 2×1-inch bars.

Makes about 5 dozen bars

TOFFEE BARS

The crisp, brown-sugar base of these milk-chocolate-topped treats will remind you of a favorite candy bar.

½ cup butter or margarine, softened
½ cup packed light brown sugar
1 egg yolk
1 teaspoon vanilla
1 cup all-purpose flour
1 cup (6 ounces) milk chocolate chips
½ cup chopped walnuts or pecans

Preheat oven to 350°F. Lightly grease a 13×9-inch pan. Cream butter and sugar in large bowl. Blend in egg yolk and vanilla. Stir in flour until well blended. Press on bottom of prepared pan. Bake 15 minutes or until golden. Remove from oven; sprinkle chocolate chips over the top. Let stand a few minutes until chips melt, then spread evenly over bars. Sprinkle nuts over chocolate. Score into 2×1½-inch bars while still warm. Cool completely in pan on wire rack before cutting and removing from pan.

Makes about 3 dozen bars

FRUIT & PECAN BROWNIES

2 squares (1 ounce each) unsweetened chocolate
½ cup butter or margarine, softened
1 cup sugar
2 eggs
1 teaspoon vanilla
½ cup all-purpose flour
1 cup chopped dried mixed fruit
1 cup coarsely chopped pecans, divided
1 cup (6 ounces) semisweet chocolate chips, divided

Preheat oven to 350°F. Butter an 8-inch square pan. Melt unsweetened chocolate in top of double boiler over hot, not boiling, water. Remove from heat; cool. Cream butter and sugar in large bowl until smooth. Mix in eggs, beating until light and fluffy. Blend in melted chocolate and vanilla. Stir in flour, fruit, ½ cup of the pecans and ½ cup of the chocolate chips. Spread batter evenly in prepared pan. Sprinkle remaining ½ cup pecans and ½ cup chocolate chips over the top. Bake 25 to 30 minutes or just until center feels firm. Do not overbake. Remove from oven; cover while still warm with waxed paper or foil. Cool completely in pan on wire rack. Cut into 2-inch squares.

Makes 16 brownies

Chocolate Chippers

Clockwise from top right: White Chocolate and Cocoa Chippers (page 62),
Aloha Chippers (page 62), Peanutty Double Chip Cookies (page 63)

CHOCOLATE CHIP
CINNAMON CRINKLES

Rolling the dough in cinnamon sugar makes these cookies crinkly on top.

½ cup butter or margarine,
    softened
½ cup packed brown sugar
¼ cup plus 2 tablespoons
    granulated sugar
1 teaspoon vanilla
1 egg
1 teaspoon cream of tartar
½ teaspoon baking soda
⅛ teaspoon salt
1⅓ cups all-purpose flour
1 cup (6 ounces) semisweet
    chocolate chips
2 teaspoons unsweetened
    cocoa
1 teaspoon ground
    cinnamon

Preheat oven to 400°F. Line cookie sheets with parchment paper or leave ungreased. Cream butter with brown sugar, the ¼ cup granulated sugar, vanilla and egg in large bowl until light and fluffy. Beat in cream of tartar, baking soda and salt. Add flour; mix until dough is blended and stiff. Stir in chocolate chips. Combine the 2 tablespoons granulated sugar, the cocoa and cinnamon in small bowl. Shape rounded teaspoonfuls of dough into balls about 1¼ inches in diameter. Roll balls in cinnamon mixture until coated on all sides. Place 2 inches apart on cookie sheets. Bake 8 to 10 minutes or until firm. Do not overbake. Remove to wire racks to cool.

Makes about 3½ dozen cookies

CHOCOLATE CHIP
WAFER COOKIES

The trick to handling these delicate cookies is to line the cookie sheets with greased foil. When the cookies are cool, it's easy to peel the foil right off them.

½ cup butter or margarine,
    softened
½ cup sugar
1 egg
1 teaspoon vanilla
½ cup all-purpose flour
    Dash salt
1 cup (6 ounces) semisweet
    chocolate chips
⅓ cup chopped pecans or
    walnuts

Preheat oven to 350°F. Line cookie sheets with foil; lightly grease foil. Cream butter and sugar in large bowl until light. Add egg; beat until creamy. Stir in vanilla, flour and salt. Add chocolate chips and nuts; mix until well blended. Drop dough by teaspoonfuls 3 inches apart onto prepared cookie sheets. Bake 7 to 10 minutes or until edges are golden and centers are set. (Cookies are soft when hot, but become crispy as they cool.) Cool completely on foil, then peel foil from cookies.

Makes about 2 dozen cookies

*Top to bottom: Mrs. J's Chip Cookies (page 63), Chocolate Chip
Wafer Cookies, Chocolate Chip Cinnamon Crinkles*

ALOHA CHIPPERS

½ cup butter or margarine,
  softened
⅓ cup granulated sugar
⅓ cup packed light brown
  sugar
1 egg
1 tablespoon dark rum or
  water
1 teaspoon vanilla
½ teaspoon baking soda
⅛ teaspoon salt
1¼ cups all-purpose flour
½ cup semisweet chocolate
  chips
1 cup (6 ounces) white
  chocolate chips
½ cup flaked coconut
½ cup coarsely chopped
  macadamia nuts
  Flaked coconut

Preheat oven to 375°F. Line cookie sheets with parchment paper or leave ungreased. Cream butter, sugars, egg, rum, vanilla, baking soda and salt in large bowl until light and fluffy. Blend in flour until dough is smooth and stiff. Stir in semisweet and white chocolate chips, ½ cup coconut and the macadamia nuts. Drop dough by teaspoonfuls 2 inches apart onto cookie sheets. Sprinkle tops of cookies with additional coconut. Bake 8 to 10 minutes or until just firm in center. Do not overbake. Remove to wire racks to cool.

Makes about 3 dozen cookies

WHITE CHOCOLATE & COCOA CHIPPERS

¾ cup butter or margarine,
  softened
½ cup granulated sugar
½ cup packed brown sugar
1 egg
2 tablespoons water
½ cup unsweetened cocoa
¾ teaspoon baking soda
½ teaspoon vanilla
¼ teaspoon salt
1⅓ cups all-purpose flour
1½ cups (10 to 12 ounces)
  large white chocolate
  chips
1 cup coarsely chopped
  pecans or walnuts

Preheat oven to 375°F. Line cookie sheets with parchment paper or leave ungreased. Cream butter, sugars, egg and water in large bowl until light and fluffy. Blend in cocoa, baking soda, vanilla and salt. Blend in flour until well mixed. Stir in white chocolate chips and nuts. Drop dough by rounded tablespoonfuls 3 inches apart onto cookie sheets. Bake 8 to 10 minutes or until firm in center. Do not overbake. Remove to wire racks to cool.

Makes about 4 dozen cookies

PEANUTTY DOUBLE CHIP COOKIES

½ cup butter or margarine, softened
¾ cup packed light brown sugar
¾ cup granulated sugar
2 eggs
1 teaspoon baking soda
1 teaspoon vanilla
2 cups all-purpose flour
1 cup chunky peanut butter
1 cup (6 ounces) semisweet or milk chocolate chips
1 cup (6 ounces) peanut butter chips

Preheat oven to 350°F. Lightly grease cookie sheets or line with parchment paper. Cream butter and sugars in large bowl until blended. Add eggs, baking soda and vanilla; beat until light. Blend in flour and peanut butter until dough is stiff and smooth. Stir in chocolate and peanut butter chips. Drop dough by teaspoonfuls 2 inches apart onto prepared cookie sheets. Press cookies down with tines of fork to flatten slightly. Bake 12 minutes or until just barely done. Do not overbake. Remove to wire racks to cool.

Makes about 5 dozen cookies

MRS. J'S CHIP COOKIES

Crispy rice cereal, pulverized into a flour, adds flavor and texture to these cookies.

4 cups crispy rice cereal
1 milk chocolate crunch bar (5 ounces), broken into squares
2 cups all-purpose flour
1 teaspoon baking powder
1 teaspoon baking soda
¼ teaspoon salt
1 cup butter or margarine, softened
1 cup granulated sugar
1 cup packed light brown sugar
2 eggs
1 teaspoon vanilla
1 package (12 ounces) semisweet chocolate chips
1½ cups chopped walnuts

Preheat oven to 375°F. Line cookie sheets with parchment paper or leave ungreased. Process cereal in blender or food processor until pulverized. Add chocolate bar; continue processing until both chocolate and cereal are completely ground. Add flour, baking powder, baking soda and salt; process until blended. Cream butter and sugars in large bowl. Add eggs; beat until light. Blend in vanilla. Add flour mixture; blend until smooth. Stir in chocolate chips and walnuts until blended. Shape dough into walnut-sized balls. Place 2 inches apart on cookie sheets. Bake 10 to 12 minutes or until firm in center. Do not overbake. Remove to wire racks to cool.

Makes about 8 dozen cookies

DOUBLE CHOCOLATE CHUNK COOKIES

2 squares (1 ounce each)
   unsweetened chocolate
3 eggs
1 cup vegetable oil
¾ cup packed brown sugar
1 teaspoon baking powder
1 teaspoon vanilla
¼ teaspoon baking soda
¼ teaspoon salt
2⅓ cups all-purpose flour
1 package (12 ounces)
   semisweet chocolate
   chunks

Preheat oven to 350°F. Lightly grease cookie sheets or line with parchment paper. Melt unsweetened chocolate in top of double boiler over hot, not boiling, water. Remove from heat; cool. Beat eggs in large bowl until foamy. Add the oil and sugar; continue beating until light and frothy. Blend in baking powder, vanilla, baking soda, salt and melted chocolate. Mix in flour until smooth. Stir in chocolate chunks. Shape dough into walnut-sized balls. Place 2 inches apart on prepared cookie sheets. Bake 10 to 12 minutes or until firm in center. Do not overbake. Remove to wire racks to cool.

Makes about 4½ dozen cookies

White Chocolate Chunk Cookies:
Substitute one package (12 ounces) white chocolate chunks *or* two white chocolate candy bars (5 to 6 ounces each), cut into chunks, for the semisweet chocolate chunks.

CHOCOLATE CHUNK COOKIES

3 eggs
1 cup vegetable oil
¾ cup packed brown sugar
1 teaspoon baking powder
1 teaspoon vanilla
¼ teaspoon baking soda
¼ teaspoon salt
2½ cups all-purpose flour
1 package (12 ounces)
   semisweet chocolate
   chunks

Preheat oven to 350°F. Lightly grease cookie sheets or line with parchment paper. Beat eggs in large bowl until foamy. Add oil and sugar; beating until light and frothy. Blend in baking powder, vanilla, baking soda and salt. Mix in flour until dough is smooth. Stir in chocolate chunks. Shape dough into walnut-sized balls. Place 2 inches apart on prepared cookie sheets. Bake 10 to 12 minutes or until lightly browned. Remove to wire racks to cool.

Makes about 4½ dozen cookies

White Chocolate Chunk Cookies

CINNAMON-MOCHA CHIP COOKIES

1 cup butter or margarine, softened
1 cup packed light brown sugar
1 tablespoon instant espresso coffee powder
1 tablespoon boiling water
1 teaspoon vanilla
1 egg
2 cups all-purpose flour
1 teaspoon baking soda
1 teaspoon ground cinnamon
¼ teaspoon salt
1 package (12 ounces) milk chocolate chips
1½ cups coarsely chopped walnuts

Preheat oven to 375°F. Line cookie sheets with parchment paper or leave ungreased. Cream butter and sugar in large bowl until smooth. Dissolve coffee powder in water. Add to creamed mixture with vanilla and egg; beat until light. Combine flour, baking soda, cinnamon and salt in small bowl. Blend into creamed mixture until smooth. Stir in chocolate chips and walnuts. Drop dough by rounded tablespoonfuls 3 inches apart onto cookie sheets. Bake 7 to 9 minutes or until just firm in center. Cool 3 minutes on cookie sheet, then remove to wire racks to cool completely.

Makes about 3 dozen cookies

ULTIMATE WHITE & DARK CHOCOLATE CHIPPERS

1 cup butter or margarine, softened
¾ cup granulated sugar
¾ cup packed light brown sugar
2 eggs
2 tablespoons almond-flavored liqueur or water
1 teaspoon baking soda
1 teaspoon vanilla
¼ teaspoon salt
2⅓ cups all-purpose flour
1 cup (6 ounces) semisweet chocolate chips
1 cup (6 ounces) white chocolate chips
1 cup coarsely chopped pecans

Preheat oven to 375°F. Line cookie sheets with parchment paper or leave ungreased. Cream butter, sugars, eggs, liqueur, baking soda, vanilla and salt in large bowl until light and fluffy. Blend in flour until dough is smooth and stiff. Stir in semisweet and white chocolate chips and pecans. Drop dough by teaspoonfuls 2 inches apart onto prepared cookie sheets. Bake 8 to 10 minutes or until just firm in center. Do not overbake. Remove to wire racks to cool.

Makes about 5 dozen cookies

PISTACHIO CHIP COOKIES

Serve these cookies for dessert as an elegant accompaniment to ice cream. Be sure to follow the instructions and bake them on greased foil.

½ cup butter or margarine
⅓ cup light corn syrup
2 tablespoons frozen orange juice concentrate, thawed
1 tablespoon grated orange zest
⅔ cup packed dark brown sugar
1 cup all-purpose flour
½ cup chopped pistachio nuts
1 cup (6 ounces) semisweet chocolate chips

Preheat oven to 375°F. Line cookie sheets with foil; lightly grease foil. Combine butter, corn syrup, orange concentrate, orange zest and sugar in medium saucepan. Bring to a boil over medium heat, stirring constantly. Remove from heat; gradually stir in flour and nuts. Cool completely. Stir in chocolate chips. Drop batter by teaspoonfuls 3 inches apart onto prepared cookie sheets. Bake 8 to 10 minutes or until golden and lacy. (Cookies are soft when hot, but become crispy as they cool.) Cool completely on foil, then peel foil from cookies.

Makes about 4 dozen cookies

OAT BRAN CHIP COOKIES

Oat bran, touted as a health food, adds a wonderful nutty flavor to cookies.

1 cup oat bran*
2 cups all-purpose flour
½ teaspoon baking soda
1 cup butter or margarine, softened
⅔ cup packed light brown sugar
½ cup granulated sugar
2 eggs
1 teaspoon vanilla
1 package (12 ounces) semisweet chocolate chips

Preheat oven to 350°F. Lightly grease baking sheets or line with parchment paper. Combine oat bran, flour and baking soda in small bowl. Cream butter with sugars, eggs and vanilla in large bowl. Blend in flour mixture; stir in chocolate chips. Drop dough by rounded teaspoonfuls 2 inches apart onto prepared cookie sheets. Bake 13 to 15 minutes or until lightly browned. Remove to wire racks to cool.

Makes about 6½ dozen cookies

*If oat bran has a coarse texture, process it in a blender or food processor until pulverized.

WHOLE GRAIN CHIPPERS

Whole wheat flour, rolled oats and sunflower seeds add nutrients, crunch and flavor to after-school cookies.

1 cup butter or margarine, softened
⅔ cup granulated sugar
1 cup packed light brown sugar
2 eggs
1 teaspoon baking soda
1 teaspoon vanilla
Pinch salt
1 cup whole wheat flour
1 cup all-purpose flour
2 cups uncooked rolled oats
1 package (12 ounces) semisweet chocolate chips
1 cup sunflower seeds

Preheat oven to 375°F. Lightly grease cookie sheets or line with parchment paper. Cream butter with sugars and eggs in large bowl until light and fluffy. Beat in baking soda, vanilla and salt. Blend in flours and oats to make a stiff dough. Stir in chocolate chips. Shape rounded teaspoonfuls of dough into balls; roll in sunflower seeds. Place 2 inches apart on prepared cookie sheets. Bake 8 to 10 minutes or until firm. Do not overbake. Cool a few minutes on cookie sheet, then remove to wire racks to cool completely.

Makes about 6 dozen cookies

WHITE CHOCOLATE CHIP & MACADAMIA COOKIES

Bake these for someone special. Macadamia nuts give them a sensational crunch.

2 squares (1 ounce each) unsweetened chocolate
½ cup butter or margarine, softened
1 cup packed light brown sugar
1 egg
1 teaspoon vanilla
1¼ cups all-purpose flour
½ teaspoon baking soda
1 cup (6 ounces) white chocolate chips
¾ cup macadamia nuts, chopped

Preheat oven to 350°F. Lightly grease cookie sheets or line with parchment paper. Melt unsweetened chocolate in top of double boiler over hot, not boiling, water. Remove from heat; cool. Cream butter, melted chocolate and sugar in large bowl until blended. Add egg and vanilla; beat until light. Blend in flour, baking soda, chocolate chips and macadamia nuts. Drop dough by rounded teaspoonfuls 2 inches apart onto prepared cookie sheets. Bake 10 to 12 minutes or until firm. Do not overbake. Remove to wire racks to cool.

Makes about 4 dozen cookies

Whole Grain Chippers

Special-Day Cookies

Top left to bottom right: Mocha Pecan Pinwheels (page 72), Chocolate Pistachio Fingers (page 84), Chocolate Cherry Cookies (page 73), Orange & Chocolate Ribbon Cookies (page 77), Chocolate Spritz (page 88)

MOCHA PECAN PINWHEELS

1 square (1 ounce)
   unsweetened chocolate
½ cup (1 stick) butter or
   margarine, softened
¾ cup packed brown sugar
1 egg
1 teaspoon vanilla
¼ teaspoon baking soda
1¾ cups all-purpose flour
½ cup chopped pecans
1 teaspoon instant espresso
   coffee powder

Melt chocolate in small bowl over hot water. Stir until smooth. Cream butter, sugar, egg, vanilla and baking soda in large bowl, blending well. Stir in flour to make a stiff dough. Remove half of the dough; place in another bowl. Blend pecans and coffee powder into half of the dough. Stir melted chocolate into remaining dough. Cover doughs; refrigerate 30 minutes. Roll out light-colored dough to a 15×8-inch rectangle between 2 sheets of plastic wrap. Roll chocolate dough out to same dimensions between 2 more sheets of plastic wrap. Remove top sheets of plastic. Place light-colored dough on top of chocolate dough. Roll up firmly, jelly-roll fashion, starting with a long side. Wrap in plastic; freeze. (Dough can be frozen up to 6 weeks.) Preheat oven to 350°F. Line cookie sheets with parchment paper or leave ungreased. Cut frozen dough into ¼-inch-thick slices; place 2 inches apart on cookie sheets. Bake 9 to 12 minutes or until set. Remove to wire racks to cool.

Makes about 5 dozen cookies

CHOCOLATE-COCONUT MACAROONS

4 egg whites
1 teaspoon vanilla
   Dash salt
1½ cups sugar
2⅔ cups flaked coconut
2 tablespoons ground
   chocolate with sugar
   added*

*This type of ground chocolate is available in specialty food stores.

Preheat oven to 325°F. Line cookie sheets with parchment paper or lightly grease and dust with flour. In large clean, dry bowl, beat egg whites with vanilla and salt until stiff, but not dry. Beat in sugar, one tablespoon at a time, until mixture becomes stiff and glossy. Gently fold in coconut and ground chocolate until blended. Drop by rounded teaspoonfuls 2 inches apart onto prepared cookie sheets. Bake 20 minutes or until firm. Remove to wire racks to cool. Store in airtight containers.

Makes about 6 dozen cookies

CHOCOLATE CHERRY COOKIES

2 squares (1 ounce each)
    unsweetened chocolate
½ cup butter or margarine,
    softened
½ cup sugar
1 egg
2 cups cake flour
1 teaspoon vanilla
¼ teaspoon salt
    Maraschino cherries, well
    drained (about 48)
1 cup (6 ounces) semisweet
    or milk chocolate chips

Melt unsweetened chocolate in top of double boiler over hot, not boiling, water. Remove from heat; cool. Cream butter and sugar in large bowl until light. Add egg and melted chocolate; beat until fluffy. Stir in cake flour, vanilla and salt until well blended. Cover; refrigerate until firm, about 1 hour.

Preheat oven to 400°F. Lightly grease cookie sheets or line with parchment paper. Shape dough into 1-inch balls. Place 2 inches apart on prepared cookie sheets. With knuckle of a finger, make a deep indentation in center of each ball. Place a cherry into each indentation. Bake 8 minutes or just until set. Meanwhile, melt chocolate chips in small bowl over hot water. Stir until melted. Remove cookies to wire racks. Drizzle melted chocolate over tops while still warm. Refrigerate until chocolate is set.

Makes about 4 dozen cookies

FUDGE KISSES

Flavored with coconut, nuts and swirls of chocolate, these meringue-based cookies are called kisses—maybe because they crumble when you bite into them.

1 cup (6 ounces) semisweet
    chocolate chips
2 egg whites
    Dash salt
½ teaspoon cider vinegar
½ teaspoon vanilla
½ cup sugar
½ cup flaked coconut
¼ cup chopped walnuts or
    pecans

Preheat oven to 350°F. Line cookie sheets with parchment paper or lightly grease and sprinkle with flour. Melt chocolate chips in top of double boiler over hot, not boiling, water. Remove from heat; cool. In large clean, dry bowl, beat egg whites with salt until frothy. Beat in vinegar and vanilla. Beat in sugar, one tablespoon at a time, until mixture becomes stiff and glossy. Gently fold in coconut, nuts and melted chocolate until mixture is marbled. Drop mixture by rounded teaspoonfuls 2 inches apart onto prepared cookie sheets. Bake 12 to 15 minutes or until dry on top. Cool completely on cookie sheets. Store in airtight containers.

Makes 3 dozen cookies

RASPBERRY-FILLED CHOCOLATE RAVIOLI

Squares of rich chocolate dough encase a surprise filling of raspberry jam.

2 squares (1 ounce each)
    bittersweet or semisweet
    chocolate
1 cup butter or margarine,
    softened
½ cup granulated sugar
1 egg
1 teaspoon vanilla
½ teaspoon chocolate extract
¼ teaspoon baking soda
    Dash salt
2½ cups all-purpose flour
1 to 1¼ cups seedless
    raspberry jam
    Powdered sugar

Melt chocolate in top of double boiler over hot, not boiling, water. Remove from heat; cool. Cream butter and granulated sugar in large bowl until blended. Add egg, vanilla, chocolate extract, baking soda, salt and melted chocolate; beat until light. Blend in flour to make a stiff dough. Divide dough in half. Cover; refrigerate until firm.

Preheat oven to 350°F. Lightly grease cookie sheets or line with parchment paper. Roll out dough, half at a time, ⅛ inch thick between 2 sheets of plastic wrap. Remove top sheet of plastic. (If dough gets too soft and sticks to plastic, refrigerate until firm.) Cut dough into 1½-inch squares. Place half of the squares 2 inches apart on prepared cookie sheets. Place about ½ teaspoon jam in center of each square; top with another square. Using fork, press edges of squares together to seal, then pierce center of each square. Bake 10 minutes or just until edges are browned. Remove to wire racks to cool. Dust lightly with powdered sugar.

Makes about 6 dozen cookies

Raspberry-Filled Chocolate Ravioli

ORANGE & CHOCOLATE RIBBON COOKIES

Use an empty 12×2×2-inch food wrap box to shape these cookies as they chill. A foil, plastic wrap, or waxed paper box is ideal.

1 cup butter or margarine, softened
½ cup sugar
3 egg yolks
2 teaspoons grated orange zest
1 teaspoon orange extract
2¼ cups all-purpose flour, divided
3 tablespoons unsweetened cocoa
1 teaspoon vanilla
1 teaspoon chocolate extract

Cream butter, sugar and egg yolks in large bowl until light and fluffy. Remove half of the mixture; place in another bowl. Add orange zest, orange extract and 1¼ cups of the flour to one half of the mixture; mix until blended and smooth. Shape into a ball. Add cocoa, vanilla and chocolate extract to second half of the mixture; beat until smooth. Stir in remaining 1 cup flour; mix until blended and smooth. Shape into a ball. Cover doughs; refrigerate 10 minutes.

Empty a 12×2×2-inch food wrap box, such as foil or plastic wrap; set aside. Roll out each dough separately on lightly floured surface to a 12×4-inch rectangle. Pat edges of dough to straighten; use rolling pin to level off thickness. Place one of the doughs on top of the other. Using a sharp knife, make a lengthwise cut through center of doughs. Lift half of the dough onto the other to make a long, 4-layer strip of dough. With hands, press dough strips together. Wrap in plastic wrap; fit into food wrap box, pressing down at the top. Close box; refrigerate at least 1 hour or up to 3 days. (For longer storage, freeze up to 6 weeks.)

Preheat oven to 350°F. Lightly grease cookie sheets or line with parchment paper. Cut dough crosswise into ¼-inch-thick slices; place 2 inches apart on prepared cookie sheets. Bake 10 to 12 minutes or until very lightly browned. Remove to wire racks to cool.

Makes about 5 dozen cookies

Orange & Chocolate Ribbon Cookies, Chocolate-Mint Sandwiches (page 78), Cinnamon-Chocolate Cutouts (page 79)

CHOCOLATE-MINT SANDWICHES

2 squares (1 ounce each) unsweetened chocolate
½ cup butter or margarine, softened
1 cup packed light brown sugar
1 teaspoon vanilla
1 egg
⅛ teaspoon baking soda
2 cups all-purpose flour
Creamy Mint Filling (recipe follows)

Melt chocolate in top of double boiler over hot, not boiling, water. Remove from heat; cool. Cream butter and brown sugar in large bowl. Beat in vanilla, egg, melted chocolate and baking soda until light and fluffy. Stir in flour to make a stiff dough. Divide dough into 4 parts. Shape each part into a roll, about 1½ inches in diameter. Wrap in plastic wrap; refrigerate at least 1 hour or up to 2 weeks. (For longer storage, freeze up to 6 weeks.)

Preheat oven to 375°F. Line cookie sheets with parchment paper or leave ungreased. Cut rolls into ⅛-inch-thick slices; place 2 inches apart on cookie sheets. Bake 6 to 7 minutes or until firm. Remove to wire racks to cool. Prepare Creamy Mint Filling. Spread filling on bottoms of half the cookies. Top with remaining cookies, bottom sides down, forming sandwiches.

Makes about 3 dozen sandwich cookies

CREAMY MINT FILLING
2 tablespoons butter or margarine, softened
1½ cups powdered sugar
3 to 4 tablespoons light cream or half-and-half
¼ teaspoon peppermint extract
Few drops green food coloring

Cream butter with powdered sugar and cream in small bowl until smooth and blended. Stir in peppermint extract and food coloring, blending well.

CINNAMON-CHOCOLATE CUTOUTS

2 squares (1 ounce each) unsweetened chocolate
½ cup butter or margarine, softened
1 cup granulated sugar
1 egg
1 teaspoon vanilla
3 cups all-purpose flour
2 teaspoons ground cinnamon
½ teaspoon baking soda
¼ teaspoon salt
½ cup sour cream
Decorator Icing (recipe follows)

Melt chocolate in top of double boiler over hot, not boiling, water. Remove from heat; cool. Cream butter, melted chocolate, granulated sugar, egg and vanilla in large bowl until light. Combine flour, cinnamon, baking soda and salt in small bowl. Stir into creamed mixture with sour cream until smooth. Cover; refrigerate at least 30 minutes.

Preheat oven to 400°F. Lightly grease cookie sheets or line with parchment paper. Roll out dough, one fourth at a time, ¼ inch thick on lightly floured surface. Cut out with cookie cutters. Place 2 inches apart on prepared cookie sheets. Bake 10 minutes or until lightly browned, but not dark. Remove to wire racks to cool. Prepare Decorator Icing. Spoon into pastry bag fitted with small tip or small heavy-duty plastic bag. (If using plastic bag, close securely. With scissors, snip off small corner from one side of bag.) Decorate cookies with icing.

Makes about 6 dozen cookies

DECORATOR ICING
1 egg white*
3½ cups powdered sugar
1 teaspoon almond or lemon extract
2 to 3 tablespoons water

Beat egg white in large bowl until frothy. Gradually beat in powdered sugar until blended. Add almond extract and enough water to moisten. Beat until smooth and glossy.

*Use clean, uncracked egg.

SPUMONI BARS

These pretty tri-colored cookies will remind you of the popular Italian ice cream.

¾ cup butter or margarine,
   softened
⅔ cup sugar
3 egg yolks
1 teaspoon vanilla
¼ teaspoon baking powder
⅛ teaspoon salt
2 cups all-purpose flour
12 maraschino cherries, well
   drained and chopped
¼ cup chopped walnuts
¼ cup mint-flavored or plain
   semisweet chocolate
   chips
2 teaspoons water, divided

Preheat oven to 350°F. Cream butter and sugar in large bowl until blended. Beat in egg yolks, vanilla, baking powder and salt until light. Stir in flour to make a stiff dough. Divide dough into 3 equal parts; place each part in small bowl. Add cherries and walnuts to one part, blending well. Melt chocolate chips in small bowl over hot water. Stir until smooth. Add melted chocolate and 1 teaspoon of the water to second part, blending well. Stir remaining 1 teaspoon water into third part. (If doughs are soft, refrigerate 10 minutes.)

Divide each color dough into 4 equal parts. Shape each part into a 6-inch rope by rolling on lightly floured surface. Place one rope of each color side by side on ungreased cookie sheet. Flatten ropes so they attach together making 1 strip of 3 colors. With rolling pin, roll strip directly on cookie sheet until it measures 12×3 inches. With straight edge of knife, score strip crosswise at 1-inch intervals. Repeat with remaining ropes to make a total of 4 tri-colored strips of dough. Bake 12 to 13 minutes or until set but not completely browned; remove from oven. While cookies are still warm, trim lengthwise edges to make them even and cut into individual cookies along score marks. (Cookies will bake together but are easy to cut apart while still warm.) Cool on cookie sheets.

Makes 4 dozen cookies

Spumoni Bars, Chocolate Pistachio Fingers (page 84),
Chocolate-Dipped Oat Cookies (page 84)

DOUBLE-DIPPED HAZELNUT CRISPS

¾ cup semisweet chocolate
   chips
1¼ cups all-purpose flour
¾ cup powdered sugar
⅔ cup whole hazelnuts,
   toasted, hulled and
   pulverized*
¼ teaspoon instant espresso
   coffee powder
   Dash salt
½ cup butter or margarine,
   softened
2 teaspoons vanilla
4 squares (1 ounce each)
   bittersweet or semisweet
   chocolate
4 ounces white chocolate
2 teaspoons shortening,
   divided

Preheat oven to 350°F. Lightly grease cookie sheets or line with parchment paper. Melt chocolate chips in top of double boiler over hot, not boiling, water. Remove from heat; cool. Blend flour, sugar, hazelnuts, coffee powder and salt in large bowl. Blend in butter, melted chocolate and vanilla until dough is stiff but smooth. (If dough is too soft to handle, cover and refrigerate until firm.) Roll out dough, one fourth at a time, ⅛ inch thick on lightly floured surface. Cut out with 2-inch scalloped round cutters. Place 2 inches apart on prepared cookie sheets. Bake 8 minutes or until not quite firm. (Cookies should not brown. They will puff up during baking and then fall again.) Remove to wire racks to cool.

Place bittersweet and white chocolates into separate small bowls. Add 1 teaspoon shortening to each bowl. Place bowls over hot water; stir until chocolate is melted and smooth. Dip cookies, one at a time, halfway into bittersweet chocolate. Place on waxed paper; refrigerate until chocolate is set. Dip other halves of cookies into white chocolate; refrigerate until set. Store cookies in airtight container in cool place. (If cookies are frozen, chocolate may discolor.)

Makes about 4 dozen cookies

*To pulverize hazelnuts, place in food processor or blender. Process until thoroughly ground with a dry, not pasty, texture.

Left to right: Double-Dipped Hazelnut Crisps, Pecan Florentines (page 85)

CHOCOLATE-DIPPED
OAT COOKIES

2 cups uncooked rolled oats
¾ cup packed brown sugar
½ cup vegetable oil
½ cup finely chopped
    walnuts
1 egg
2 teaspoons grated orange
    rind
¼ teaspoon salt
1 package (12 ounces) milk
    chocolate chips

Combine oats, sugar, oil, walnuts, egg, orange rind and salt in large bowl until blended. Cover; refrigerate overnight. Preheat oven to 350°F. Lightly grease cookie sheets or line with parchment paper. Melt chocolate chips in top of double boiler over hot, not boiling, water; set aside. Shape oat mixture into large-marble-sized balls. Place 2 inches apart on prepared cookie sheets. Bake 10 to 12 minutes or until golden and crisp. Cool 10 minutes on wire racks. Dip tops of cookies, one at a time, into melted chocolate. Place on waxed paper; cool until chocolate is set.

Makes about 6 dozen cookies

CHOCOLATE PISTACHIO
FINGERS

Both ends of these buttery, finger-shaped cookies are dipped into melted chocolate. Then, for an elegant finish, the chocolate ends are covered with chopped pistachios.

¾ cup butter or margarine,
    softened
⅓ cup sugar
3 ounces (about ⅓ cup)
    almond paste
1 egg yolk
1⅔ cups all-purpose flour
1 cup (6 ounces) semisweet
    chocolate chips
½ cup finely chopped
    natural pistachios

Preheat oven to 350°F. Line cookie sheets with parchment paper or lightly grease and dust with flour. Cream butter and sugar in large bowl until blended. Add almond paste and egg yolk; beat until light. Blend in flour to make a smooth dough. (If dough is too soft to handle, cover and refrigerate until firm.) Turn out onto lightly floured board. Divide into 8 equal pieces; divide each piece in half. Roll each half into a 12-inch rope; cut each rope into 2-inch lengths. Place 2 inches apart on prepared cookie sheets. Bake 10 to 12 minutes or until edges just begin to brown. Remove to wire racks to cool. Melt chocolate chips in small bowl over hot water. Stir until smooth. Dip both ends of cookies about ½ inch into melted chocolate, then dip the chocolate ends into pistachios. Place on waxed paper; let stand until chocolate is set.

Makes 8 dozen cookies

PECAN FLORENTINES

Florentines are lacy confections that require a bit more skill than the average drop cookie. When baked on foil as directed, they are much easier to handle.

¾ cup pecan halves,
    pulverized*
½ cup all-purpose flour
⅓ cup packed brown sugar
¼ cup light corn syrup
¼ cup butter or margarine
 2 tablespoons milk
⅓ cup semisweet chocolate
    chips

Preheat oven to 350°F. Line cookie sheets with foil; lightly grease foil. Combine pecans and flour in small bowl. Combine sugar, syrup, butter and milk in medium saucepan. Stir over medium heat until mixture comes to a boil. Remove from heat; stir in flour mixture. Drop batter by teaspoonfuls about 3 inches apart onto prepared cookie sheets. Bake 10 to 12 minutes or until lacy and golden brown. (Cookies are soft when hot, but become crispy as they cool.) Cool completely on foil. Place chocolate chips in small heavy-duty plastic bag; close securely. Set bag in bowl of hot water until chips are melted, being careful not to let any water into bag. (Knead bag lightly to check that chips are completely melted.) Pat bag dry. With scissors, snip off a small corner from one side of bag. Squeeze melted chocolate over cookies to decorate. Let stand until chocolate is set. Peel foil off cookies.

Makes about 3 dozen cookies

*To pulverize pecans, place in food processor or blender. Process until thoroughly ground with a dry, not pasty, texture.

TRIPLE CHOCOLATE PRETZELS

Buttery pretzel-shaped chocolate cookies are glazed with dark chocolate, then decorated with white chocolate for a triple chocolate treat.

2 squares (1 ounce each) unsweetened chocolate
½ cup butter or margarine, softened
½ cup granulated sugar
1 egg
2 cups cake flour
1 teaspoon vanilla
¼ teaspoon salt
    Mocha Glaze (recipe follows)
2 ounces white chocolate, chopped

Melt unsweetened chocolate in top of double boiler over hot, not boiling, water. Remove from heat; cool. Cream butter and granulated sugar in large bowl until light. Add egg and melted chocolate; beat until fluffy. Stir in cake flour, vanilla and salt until well blended. Cover; refrigerate until firm, about 1 hour.

Preheat oven to 400°F. Lightly grease cookie sheets or line with parchment paper. Divide dough into 4 equal parts. Divide each part into 12 pieces. To form pretzels, knead each piece briefly to soften dough. Roll into a rope about 6 inches long. Form each rope on prepared cookie sheet into a pretzel shape. Repeat with all pieces of dough, spacing cookies 2 inches apart. Bake 7 to 9 minutes or until firm. Remove to wire racks to cool. Prepare Mocha Glaze. Dip pretzels, one at a time, into glaze to coat completely. Place on waxed paper, right side up. Let stand until glaze is set. Melt white chocolate in small bowl over hot water. Squeeze melted chocolate through pastry bag or drizzle over pretzels to decorate. Let stand until chocolate is completely set.

Makes 4 dozen cookies

MOCHA GLAZE
1 cup (6 ounces) semisweet chocolate chips
1 teaspoon light corn syrup
1 teaspoon shortening
1 cup powdered sugar
3 to 5 tablespoons hot coffee or water

Combine chocolate chips, corn syrup and shortening in small heavy saucepan. Stir over low heat until chocolate is melted. Stir in powdered sugar and enough coffee to make a smooth glaze.

Top: Chocolate Spritz (page 88) and Chocolate Cherry Cookies (page 73), bottom: Triple Chocolate Pretzels

CHOCOLATE SPRITZ

2 squares (1 ounce each) unsweetened chocolate
1 cup butter, softened
½ cup granulated sugar
1 egg
1 teaspoon vanilla
¼ teaspoon salt
2¼ cups all-purpose flour
Powdered sugar

Preheat oven to 400°F. Line cookie sheets with parchment paper or leave ungreased. Melt chocolate in top of double boiler over hot, not boiling, water. Remove from heat; cool. Cream butter, granulated sugar, egg, vanilla and salt in large bowl until light. Blend in melted chocolate and flour until stiff. Fit cookie press with your choice of plate. Load press with dough; press cookies out onto cookie sheets, spacing 2 inches apart. Bake 5 to 7 minutes or just until very slightly browned around edges. Remove to wire racks to cool. Dust with powdered sugar.

Makes about 5 dozen cookies

CHOCOLATE-FROSTED ALMOND SHORTBREAD

This shortbread keeps quite well in the refrigerator. Simply slip the whole pan into a plastic bag and seal securely.

¾ cup butter, softened
¼ cup packed light brown sugar
¼ cup powdered sugar
1 egg yolk
1 teaspoon almond extract
1½ cups all-purpose flour
⅛ teaspoon baking soda
7 ounces (about 1 cup) almond paste
½ cup granulated sugar
1 egg
½ cup milk chocolate chips

Preheat oven to 350°F. Cover bottom of a 9-inch pie pan with parchment or waxed paper. Cream butter, brown sugar, powdered sugar, egg yolk and almond extract in large bowl. Blend in flour and baking soda until smooth. Press half of the dough into prepared pie pan. Beat almond paste, granulated sugar and whole egg in small bowl until smooth. Spread over dough in pan. Roll out remaining half of dough on lightly floured surface into a circle to fit top of almond layer. Place over almond layer; press down to make smooth top. Bake 30 to 40 minutes or until top appears very lightly browned and feels firm. Remove from oven; sprinkle chocolate chips over the top. Let stand a few minutes until chips melt, then spread evenly over shortbread. Refrigerate until chocolate is set. Cut into slim wedges to serve.

Makes 16 to 20 cookies

DANISH RASPBERRY COOKIES

These fancy cookies look like you fussed all day making them. Only you know how easy and fun they were to prepare.

2 squares (1 ounce each) unsweetened chocolate
½ cup butter or margarine, softened
½ cup sugar
1 egg
2 cups cake flour
1 teaspoon vanilla
¼ teaspoon salt
1 cup (6 ounces) milk chocolate or white chocolate chips *or* ½ cup of each
1 to 1¼ cups seedless raspberry preserves or jam

Melt unsweetened chocolate in top of double boiler over hot, not boiling, water. Remove from heat; cool. Cream butter and sugar in large bowl until light. Add egg and melted chocolate; beat until fluffy. Stir in cake flour, vanilla and salt until well blended. Cover; refrigerate until firm, about 1 hour.

Preheat oven to 400°F. Lightly grease cookie sheets or line with parchment paper. Divide dough into 4 equal parts. Divide each part into 2 pieces. Roll each piece into a rope 12 inches long on lightly floured board. (The ropes should be about the thickness of a finger.) Place 2 inches apart on prepared cookie sheets. With side of finger, make an indentation along length of each rope. Bake 8 minutes or until firm. Meanwhile, melt chocolate chips in small bowl over hot water. Stir until smooth. (If using both kinds of chips, melt separately.) Stir preserves; spoon into pastry bag fitted with ¼-inch tip or into small heavy-duty plastic bag. (If using plastic bag, snip off a small corner from one side of bag.) Remove cookies from oven. Press preserves down length of each cookie strip. Return to oven for 2 minutes, then remove to wire racks. While cookies are still warm, drizzle melted chocolate over the tops, then cut strips into 1-inch diagonal pieces. Refrigerate until chocolate is set.

Makes 8 dozen cookies

CHOCOLATE COOKIE PRINTS

Cookie stamps imprint cookies with a raised design. Usually made of ceramic or glass, they are available in specialty shops or large department stores.

2 squares (1 ounce each) unsweetened chocolate
½ cup butter or margarine, softened
¾ cup sugar
1 egg
2 cups cake flour
1 teaspoon vanilla
¼ teaspoon salt
    Sugar

Melt chocolate in top of double boiler over hot, not boiling, water. Remove from heat; cool. Cream butter and ¾ cup sugar in large bowl until light. Add egg and melted chocolate; beat until fluffy. Stir in cake flour, vanilla and salt until well blended. Cover; refrigerate until firm, about 1 hour.

Preheat oven to 400°F. Lightly grease cookie sheets or line with parchment paper. Divide dough into 4 equal parts. Divide each part into 12 pieces. Roll each piece into a smooth round ball. Place 2 inches apart on prepared cookie sheets. Dip cookie stamp into water, then into sugar. Press down firmly onto a dough ball; remove. (Cookie will have imprint of stamp on it.) Repeat for each cookie, dipping stamp into water and sugar each time. Bake 7 to 9 minutes or until firm. Remove to wire racks to cool.

Makes 4 dozen cookies

CHOCOLATE RUM BALLS

½ cup butter or margarine, softened
⅓ cup granulated sugar
1 egg yolk
1 tablespoon dark rum
1 teaspoon vanilla
1 cup all-purpose flour
¼ cup unsweetened cocoa
1 cup finely chopped walnuts or pecans
    Powdered sugar

Cream butter, granulated sugar and egg yolk in large bowl until light and fluffy. Blend in rum and vanilla. Stir in flour, cocoa and nuts; mix well. Cover; refrigerate until firm, about 1 hour. Preheat oven to 350°F. Lightly grease cookie sheets or line with parchment paper. Shape dough into 1-inch balls. Place 2 inches apart on prepared cookie sheets. Bake 15 to 20 minutes or until firm. Remove to wire racks to cool. Roll in powdered sugar.

Makes about 3 dozen cookies

Clockwise from center: Chocolate Tassies (page 93),
Chocolate-Dipped Almond Crescents (page 92), Chocolate Cookie Prints

CHOCOLATE-DIPPED ALMOND CRESCENTS

One end of these crescent-shaped cookies is dipped into melted chocolate—a decorative touch that makes them look special.

1 cup butter or margarine, softened
1 cup powdered sugar
2 egg yolks
2½ cups all-purpose flour
1½ teaspoons almond extract
1 cup (6 ounces) semisweet chocolate chips

Preheat oven to 375°F. Line cookie sheets with parchment paper or leave ungreased. Cream butter, sugar and egg yolks in large bowl. Beat in flour and almond extract until well mixed. Shape dough into 1-inch balls. (If dough is too soft to handle, cover and refrigerate until firm.) Roll balls into 2-inch long ropes, tapering both ends. Curve ropes into crescent shapes. Place 2 inches apart on cookie sheets. Bake 8 to 10 minutes or until set, but not browned. Remove to wire racks to cool. Melt chocolate chips in top of double boiler over hot, not boiling, water. Dip one end of each crescent in melted chocolate. Place on waxed paper; cool until chocolate is set.

Makes about 5 dozen cookies

COCOA GINGERBREAD COOKIES

¼ cup butter or margarine, softened
2 tablespoons shortening
⅓ cup packed brown sugar
¼ cup dark molasses
1 egg
1½ cups all-purpose flour
¼ cup unsweetened cocoa
½ teaspoon baking soda
½ teaspoon ground ginger
½ teaspoon ground cinnamon
¼ teaspoon salt
¼ teaspoon ground nutmeg
⅛ teaspoon ground cloves
Decorator Icing (page 79)

Preheat oven to 400°F. Lightly grease cookie sheets or line with parchment paper. Cream butter, shortening, brown sugar and molasses in large bowl. Add egg; beat until light. Combine flour, cocoa, baking soda, ginger, cinnamon, salt, nutmeg and cloves in small bowl. Blend into creamed mixture until smooth. (If dough is too soft to handle, cover and refrigerate until firm.) Roll out dough ¼ inch thick on lightly floured surface. Cut out with cookie cutters. Place 2 inches apart on prepared cookie sheets. Bake 8 to 10 minutes or until firm. Remove to wire racks to cool. Prepare Decorator Icing. Spoon into pastry bag fitted with small tip. Decorate cookies with icing.

Makes about 6 dozen cookies

CHOCOLATE TASSIES

Tassies are old-fashioned cookies that resemble miniature pecan tarts. Here, the pecan filling is enriched with chocolate.

PASTRY
- 2 cups all-purpose flour
- 2 packages (3 ounces each) cream cheese, cold, cut into chunks
- 1 cup butter or margarine, cold, cut into chunks

FILLING
- 2 tablespoons butter or margarine
- 2 squares (1 ounce each) unsweetened chocolate
- 1½ cups packed brown sugar
- 2 teaspoons vanilla
- 2 eggs, beaten
  Dash salt
- 1½ cups chopped pecans

To prepare Pastry: Place flour in large bowl. Cut in cream cheese and butter. Continue to mix until dough can be shaped into a ball. Wrap dough in plastic wrap; refrigerate 1 hour. Shape dough into 1-inch balls. Press each ball into ungreased miniature (1¾-inch) muffin pan cup, covering bottom and side of cup with dough. Preheat oven to 350°F.

To prepare Filling: Melt butter and chocolate in medium-sized heavy saucepan over low heat. Remove from heat. Blend in sugar, vanilla, eggs and salt; beat until thick. Stir in pecans. Spoon about 1 teaspoon filling into each unbaked pastry shell. Bake 20 to 25 minutes or until lightly browned and filling is set. Cool in pans on wire racks. Remove from pans; store in airtight containers.

Makes about 5 dozen cookies

ALMOND FUDGE CUPS

PASTRY
- ¾ cup butter or margarine, softened
- ⅓ cup sugar
- 2 cups all-purpose flour
- 1 tablespoon almond- or fruit-flavored liqueur *or* water
- 1 teaspoon vanilla

FILLING
- 1 cup (6 ounces) semisweet chocolate chips
- ¾ cup blanched almonds
- 2 eggs
- ½ cup sugar
  Dash salt

To prepare Pastry: Lightly grease 3 dozen miniature (1¾-inch) muffin pan cups or small tart shells. Cream butter and sugar in large bowl until blended. Add flour, liqueur and vanilla; stir to make moist crumbs. Divide crumbs evenly among muffin cups; press to cover bottoms and sides of cups completely. Preheat oven to 350°F.

To prepare Filling: Place chocolate chips and almonds in food processor or blender. Process until finely ground. Beat eggs in medium bowl until thick; stir in sugar and salt. Blend in chocolate mixture. Spoon filling into unbaked pastry shells. Bake 20 minutes or until filling is set. Cool in pans on wire racks. Store in airtight containers.

Makes 3 dozen cookies

CHOCOLATE-FROSTED MARSHMALLOW COOKIES

COOKIES

½ cup butter or margarine
2 squares (1 ounce each)
  unsweetened chocolate
1 egg
1 cup packed brown sugar
1 teaspoon vanilla
½ teaspoon baking soda
1½ cups all-purpose flour
½ cup milk
1 package (16 ounces) large
  marshmallows, halved
  crosswise

FROSTING

1½ squares (1½ ounces)
  unsweetened chocolate
¼ cup butter or margarine
1½ cups powdered sugar
1 egg white*
1 teaspoon vanilla

To prepare Cookies: Preheat oven to 350°F. Lightly grease cookie sheets or line with parchment paper. Melt butter and chocolate in small heavy saucepan over low heat; stir to blend. Remove from heat; cool. Beat egg, brown sugar, vanilla and baking soda in large bowl until light and fluffy. Blend in chocolate mixture and flour until smooth. Slowly beat in milk to make a light, cake-batter-like dough. Drop dough by teaspoonfuls 2 inches apart onto prepared cookie sheets. Bake 10 to 12 minutes or until firm in center. Immediately place a halved marshmallow, cut side down, onto each baked cookie. Return to oven 1 minute or just until marshmallow is warm enough to stick to cookie. Remove to wire racks to cool.

To prepare Frosting: Melt chocolate and butter in small heavy saucepan over low heat; stir to blend. Beat in powdered sugar. Beat in egg white and vanilla, adding a little water, if necessary, to make a smooth, slightly soft frosting. Spoon frosting over cookies to cover marshmallows.

Makes about 5 dozen cookies

*Use clean, uncracked egg.

I N D E X

HERSHEY'S®
FABULOUS
DESSERTS

HERSHEY'S®
FABULOUS
DESSERTS

PUBLICATIONS INTERNATIONAL, LTD.

All recipes developed and tested by the Hershey Kitchens.

This edition published by Publications International, Ltd., 7373 North Cicero Avenue, Lincolnwood, IL 60646

ISBN: 1-56173-529-9

Pictured on the front cover: Chocolatetown Special Cake (*see page 26*).

First published in the United States.

Manufactured in U.S.A.

8 7 6 5 4 3 2 1

Microwave cooking times given in this book are approximate. Numerous variables, such as the microwave oven's rated wattage and starting temperature, shape, amount and depth of the food, can affect cooking time. Use the cooking times as a guideline and check doneness before adding more time. Lower wattage ovens may consistently require longer cooking times.

If you have any questions or comments about the recipes in this book, or about any of our fine Hershey products, please write us at The Hershey Kitchens, P.O. Box 815, Hershey, PA 17033-0815, or call us, toll-free, weekdays 9am - 4pm Eastern time, at 1-800-468-1714.

CONTENTS

FABULOUS DESSERTS

What comes to mind when you think about chocolate? Perhaps it's chocolate's irresistibly rich and luxurious flavor. That's why millions of us across the country are devoted chocolate lovers. Milton S. Hershey was devoted to chocolate too. When he made his first milk chocolate bar in 1894, little did he know that Hershey would become "America's Chocolate Authority"™.

Today Hershey offers a rich heritage in fine quality chocolates from HERSHEY'S milk chocolate bars and HERSHEY'S KISSES chocolates to the very best for baking with HERSHEY'S cocoa, chocolate chips and baking chocolate. What better way to enjoy the very best chocolate desserts than with Hershey's!

If you've made a batch of Great American Chocolate Chip Cookies from the recipe found on every bag of HERSHEY'S chocolate chips, or seen a recipe in your favorite magazine, then you're familiar with the kind of work we do in the Hershey Kitchens. For over 30 years, we've been developing new chocolate snacks and desserts for all occasions as well as updating popular classics to fit today's lifestyles.

The *HERSHEY'S Fabulous Desserts* cookbook has been designed for all chocolate-loving cooks. The key ingredient in all our recipes is chocolate, of course, and 100% pure HERSHEY'S, too. The easy-to-follow recipe instructions and special hints throughout will help eliminate

guesswork. And for extra convenience, many of the recipes come with microwave cooking instructions as well. With page after page of beautiful color photos, the *HERSHEY'S Fabulous Desserts* cookbook will show you just how tempting your chocolate creations will look.

Turn the pages and find popular Hershey classics and tantalizing new desserts that are quick, easy and taste like you've baked all day! From everyday family favorites and chocolate snacking treats to elegant endings and indulgent rewards, *HERSHEY'S Fabulous Desserts* was designed to make your dessert selections easier and better than ever before.

The Hershey Kitchens

CAKES & CHEESECAKES

From elegant to easy, indulge yourself with any one of these wonderful cakes.

From left to right: Devil's Delight Cake, Peanut Butter-Fudge Marble Cake (recipes page 8) and Chocolate Sour Cream Cake (recipe page 11)

Devil's Delight Cake

1 package (18.25 ounces) devil's
    food cake mix (with pudding
    in the mix)
4 eggs
1 cup water
1/2 cup vegetable oil
1 cup chopped nuts
1 cup miniature marshmallows
1 cup HERSHEY'S Semi-Sweet
    Chocolate Chips
1/2 cup raisins
    Confectioners' sugar or
    Chocolate Chip Glaze
    (recipe follows)

Heat oven to 350°. Grease and flour
12-cup Bundt pan. In large mixer
bowl combine cake mix, eggs, water
and oil; beat on low speed just until
blended. Increase speed to medium;
beat 2 minutes. Stir in nuts,
marshmallows, chocolate chips and
raisins. Pour batter into prepared
pan. Bake 45 to 50 minutes or until
wooden pick inserted in center
comes out clean. Cool 10 minutes;
remove from pan to wire rack. Cool
completely. Sprinkle confectioners'
sugar over top or drizzle Chocolate
Chip Glaze over top.

12 to 16 servings

Chocolate Chip Glaze

In small saucepan combine
2 tablespoons butter or margarine, 2
tablespoons light corn syrup and 2
tablespoons water. Cook over low
heat, stirring constantly, until mixture
begins to boil. Remove from heat;
add 1 cup HERSHEY'S Semi-Sweet
Chocolate Chips. Stir until chips are
melted and mixture is smooth.
Continue stirring until glaze is
desired consistency.

About 1 cup glaze

Peanut Butter-Fudge Marble Cake

1 package (18.25 or 19.75
    ounces) fudge marble cake
    mix
3 eggs
1/3 cup plus 2 tablespoons
    vegetable oil, divided
    Water
1 cup REESE'S Peanut Butter Chips

Heat oven to 350°. Grease and flour
two 8- or 9-inch round baking pans.
Prepare cake batters according to
package directions using eggs, 1/3
cup oil and water. In top of double
boiler over hot, not boiling, water
melt peanut butter chips with
remaining 2 tablespoons oil, stirring
constantly. OR, in small microwave-
safe bowl place chips and oil.
Microwave at HIGH (100%) 45
seconds; stir. (If necessary, microwave
at HIGH additional 15 seconds or
until melted and smooth when
stirred.) Gradually add peanut butter
mixture to vanilla batter, blending
well. Pour peanut butter batter into
prepared pans. Randomly place
spoonfuls of chocolate batter on top;
swirl as directed on package. Bake
30 to 40 minutes or until wooden pick
inserted in center comes out clean.
Cool 15 minutes; remove from pans.
Cool completely on wire rack; frost
as desired.   *10 to 12 servings*

Collector's Cocoa Cake

    ³/₄ cup butter or margarine
1 ³/₄ cups sugar
    2 eggs
    1 teaspoon vanilla extract
    2 cups all-purpose flour
    ³/₄ cup HERSHEY'S Cocoa
1 ¹/₄ teaspoons baking soda
    ¹/₂ teaspoon salt
1 ¹/₃ cups water
        Peanut Butter Cream Frosting
        (recipe follows)

Heat oven to 350°. Grease and flour two 8- or 9-inch round baking pans. In large mixer bowl cream butter and sugar. Add eggs and vanilla; beat 1 minute at medium speed. Combine flour, cocoa, baking soda and salt; add alternately with water to creamed mixture, beating after each addition. Pour batter into prepared pans. Bake 35 to 40 minutes for 8-inch rounds, 30 to 35 minutes for 9-inch rounds, or until wooden pick inserted in center comes out clean. Cool 10 minutes; remove from pans. Cool completely. Frost with Peanut Butter Cream Frosting. Cover; refrigerate frosted cake.   *8 to 10 servings*

Creamy Peanut Butter Frosting

    1 package (8 ounces) cream
        cheese, softened
    ¹/₂ cup REESE'S Peanut Butter
    ¹/₄ cup butter or margarine,
        softened
3 ²/₃ cups (1-pound box)
        confectioners' sugar
    1 teaspoon vanilla extract

In large mixer bowl beat cream cheese, peanut butter and butter until creamy. Gradually add confectioners' sugar and vanilla, beating until well blended.
                    About 3 cups frosting

Cocoa Cheesecake

Graham Crust (recipe follows)
2 packages (8 ounces each)
  cream cheese, softened
3/4 cup plus 2 tablespoons sugar,
  divided
1/2 cup HERSHEY'S Cocoa
2 teaspoons vanilla extract,
  divided
2 eggs
1 cup dairy sour cream

Prepare Graham Crust; set aside.
Heat oven to 375°. In large mixer
bowl beat cream cheese, 3/4 cup
sugar, cocoa and 1 teaspoon vanilla
until light and fluffy. Add eggs; blend
well. Pour batter into prepared crust.
Bake 20 minutes. Remove from oven;
cool 15 minutes. Increase oven
temperature to 425°. In small bowl
combine sour cream, remaining
2 tablespoons sugar and remaining
1 teaspoon vanilla; stir until smooth.
Spread evenly over baked filling.
Bake 10 minutes. Cool; chill several
hours or overnight.
10 to 12 servings

Graham Crust

In small bowl combine 1 1/2 cups
graham cracker crumbs, 1/3 cup
sugar and 1/3 cup melted butter or
margarine. Press mixture onto bottom
and halfway up side of 9-inch
springform pan.

Chocolate Lover's Cheesecake:
Prepare as above, adding 1 cup
HERSHEY'S Semi-Sweet Chocolate
Chips after eggs have been blended
into mixture. Bake and serve as
directed.

Chocolate Sour Cream Cake

1 3/4 cups all-purpose flour
1 3/4 cups sugar
3/4 cup HERSHEY'S Cocoa
1 1/2 teaspoons baking soda
1 teaspoon salt
2/3 cup butter or margarine,
  softened
2 cups dairy sour cream
2 eggs
1 teaspoon vanilla extract
Fudge Frosting (recipe follows)

Heat oven to 350°. Grease and flour
13 x 9 x 2-inch baking pan. In large
mixer bowl combine flour, sugar,
cocoa, baking soda and salt. Blend
in butter, sour cream, eggs and
vanilla. Beat 3 minutes on medium
speed. Pour batter into prepared
pan. Bake 40 to 45 minutes or until
wooden pick inserted in center
comes out clean. Cool completely in
pan on wire rack. Frost with Fudge
Frosting.   *12 to 15 servings*

Fudge Frosting

3 tablespoons butter or
  margarine
1/3 cup HERSHEY'S Cocoa
1 1/3 cups confectioners' sugar
2 to 3 tablespoons milk
1/2 teaspoon vanilla extract

In small saucepan over low heat
melt butter. Add cocoa; cook, stirring
constantly, just until mixture begins to
boil. Pour mixture into small mixer
bowl; cool completely. To cocoa
mixture, add confectioners' sugar
alternately with milk, beating to
spreading consistency. Blend in
vanilla.

About 1 cup frosting

Cocoa Cheesecake

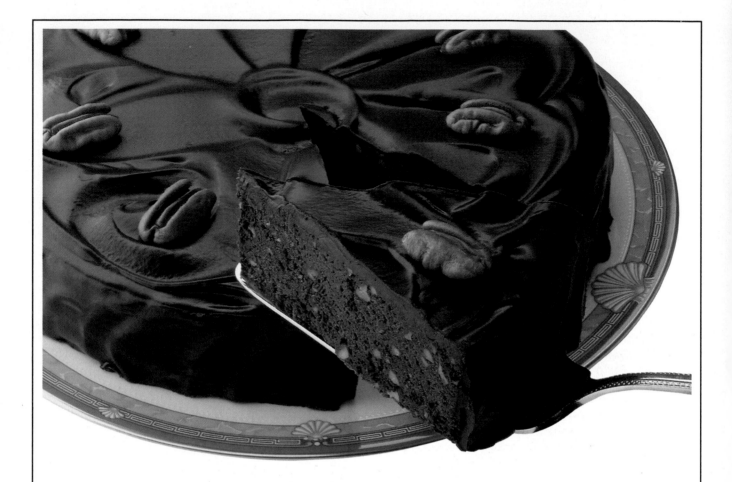

*F*udgey Pecan Cake

1 cup butter or margarine,
    melted
1¹/₂ cups sugar
1¹/₂ teaspoons vanilla extract
   3 eggs, separated
  ²/₃ cup HERSHEY'S Cocoa
  ¹/₂ cup all-purpose flour
   3 tablespoons water
  ³/₄ cup finely chopped pecans
  ¹/₈ teaspoon cream of tartar
  ¹/₈ teaspoon salt
    Royal Glaze (recipe follows)
    Pecan halves (optional)

Line bottom of 9-inch springform pan
with aluminum foil; butter foil and
side of pan. Heat oven to 350°. In
large mixer bowl combine butter,
sugar and vanilla; beat well. Add
egg yolks, one at a time, beating
well after each addition. Blend in
cocoa, flour and water; beat well.
Stir in chopped pecans. In small
mixer bowl beat egg whites, cream
of tartar and salt until stiff peaks form;
carefully fold into chocolate mixture.
Pour into prepared pan. Bake 45
minutes or until top begins to crack
slightly. (Cake will not test done in
center.) Cool in pan on wire rack
1 hour. Cover; chill until firm. Remove
side of pan. Pour Royal Glaze over
cake, allowing glaze to run down
side. Spread glaze evenly on top
and side. Allow to set. Garnish with
pecan halves, if desired.

10 to 12 servings

Royal Glaze
In small saucepan combine 1¹/₃
cups HERSHEY'S Semi-Sweet
Chocolate Chips and ¹/₂ cup
whipping cream. Cook over low
heat, stirring constantly, until chips
are melted and mixture begins to
thicken.

Jubilee Chocolate Cake

3/4 teaspoon baking soda
1 cup buttermilk or sour milk*
1 1/2 cups cake flour or 1 1/4 cups all-purpose flour
1 1/2 cups sugar, divided
1/2 cup HERSHEY'S Cocoa
1/2 teaspoon salt
1/2 cup vegetable oil
2 eggs, separated
1/2 teaspoon vanilla extract
Vanilla ice cream
Flaming Cherry Sauce (recipe follows)

In medium bowl stir baking soda into buttermilk until dissolved; set aside. Heat oven to 350°. Grease and flour 13 x 9 x 2-inch baking pan. In large mixer bowl combine flour, 1 cup sugar, cocoa and salt. Add oil, buttermilk mixture, egg yolks and vanilla; beat until smooth. In small mixer bowl beat egg whites until foamy; gradually add remaining 1/2 cup sugar, beating until stiff peaks form. Gently fold egg whites into chocolate batter. Pour batter into prepared pan. Bake 30 to 35 minutes or until cake springs back when touched lightly in center. Cool in pan on wire rack. Cut into squares; top each square with scoop of ice cream and serving of Flaming Cherry Sauce.   *10 to 12 servings*

*To sour milk: Use 1 tablespoon white vinegar plus milk to equal 1 cup.

Flaming Cherry Sauce

1 can (16 or 17 ounces) pitted dark or light sweet cherries, drained (reserve 3/4 cup liquid)
1 1/2 tablespoons sugar
1 tablespoon cornstarch
Dash salt
1/2 teaspoon grated orange peel
1/4 cup kirsch or brandy

In saucepan or chafing dish stir together reserved cherry liquid, sugar, cornstarch and salt. Cook over medium heat, stirring constantly, until mixture boils; boil 1 minute. Add cherries and orange peel; heat thoroughly. In small saucepan over low heat gently heat kirsch or brandy; pour over cherry mixture. Carefully ignite with match. Stir gently; serve as directed. (Repeat procedure for sufficient amount of sauce for entire cake.)

4 to 6 servings

Filled Rich Chocolate Cupcakes

　　Filling (recipe follows)
　3 cups all-purpose flour
　2 cups sugar
　2/3 cup HERSHEY'S Cocoa
　2 teaspoons baking soda
　1 teaspoon salt
　2 cups water
　2/3 cup vegetable oil
　2 tablespoons white vinegar
　2 teaspoons vanilla extract

Prepare Filling; set aside. Heat oven to 350°. In large mixer bowl combine flour, sugar, cocoa, baking soda and salt. Add water, oil, vinegar and vanilla; beat on medium speed 2 minutes or until well combined. Fill paper-lined muffin cups (2½ inches in diameter) 2/3 full with batter. Spoon 1 level tablespoon Filling into center of each cupcake. Bake 20 to 25 minutes or until wooden pick inserted in cake portion comes out clean. Remove to wire rack. Cool completely.

About 2½ dozen cupcakes

Filling

　1 package (8 ounces) cream
　　　cheese, softened
　1/3 cup sugar
　1 egg
　1/8 teaspoon salt
　1 cup HERSHEY'S Semi-Sweet
　　　Chocolate Chips or MINI
　　　CHIPS

In small mixer bowl combine cream cheese, sugar, egg and salt; beat until smooth and creamy. Stir in chocolate chips.

VARIATIONS
Goblin's Delight Filling: Add 2 teaspoons grated orange peel, 4 drops yellow food color and 3 drops red food color to Filling before stirring in chips.

Valentine Filling: Add 4 to 5 drops red food color to Filling.

Easy Peanut Butter-Chocolate Chip Cake (left) and Double Marble Cake

Easy Peanut Butter-Chocolate Chip Cake

1 package (18.5 ounces) yellow cake mix (with pudding in the mix)
4 eggs
³/₄ cup water
¹/₃ cup vegetable oil
¹/₃ cup creamy peanut butter
1¹/₂ cups HERSHEY'S Semi-Sweet Chocolate Chips, divided
¹/₄ cup chopped, unsalted peanuts

Heat oven to 350°. Grease and lightly flour 13 × 9 × 2-inch baking pan. Prepare cake batter according to package directions using eggs, water and oil. Blend in peanut butter. Spoon half of batter into prepared pan. Sprinkle ³/₄ cup chocolate chips over batter. Gently spread remaining batter over top. Sprinkle remaining ³/₄ cup chips and peanuts over batter. Bake 45 minutes or until wooden pick inserted in center comes out clean. Cool in pan on wire rack. *12 to 15 servings*

Double Marble Cake

1 package (18.25 or 19.75 ounces) fudge marble cake mix
3 eggs
¹/₃ cup vegetable oil
Water
1 cup HERSHEY'S Semi-Sweet Chocolate Chips, divided
1 jar (7 ounces) marshmallow creme

Heat oven to 350°. Grease and flour 13 × 9 × 2-inch baking pan. Prepare cake batters according to package directions, using eggs, oil and water. Stir ¹/₂ cup chocolate chips into chocolate batter. Spoon vanilla and chocolate batters into prepared pan; swirl as directed on package. Bake 33 to 38 minutes or until wooden pick inserted in center comes out clean. Cool in pan on wire rack 5 minutes. Gently spread marshmallow creme over warm cake. In small saucepan over low heat melt remaining ¹/₂ cup chips; swirl through marshmallow creme. Cool thoroughly. *12 to 15 servings*

Black Forest Torte

Deep Dark Chocolate Cake
(recipe page 18)
1 can (21 ounces) cherry pie
filling, chilled
1 container (4 ounces) frozen
whipped topping, thawed

Bake cake in two 9-inch round baking pans as directed. Cool 10 minutes; remove from pans to wire rack. Cool completely. Place one layer on serving plate. Spoon half of pie filling in center and spread to within 1/2 inch of edge. Spoon or pipe border of whipped topping around edge. Top with second layer. Spoon remaining pie filling to within 1/2 inch of edge. Make border around top edge with remaining topping. Chill.   *10 to 12 servings*

Triple Layer Chocolate Mousse Cake

Deep Dark Chocolate Cake
(recipe page 18)
Chocolate Mousse, Double
Recipe (recipe page 39)
Sliced almonds (optional)
Chocolate curls (optional)

Bake cake in three 8-inch round baking pans at 350° for 30 to 35 minutes. Cool 10 minutes; remove from pans to wire rack. Cool completely. Prepare Chocolate Mousse, Double Recipe, as directed. Fill and frost layers with mousse. Garnish with sliced almonds and chocolate curls, if desired. Chill at least 1 hour. Cover; refrigerate cake.
10 to 12 servings

Chocolate Chip Orange Pound Cake

1/2 cup butter, softened
4 ounces (1/2 of 8-ounce
package) cream cheese,
softened
3/4 cup granulated sugar
2 eggs
1 teaspoon vanilla extract
1/4 teaspoon grated orange peel
1 cup all-purpose flour
1 teaspoon baking powder
1 cup HERSHEY'S MINI CHIPS Semi-
Sweet Chocolate
Confectioners' sugar

Heat oven to 325°. Grease and flour 9 x 5 x 3-inch loaf pan. Cut butter and cream cheese into 1-inch slices; place in bowl of food processor. Add granulated sugar; process until smooth, about 30 seconds. Add eggs, vanilla and orange peel; process until blended, about 10 seconds. Add flour and baking powder; process until blended, about 10 seconds. Stir in MINI CHIPS Chocolate. Pour batter into prepared pan. Bake 45 to 50 minutes or until cake pulls away from sides of pan. Cool 10 minutes; remove from pan. Cool completely on wire rack. Sprinkle confectioners' sugar over cake.   *About 10 servings*

Black Forest Torte (top) and Triple Layer Chocolate Mousse Cake

Deep Dark Chocolate Cake

Deep Dark Chocolate Cake

    2 cups sugar
1 3/4 cups all-purpose flour
    3/4 cup HERSHEY'S Cocoa
1 1/2 teaspoons baking powder
1 1/2 teaspoons baking soda
    1 teaspoon salt
    2 eggs
    1 cup milk
    1/2 cup vegetable oil
    2 teaspoons vanilla extract
    1 cup boiling water
        One-Bowl Buttercream Frosting
        (recipe page 26)

Heat oven to 350°. Grease and flour two 9-inch round baking pans or 13 x 9 x 2-inch baking pan. In large mixer bowl combine sugar, flour, cocoa, baking powder, baking soda and salt. Add eggs, milk, oil and vanilla; beat on medium speed 2 minutes. Remove from mixer; stir in boiling water (batter will be thin). Pour into prepared pan(s). Bake 30 to 35 minutes for round pans, 35 to 40 minutes for rectangular pan, or until wooden pick inserted in center comes out clean. Cool 10 minutes; remove from pan(s) to wire rack. Cool completely. (Cake may be left in rectangular pan, if desired.) Frost with One-Bowl Buttercream Frosting.

10 to 12 servings

VARIATION

Chocolate Cupcakes: Prepare Deep Dark Chocolate Cake as directed. Fill paper-lined muffin cups (2 1/2 inches in diameter) 2/3 full with batter. Bake at 350° for 18 to 22 minutes or until wooden pick inserted in center comes out clean. Cool; frost as desired.

About 3 dozen cupcakes

Hot Fudge Pudding Cake

1 1/4 cups granulated sugar, divided
    1 cup all-purpose flour
    7 tablespoons HERSHEY'S Cocoa,
        divided
    2 teaspoons baking powder
    1/4 teaspoon salt
    1/2 cup milk
    1/3 cup butter or margarine,
        melted
1 1/2 teaspoons vanilla extract
    1/2 cup packed light brown sugar
1 1/4 cups hot water
        Whipped topping

Heat oven to 350°. In large mixer bowl combine 3/4 cup granulated sugar, flour, 3 tablespoons cocoa, baking powder and salt. Stir in milk, butter and vanilla; beat until smooth. Pour into 8- or 9-inch square baking pan. Combine remaining 1/2 cup granulated sugar, brown sugar and remaining 4 tablespoons cocoa; sprinkle mixture evenly over batter. Pour hot water over top; *do not stir*. Bake 35 to 40 minutes or until center is almost set. Let stand 15 minutes; spoon into dessert dishes, spooning sauce from bottom of pan over top. Garnish with whipped topping.

About 8 servings

No-Bake Chocolate Cheesecake

1 1/2 cups HERSHEY'S Semi-Sweet
      Chocolate Chips
  1 package (8 ounces) cream
      cheese, softened
  1 package (3 ounces) cream
      cheese, softened
1/2 cup sugar
1/4 cup butter or margarine,
      softened
  2 cups frozen non-dairy whipped
      topping, thawed
    8-inch (6 ounces) packaged
      graham cracker crumb crust

Microwave Directions: In small microwave-safe bowl place chocolate chips. Microwave at HIGH (100%) 1 to 1 1/2 minutes or until chips are melted and mixture is smooth when stirred. Set aside to cool. In large mixer bowl beat cream cheese, sugar and butter until smooth. On low speed blend in melted chocolate. Fold in whipped topping until blended; spoon into crust. Cover; chill until firm. Garnish as desired.   *About 8 servings*

German Chocolate Cake

¼ cup HERSHEY'S Cocoa
½ cup boiling water
1 cup plus 3 tablespoons butter
    or margarine, softened
2¼ cups sugar
1 teaspoon vanilla extract
4 eggs
2 cups all-purpose flour
1 teaspoon baking soda
½ teaspoon salt
1 cup buttermilk or sour milk*
    Coconut Pecan Frosting
    (recipe page 21)
    Pecan halves (optional)

In small bowl combine cocoa and water; stir until smooth. Set aside to cool. Heat oven to 350°. Grease three 9-inch round baking pans; line bottoms with wax paper. In large mixer bowl cream butter. Add sugar and vanilla; beat until light and fluffy. Add eggs, one at a time, beating well after each addition. Combine flour, baking soda and salt; add alternately with chocolate mixture and buttermilk to creamed mixture. Mix only until smooth. Pour batter into prepared pans. Bake 25 to 30 minutes or until top springs back when touched lightly in center. Cool 5 minutes; remove from pans and peel off paper. Cool completely. Spread Coconut Pecan Frosting between layers and over top. Garnish with pecan halves, if desired. Cover; refrigerate frosted cake.

10 to 12 servings

*To sour milk: Use 1 tablespoon white vinegar plus milk to equal 1 cup.

Coconut Pecan Frosting

1 can (14 ounces) sweetened
    condensed milk
3 egg yolks, beaten
1/2 cup butter or margarine
1 teaspoon vanilla extract
1 can (3 1/2 ounces) flaked
    coconut (about 1 1/3 cups)
1 cup chopped pecans

In heavy 2-quart saucepan combine sweetened condensed milk, egg yolks and butter. Cook, stirring constantly, over medium heat until mixture is thickened and bubbly, about 10 minutes. Remove from heat; stir in vanilla, coconut and pecans. Cool about 15 minutes.

About 2 3/4 cups frosting

Microwave Chocolate Cake

1/4 cup HERSHEY'S Cocoa
2/3 cup hot water, divided
3/4 cup plus 2 tablespoons all-
    purpose flour
1 cup sugar
1/2 teaspoon baking soda
1/4 teaspoon baking powder
1/4 teaspoon salt
1/4 cup plus 2 tablespoons
    vegetable oil
1 egg
2 teaspoons vanilla extract
    Easy Cocoa Frosting (recipe
    follows)

Microwave Directions: Grease microwave-safe 7 1/4 x 2 1/4-inch or 8 x 1 1/2-inch round baking dish. Line bottom of dish with plastic wrap. In small microwave-safe bowl combine cocoa and 1/3 cup water; microwave at HIGH (100%) 40 to 50 seconds or until very hot and slightly thickened. In medium bowl combine flour, sugar, baking soda, baking powder and salt. Add oil, remaining 1/3 cup hot water, egg, vanilla and chocolate mixture; beat with whisk 40 to 50 strokes or until batter is smooth and well blended. Pour batter into prepared pan. Microwave at HIGH 5 to 6 minutes,* without turning, until cake begins to pull away from sides (some moist spots may remain but will disappear on standing). Let stand 5 minutes; invert onto serving plate. Peel off plastic wrap; cool. Frost with Easy Cocoa Frosting. *About 8 servings*

*Time is for 600-700 watt microwave ovens. Increase baking time for lower wattage ovens.

Easy Cocoa Frosting

3 tablespoons butter or
    margarine, softened
1/4 cup HERSHEY'S Cocoa
1 1/3 cups confectioners' sugar
2 to 3 tablespoons milk
1/2 teaspoon vanilla extract

In small mixer bowl combine all ingredients; beat to spreading consistency. *About 1 cup frosting*

Marbled Angel Cake

1 box (14.5 ounces) angel food
    cake mix
1/4 cup HERSHEY'S Cocoa
    Chocolate Glaze (recipe
    follows)

Adjust oven rack to lowest position. Heat oven to 375°. Prepare cake batter according to package directions. Measure 4 cups batter into separate bowl; gradually fold cocoa into this batter until well blended, being careful not to deflate batter. Alternately pour vanilla and chocolate batters into ungreased 10-inch tube pan. Cut through batter with knife or spatula to marble batter. Bake 30 to 35 minutes or until top crust is firm and looks very dry. Do not underbake. Invert pan on heat-proof funnel or bottle; cool at least 1 1/2 hours. Carefully run knife along side of pan to loosen cake. Place on serving plate; drizzle with Chocolate Glaze.
12 to 16 servings

Chocolate Glaze

In small saucepan bring 1/3 cup sugar and 1/4 cup water to full boil, stirring until sugar dissolves. Remove from heat; add 1 cup HERSHEY'S MINI CHIPS Semi-Sweet Chocolate. Stir with wire whisk until chips are melted and mixture is smooth. Cool to desired consistency; use immediately.
About 2/3 cup glaze

Chocolate Cake with Crumb Topping

    Crumb Topping (recipe follows)
1 1/2 cups all-purpose flour
1 cup sugar
1/4 cup HERSHEY'S Cocoa
1 teaspoon baking soda
1/2 teaspoon salt
1 cup water
1/4 cup plus 2 tablespoons
    vegetable oil
1 tablespoon white vinegar
1 teaspoon vanilla extract
    Whipped topping or ice cream
    (optional)

Prepare Crumb Topping; set aside. Heat oven to 350°. Grease and flour 9-inch square baking pan. In medium bowl combine flour, sugar, cocoa, baking soda and salt. Add water, oil, vinegar and vanilla; beat with spoon or wire whisk just until batter is smooth and ingredients are well blended. Pour batter into prepared pan. Sprinkle topping over batter. Bake 35 minutes or until wooden pick inserted in center comes out clean. Cool in pan on wire rack. Serve with whipped topping or ice cream, if desired.
About 9 servings

Crumb Topping

In small bowl combine 1/2 cup graham cracker crumbs, 1/4 cup chopped nuts and 2 tablespoons melted butter or margarine. Stir in 1/2 cup HERSHEY'S Semi-Sweet Chocolate Chips.

Marbled Angel Cake (top) and Chocolate Cake with Crumb Topping

All-Chocolate Boston Cream Pie

    1 cup all-purpose flour
    1 cup sugar
    1/3 cup HERSHEY'S Cocoa
    1/2 teaspoon baking soda
    6 tablespoons butter or
       margarine, softened
    1 cup milk
    1 egg
    1 teaspoon vanilla extract
       Chocolate Filling (recipe
          follows)
       Satiny Chocolate Glaze (recipe
          follows)

Heat oven to 350°. Grease and flour 9-inch round baking pan. In large mixer bowl combine flour, sugar, cocoa and baking soda. Add butter, milk, egg and vanilla. Blend on low speed until all ingredients are moistened. Beat on medium speed 2 minutes or until mixture is smooth. Pour into prepared pan. Bake 30 to 35 minutes or until wooden pick inserted in center comes out clean. Cool 10 minutes; remove from pan. Cool completely. Meanwhile, prepare Chocolate Filling. Cut cake horizontally into two thin layers. Spread filling over one cake layer; top with remaining layer. Cover; chill. Pour Satiny Chocolate Glaze on top of cake, allowing some to drizzle down side. Cover; chill several hours. Garnish as desired. *8 servings*

Chocolate Filling

    1/2 cup sugar
    1/4 cup HERSHEY'S Cocoa
    2 tablespoons cornstarch
    1 1/2 cups light cream or half-and-
          half
    1 tablespoon butter or
          margarine
    1 teaspoon vanilla extract

In medium saucepan combine sugar, cocoa and cornstarch; gradually add light cream. Cook and stir over medium heat until mixture thickens and begins to boil; boil and stir 1 minute. Remove from heat; blend in butter and vanilla. Press plastic wrap directly onto surface. Cool completely.

Satiny Chocolate Glaze

    2 tablespoons butter or
       margarine
    3 tablespoons HERSHEY'S Cocoa
    2 tablespoons water
    1/2 teaspoon vanilla extract
    1 cup confectioners' sugar

In small saucepan over low heat melt butter. Add cocoa and water. Cook, stirring constantly, until mixture thickens; *do not boil*. Remove from heat; add vanilla. Gradually add confectioners' sugar, beating with wire whisk until smooth. Add additional water, 1/2 teaspoon at a time, until desired consistency.

About 3/4 cup glaze

Marble Cheesecake

       Chocolate Crumb Crust
          (recipe follows)
    3 packages (8 ounces each)
          cream cheese, softened
    1 cup sugar, divided
    1/2 cup dairy sour cream
    2 1/2 teaspoons vanilla extract,
          divided
    3 tablespoons all-purpose flour
    3 eggs
    1/4 cup HERSHEY'S Cocoa
    1 tablespoon vegetable oil

Prepare Chocolate Crumb Crust; set aside. Heat oven to 450°. In large mixer bowl combine cream cheese, 3/4 cup sugar, sour cream and 2 teaspoons vanilla; beat on medium speed until smooth. Gradually add flour; blend well. Add eggs and beat well; set aside. In small bowl combine cocoa and remaining $1/4$ cup sugar. Add oil, remaining $1/2$ teaspoon vanilla and $1^1/2$ cups of cream cheese mixture; blend well. Spoon plain and chocolate mixtures alternately into cooled crust, ending with dollops of chocolate on top. Swirl gently with metal spatula or knife to marble. Bake 10 minutes. Without opening oven door, decrease temperature to 250° and continue to bake 30 minutes. Turn off oven; leave cheesecake in oven 30 minutes without opening door. Remove from oven; loosen cake from side of pan. Cool completely. Cover; chill.   *10 to 12 servings*

Chocolate Crumb Crust

   1 cup vanilla wafer crumbs
       (about 30 wafers)
   $1/4$ cup confectioners' sugar
   $1/4$ cup HERSHEY'S Cocoa
   $1/4$ cup butter or margarine,
       melted

Heat oven to 350°. In medium bowl stir together crumbs, confectioners' sugar and cocoa. Stir in butter. Press mixture onto bottom and $1/2$ inch up side of 9-inch springform pan. Bake 8 minutes; cool.

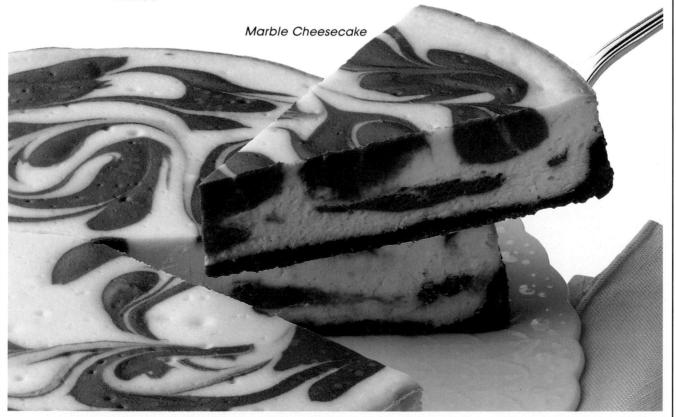

Marble Cheesecake

Chocolatetown Special Cake

¹/₂ cup HERSHEY'S Cocoa
¹/₂ cup boiling water
²/₃ cup shortening
1³/₄ cups sugar
1 teaspoon vanilla extract
2 eggs
2¹/₄ cups all-purpose flour
1¹/₂ teaspoons baking soda
¹/₂ teaspoon salt
1¹/₃ cups buttermilk or sour milk*
One-Bowl Buttercream Frosting
(recipe follows)

In small bowl stir together cocoa and boiling water until smooth; set aside. Heat oven to 350°. Grease and flour two 9-inch round baking pans. In large mixer bowl cream shortening, sugar and vanilla until light and fluffy. Add eggs; beat well. Combine flour, baking soda and salt; add alternately with buttermilk to creamed mixture. Blend in cocoa mixture. Pour into prepared pans. Bake 35 to 40 minutes or until wooden pick inserted in center comes out clean. Cool 10 minutes; remove from pans. Cool completely; frost with One-Bowl Buttercream Frosting. Garnish as desired.

10 to 12 servings

*To sour milk: Use 1 tablespoon plus 1 teaspoon white vinegar plus milk to equal 1¹/₃ cups.

One-Bowl Buttercream Frosting

6 tablespoons butter or
    margarine, softened
HERSHEY'S Cocoa:
    ¹/₃ cup for light flavor
    ¹/₂ cup for medium flavor
    ³/₄ cup for dark flavor
2²/₃ cups confectioners' sugar
¹/₃ cup milk
1 teaspoon vanilla extract

In small mixer bowl cream butter. Add cocoa and confectioners' sugar alternately with milk; beat to spreading consistency (additional milk may be needed). Blend in vanilla.

About 2 cups frosting

Chocolate Cherry Upside-Down Cake

1 tablespoon cold water
1 tablespoon cornstarch
1/4 to 1/2 teaspoon almond extract (optional)
1 can (21 ounces) cherry pie filling
1 2/3 cups all-purpose flour
1 cup sugar
1/4 cup HERSHEY'S Cocoa
1 teaspoon baking soda
1/2 teaspoon salt
1 cup water
1/3 cup vegetable oil
1 teaspoon white vinegar
1/2 teaspoon vanilla extract

Heat oven to 350°. In medium bowl combine cold water, cornstarch and almond extract, if desired. Stir in cherry pie filling; blend well. Spread evenly on bottom of ungreased 9-inch square baking pan; set aside. In medium bowl combine flour, sugar, cocoa, baking soda and salt. Add water, oil, vinegar and vanilla; beat with spoon or wire whisk until batter is smooth and well blended. Pour evenly over cherries. Bake 40 to 45 minutes or until wooden pick inserted in center comes out clean. Cool 10 minutes; invert onto serving plate. Serve warm.

About 9 servings

Chocolate Stripe Cake

1 package (about 18.25 ounces) white cake mix
1 envelope unflavored gelatin
1/4 cup cold water
1/4 cup boiling water
1 cup HERSHEY'S Syrup
Whipped topping

Heat oven to 350°F. Line 13 x 9 x 2-inch baking pan with foil; grease and flour foil. Prepare cake batter and bake according to package directions. Cool 15 minutes; do *not* remove cake from pan. With end of drinking straw, carefully pierce down through cake to bottom of pan, making rows about 1 inch apart covering length and width of cake. In small bowl, sprinkle gelatin over cold water; let stand 1 minute to soften. Add boiling water; stir until gelatin is completely dissolved and mixture is clear. Stir in syrup. Pour chocolate mixture evenly over cooled cake, making sure entire top is covered and mixture has flowed into holes. Cover; refrigerate about 5 hours or until set. Remove cake from pan; peel off foil. Spread with whipped topping. Cover; refrigerate leftovers.

12 to 15 servings

Cocoa Bundt Cake

1 2/3 cups all-purpose flour
1 1/2 cups sugar
1/2 cup HERSHEY'S Cocoa
1 1/2 teaspoons baking soda
1 teaspoon salt
1/2 teaspoon baking powder
2 eggs
1/2 cup shortening
1 1/2 cups buttermilk or sour milk*
1 teaspoon vanilla extract
Cocoa Glaze (recipe follows)

Heat oven to 350°. Generously grease and flour 12-cup Bundt pan. In large mixer bowl blend flour, sugar, cocoa, baking soda, salt and baking powder; add remaining ingredients except Cocoa Glaze. Beat on low speed 1 minute, scraping bowl constantly. Beat on high speed 3 minutes, scraping bowl occasionally. Pour into prepared pan. Bake 50 to 55 minutes or until wooden pick inserted in center comes out clean. Cool 10 minutes; remove from pan to wire rack. Cool completely. Drizzle with Cocoa Glaze. Garnish as desired.

12 to 16 servings

*To sour milk: Use 1 tablespoon plus 1 1/2 teaspoons white vinegar plus milk to equal 1 1/2 cups.

Cocoa Glaze

2 tablespoons butter or margarine
2 tablespoons HERSHEY'S Cocoa
2 tablespoons water
1 cup confectioners' sugar
1/2 teaspoon vanilla extract

In small saucepan over low heat melt butter; add cocoa and water, stirring constantly, until mixture thickens. *Do not boil.* Remove from heat; gradually add confectioners' sugar and vanilla, beating with wire whisk until smooth. Add additional water, 1/2 teaspoon at a time, until desired consistency.

About 3/4 cup glaze

VARIATION
Cocoa Sheet Cake: Prepare batter as directed; pour into greased and floured 13 x 9 x 2-inch baking pan. Bake at 350° for 35 to 40 minutes or until wooden pick inserted in center comes out clean. Cool completely; frost with One-Bowl Buttercream Frosting (recipe page 26).

Cocoa Bundt Cake

Cool DESSERTS

Soothing, refreshing desserts for everyday or for entertaining guests.

From left to right: Easy Double Chocolate Ice Cream, Creamy Smooth Choco-Blueberry Parfaits and Chocolate Mint Dessert (recipes page 32)

Chocolate Mint Dessert

1 cup all-purpose flour
1 cup sugar
1/2 cup butter or margarine, softened
4 eggs
1 1/2 cups (16-ounce can) HERSHEY'S Syrup
　 Mint Cream Center (recipe follows)
　 Chocolate Topping (recipe follows)

Heat oven to 350°. Grease 13 x 9 x 2-inch baking pan. In large mixer bowl combine flour, sugar, butter, eggs and syrup; beat until smooth. Pour into prepared pan; bake 25 to 30 minutes or until top springs back when touched lightly. Cool completely in pan. Spread Mint Cream Center on cake; cover and chill. Pour Chocolate Topping over chilled dessert. Cover; chill at least 1 hour before serving. Garnish as desired.　*About 12 servings*

Mint Cream Center

2 cups confectioners' sugar
1/2 cup butter or margarine, softened
2 tablespoons green creme de menthe*

In small mixer bowl combine confectioners' sugar, butter and creme de menthe; beat until smooth.

*1 tablespoon water, 1/2 to 3/4 teaspoon mint extract and 3 drops green food color may be substituted for creme de menthe.

Chocolate Topping

6 tablespoons butter or margarine
1 cup HERSHEY'S Semi-Sweet Chocolate Chips

In small saucepan over very low heat melt butter and chocolate chips. Remove from heat; stir until smooth. Cool slightly.

Creamy Smooth Choco-Blueberry Parfaits

1 package (6 ounces) instant chocolate pudding and pie filling
2 cups milk
1/2 cup HERSHEY'S Syrup
3 1/2 cups (8-ounce container) frozen non-dairy whipped topping, thawed
1 3/4 cups canned blueberry pie filling, chilled

In large mixer bowl combine pudding mix, milk and syrup; mix well. In separate bowl fold whipped topping into blueberry pie filling; reserve about 1 cup for garnish. Beginning with chocolate mixture, alternately layer with blueberry topping in parfait glasses. Cover and chill. Top with reserved blueberry topping. Garnish as desired.
　6 to 8 parfaits

Easy Double Chocolate Ice Cream

2 cups chilled whipping cream
2 tablespoons HERSHEY'S Cocoa
1 can (14 ounces) sweetened condensed milk
1/3 cup HERSHEY'S Syrup

Line 9 x 5 x 3-inch loaf pan with foil. In large mixer bowl beat whipping cream and cocoa until stiff. Combine sweetened condensed milk and syrup; fold into whipped cream mixture. Pour into prepared pan. Cover; freeze 6 hours or until firm.　*About 6 servings*

*C*hocolate Frozen Dessert

1 package (16 ounces)
    chocolate sandwich cookies,
    crushed (about 1 3/4 cups)
1/2 cup butter or margarine,
    melted
1/2 gallon vanilla ice cream (in
    rectangular block)
    Chocolate Sauce (recipe
    follows)
2/3 cup pecan pieces (optional)

In medium bowl combine crushed
cookies and butter. Press mixture onto
bottom of 13 × 9 × 2-inch pan or two 8-
inch square pans. Cut ice cream into
1/2-inch slices; place over crust.
Cover; freeze 1 to 2 hours or until firm.
Uncover pan(s); pour Chocolate
Sauce over ice cream. Sprinkle
pecan pieces over top, if desired.
Cover; freeze until firm.

About 16 to 18 servings

Chocolate Sauce

2 cups confectioners' sugar
1/2 cup butter or margarine
1 1/2 cups (12-ounce can)
    evaporated milk
1 cup HERSHEY'S Semi-Sweet
    Chocolate Chips

In medium saucepan combine
confectioners' sugar, butter,
evaporated milk and chocolate
chips. Cook over medium heat,
stirring constantly, until mixture boils;
boil and stir 8 minutes. Remove from
heat; cool slightly.

About 2 1/2 cups sauce

No-Bake Chocolate Cake Roll

1 package (3½ ounces) instant vanilla pudding and pie filling
3 tablespoons HERSHEY'S Cocoa, divided
1 cup milk
3½ cups (8-ounce container) frozen non-dairy whipped topping, thawed and divided
1 package (8½ ounces) crisp chocolate wafers (about 36)

In small mixer bowl combine pudding mix and 2 tablespoons cocoa. Add milk; beat on low speed until smooth and thickened. Fold in 1 cup whipped topping; blend well. Spread about 1 tablespoon pudding mixture onto each chocolate wafer. On foil, stack wafers on edges to form one long roll. Wrap tightly; chill at least 5 hours or overnight. Sift remaining 1 tablespoon cocoa over remaining 2½ cups whipped topping; blend well. Cover; refrigerate until just before serving. Unwrap roll; place on serving tray. Spread reserved whipped topping mixture over entire roll. To serve, cut diagonally in slices. Store, covered, in refrigerator. Garnish as desired.
About 8 servings

Chocolate-Marshmallow Mousse

1 bar (7 ounces) HERSHEY'S Milk Chocolate Bar
1½ cups miniature marshmallows
⅓ cup milk
1 cup chilled whipping cream

Microwave Directions: Break chocolate bar into pieces; place in medium microwave-safe bowl with marshmallows and milk. Microwave at HIGH (100%) 1 to 1½ minutes or just until mixture is smooth when stirred; cool to room temperature. In small mixer bowl beat whipping cream until stiff; fold into cooled chocolate mixture. Pour into dessert dishes. Cover; chill 1 to 2 hours or until set.
6 servings

VARIATIONS
Chocolate-Marshmallow Mousse Parfaits: Prepare Chocolate-Marshmallow Mousse according to directions. Alternately spoon mousse and sweetened whipped cream or whipped topping into parfait glasses. Cover; chill about 1 hour.
4 to 6 servings

Chocolate-Marshmallow Mousse Pie: Prepare Microwave Chocolate Crumb Crust (recipe follows) or use 8-inch (6 ounces) packaged chocolate flavored crumb crust. Prepare Chocolate-Marshmallow Mousse according to directions. Pour into crust. Cover; chill 2 to 3 hours or until firm. Garnish as desired.
8 servings

Microwave Chocolate Crumb Crust

Grease microwave-safe 9-inch pie plate. In small microwave-safe bowl place ½ cup butter or margarine. Microwave at HIGH (100%) about 1 minute or until melted. Stir in 1½ cups graham cracker crumbs, 6 tablespoons HERSHEY'S Cocoa and ⅓ cup confectioners' sugar until well blended. Press onto bottom and up sides of prepared pie plate. Microwave at HIGH 1 to 1½ minutes or until blistered; *do not overcook.* Cool completely before filling.

No-Bake Chocolate Cake Roll

Chocolate Butter Pecan Ice Cream

1/2 cup coarsely chopped pecans
1 tablespoon butter
1/2 cup HERSHEY'S Cocoa
2/3 cup water
1 can (14 ounces) sweetened condensed milk
2 teaspoons vanilla extract
2 cups chilled whipping cream

In small skillet over medium heat saute pecans in butter 2 minutes; set aside to cool. In small saucepan combine cocoa and water. Cook over medium heat, stirring constantly, until mixture boils. Remove from heat; stir in sweetened condensed milk and vanilla. Pour into 9-inch square pan; freeze until slushy. In large mixer bowl beat cream until stiff. In small chilled bowl whip chocolate mixture; fold into whipped cream. Stir in pecans. Return to square pan; cover and return to freezer. Freeze until firm, 2 to 3 hours, stirring frequently during first hour.

About 1 1/2 quarts ice cream

Chocolate Butter Pecan Ice Cream

Chocolate Coeur a la Creme with Strawberry Sauce

1/2 cup whipping cream, divided
3 tablespoons HERSHEY'S Cocoa
1 tablespoon butter
1 package (3 ounces) cream cheese, softened
1/2 cup confectioners' sugar
1/2 teaspoon vanilla extract
   Strawberry Sauce (recipe follows)

Line two 1/2-cup coeur a la creme molds or two 6-ounce custard cups with double thickness of dampened cheese cloth, extending far enough beyond edges to enclose filling completely. In small saucepan combine 1/4 cup whipping cream, cocoa and butter; cook over low heat, stirring constantly, until smooth. Remove from heat; cool. In small mixer bowl beat cream cheese, confectioners' sugar and vanilla until smooth. Add cocoa mixture, blending well. Beat in remaining 1/4 cup whipping cream. Spoon mixture into prepared molds. Fold cheesecloth over top. Place molds on wire rack set in tray or deep plate. Refrigerate 8 hours or overnight. To serve, pull back cheesecloth and invert each mold onto a chilled dessert plate; carefully remove cheesecloth. Serve with Strawberry Sauce.   *8 servings*

Strawberry Sauce

1 package (10 ounces) frozen strawberries in lite syrup, thawed
1 tablespoon kirsch (optional)

In food processor or blender container puree strawberries. Strain through fine sieve into small bowl. Stir in kirsch, if desired.

About 1 cup sauce

Peanut Butter Sundae Pie

No-Bake Chocolate Crumb
Crust (recipe follows)
1 quart vanilla ice cream
Peanut Butter Chip Ice Cream
Sauce (recipe follows)

Prepare No-Bake Chocolate Crumb
Crust. Cover; freeze. Place scoops of
ice cream into crust. Cover; freeze
until just before serving. Serve with
Peanut Butter Chip Ice Cream Sauce.
8 servings

No-Bake Chocolate Crumb Crust

In small bowl combine 1 cup
graham cracker crumbs, 1/4 cup
HERSHEY'S Cocoa, 1/4 cup sugar and
1/3 cup melted butter or margarine.
Press mixture onto bottom and up
sides of buttered 9-inch pie plate.

Peanut Butter Chip Ice Cream Sauce

1 cup REESE'S Peanut Butter Chips
1/3 cup evaporated milk
2 tablespoons light corn syrup
1 tablespoon butter or
margarine
1 teaspoon vanilla extract

Microwave Directions: In small
microwave-safe bowl combine
peanut butter chips, evaporated
milk, corn syrup and butter; stir.
Microwave at HIGH (100%) 1 to 1 1/2
minutes or until chips are softened;
stir with whisk until chips are melted
and mixture is smooth. Stir in vanilla.
Cool slightly.
About 3/4 cup sauce

Conventional Directions: In small
saucepan combine all ingredients
except vanilla. Cook over low heat,
stirring constantly, until chips are
melted and mixture is smooth. Stir in
vanilla. Cool slightly.

Chocolate Rum Ice Cream

Chocolate Rum Ice Cream

1 cup sugar
2 tablespoons all-purpose flour
1 cup milk
1 egg, slightly beaten
2 bars (2 ounces) HERSHEY'S
Unsweetened Baking
Chocolate, broken into
pieces
1/2 teaspoon rum extract
2 cups chilled light cream

Microwave Directions: In large
microwave-safe bowl combine sugar
and flour; gradually stir in milk. Blend
in egg and baking chocolate
pieces. Microwave at HIGH (100%) 2
to 2 1/2 minutes, stirring frequently, just
until mixture boils and thickens. Add
rum extract; blend with wire whisk
until mixture is smooth. Chill
thoroughly. Add light cream to
chilled mixture; blend well. Freeze in
2-quart ice cream freezer according
to manufacturer's directions.
About 8 servings

Choco-Berry Frozen Dessert (left) and Cherry-Crowned Cocoa Pudding

Choco-Berry Frozen Dessert

3 packages (3 ounces each) cream cheese, softened and divided
1 cup HERSHEY'S Syrup
1/2 cup water
4 1/2 cups (about 12 ounces) frozen non-dairy whipped topping, thawed and divided
3/4 cup pureed strawberries (fresh, sweetened OR frozen, thawed and drained berries)

Line 9 x 5 x 3-inch loaf pan with foil. In large mixer bowl beat 2 packages cream cheese. Blend in syrup and water; beat until smooth. Fold in 3 cups whipped topping. Spoon half of chocolate mixture into prepared pan; freeze 15 minutes. Chill remaining chocolate mixture. In small mixer bowl beat remaining package cream cheese. Blend in strawberries until smooth. Fold in remaining 1 1/2 cups whipped topping. Spoon strawberry mixture over chocolate layer in pan. Top with chilled chocolate mixture. Cover; freeze several hours or overnight until firm. Unmold about 10 minutes before serving. Peel off foil before slicing.
About 10 servings

Chocolate Mousse

1 teaspoon unflavored gelatin
1 tablespoon cold water
2 tablespoons boiling water
1/2 cup sugar
1/4 cup HERSHEY'S Cocoa
1 cup chilled whipping cream
1 teaspoon vanilla extract

In custard cup sprinkle gelatin over cold water; let stand 1 minute to soften. Add boiling water; stir until gelatin is completely dissolved and mixture is clear. Cool slightly. In small mixer bowl stir together sugar and cocoa; add whipping cream and vanilla. Beat at medium speed, scraping bottom of bowl occasionally, until stiff peaks form; pour in gelatin mixture and beat until well blended. Spoon into serving dishes. Chill about 1/2 hour.
Four 1/2 cup servings

Double Recipe: Use 1 envelope gelatin; double remaining ingredients. Follow directions above; use large mixer bowl.

Cherry-Crowned Cocoa Pudding

1 cup sugar
1/2 cup HERSHEY'S Cocoa
1/3 cup all-purpose biscuit baking mix
2 cups milk
1 cup water
1 can (21 ounces) cherry pie filling, chilled

In medium saucepan combine sugar, cocoa and baking mix. Stir in milk and water. Cook over medium heat, stirring constantly, until mixture comes to full boil; remove from heat. Pour into dessert dishes. Press plastic wrap directly onto surface. Chill several hours or until set. Garnish with cherry pie filling. *6 servings*

Fruited Chocolate Sorbet

1 ripe, medium banana
1 1/2 cups orange juice
1/2 cup sugar
1/4 cup HERSHEY'S Cocoa
1 cup chilled whipping cream

Slice banana into blender container. Add orange juice; blend until smooth. Add sugar and cocoa; blend until thoroughly combined. Add whipping cream; blend well. Pour mixture into 9-inch square pan. Freeze until hard around edges. Spoon mixture into large mixer bowl or blender container; blend until smooth. Pour into 1-quart mold. Freeze 4 to 6 hours or until firm. To serve, unmold onto chilled plate; cut into slices. *About 8 servings*

Fast Fudge Pots de Creme

1 package (3 1/2 ounces) chocolate pudding and pie filling
2 cups milk
1 cup HERSHEY'S Semi-Sweet Chocolate Chips or MINI CHIPS

In medium saucepan combine pudding mix and milk. Cook over medium heat, stirring constantly, until mixture comes to full boil; remove from heat. Stir in chocolate chips until melted and mixture is smooth. Spoon into 8 creme pots or demitasse cups. Press plastic wrap directly onto surface. Serve slightly warm or chilled. Garnish as desired.
8 servings

Peel bananas; cut each into thirds. Insert wooden stick into each banana piece; place on wax paper-covered tray. Cover; freeze until firm. In top of double boiler over hot, not boiling, water melt chocolate chips and shortening. Remove bananas from freezer just before dipping. Dip each piece into warm chocolate, covering completely; allow excess to drip off. Immediately roll in peanuts. Cover; return to freezer. Serve frozen.

9 pops

Chocolate-Covered Banana Pops

Chocolate-Covered Banana Pops

3 ripe, large bananas
9 wooden ice cream sticks or skewers
2 cups (12-ounce package) HERSHEY'S Semi-Sweet Chocolate Chips
2 tablespoons shortening
1 1/2 cups coarsely chopped unsalted, roasted peanuts

Chocolate Cream Squares

Chocolate Graham Crust (recipe follows)
1 package (3 ounces) cream cheese, softened
2/3 cup sugar
1 teaspoon vanilla extract
1/3 cup HERSHEY'S Cocoa
1/3 cup milk
1 container (8 ounces) frozen non-dairy whipped topping, thawed

Prepare Chocolate Graham Crust; reserve 1/4 cup crumb mixture. Press remaining crumbs onto bottom of 9-inch square pan; set aside. In small mixer bowl beat cream cheese, sugar and vanilla until well blended. Add cocoa alternately with milk, beating until smooth. Gradually fold in whipped topping until well combined. Spoon mixture over crust. Sprinkle reserved crumbs over top. Cover; chill 6 to 8 hours or until set. Cut into squares. *6 to 9 servings*

Chocolate Graham Crust

In medium bowl, stir together 1 1/4 cups graham cracker crumbs, 1/4 cup HERSHEY'S Cocoa, 1/4 cup sugar and 1/3 cup melted butter or margarine.

Three-In-One Chocolate Pudding & Pie Filling

- ³/₄ cup sugar
- ¹/₃ cup HERSHEY'S Cocoa
- 2 tablespoons cornstarch
- 2 tablespoons all-purpose flour
- ¹/₄ teaspoon salt
- 2 cups milk
- 2 egg yolks, slightly beaten
- 2 tablespoons butter or margarine
- 1 teaspoon vanilla extract

In medium saucepan combine sugar, cocoa, cornstarch, flour and salt; blend in milk and egg yolks. Cook over medium heat, stirring constantly, until mixture boils; boil and stir 1 minute. Remove from heat; blend in butter and vanilla. Pour into medium bowl or individual serving dishes; press plastic wrap directly onto surface. Cool; chill.

4 servings

Pie: Reduce milk to 1³/₄ cups; cook as directed. Pour hot pudding into 8-inch (6 ounces) packaged graham crumb crust; press plastic wrap onto surface. Chill; top with sweetened whipped cream or whipped topping before serving. *6 servings*

Parfaits: Alternate layers of cold pudding and sweetened whipped cream in parfait glasses.

4 to 6 servings

Microwave Directions: In 2-quart microwave-safe bowl combine sugar, cocoa, cornstarch, flour and salt; blend in milk and egg yolks. Microwave at HIGH (100%) 5 minutes, stirring several times, or until mixture boils. Microwave at HIGH 1 to 2 additional minutes or until mixture is smooth and thickened. Stir in butter and vanilla. Cool as directed above.

PIES

A tantalizing
selection of pies—
all easy to make,
and easy to enjoy.

Chocolate Grasshopper Pie (recipe
page 44)

43

Chocolate Grasshopper Pie

Microwave Chocolate Crumb
  Crust (recipe follows) or
  8-inch (6 ounces) packaged
  chocolate flavored crumb
  crust
3 cups miniature marshmallows
1/2 cup milk
1/4 cup HERSHEY'S Cocoa
2 tablespoons white creme de
  menthe
2 tablespoons white creme de
  cacao
1 cup chilled whipping cream
2 tablespoons confectioners'
  sugar

Prepare crust, if desired; set aside. In
medium saucepan combine
marshmallows, milk and cocoa. Stir
constantly over low heat until
marshmallows are melted; remove
from heat. Stir in creme de menthe
and creme de cacao; cool to room
temperature. In small mixer bowl
beat whipping cream with
confectioners' sugar until stiff. Fold in
cooled chocolate mixture. Spoon
into crust. Cover and freeze several
hours or overnight. Garnish as
desired.   *6 to 8 servings*

Microwave Chocolate Crumb Crust

Grease microwave-safe 9-inch pie
plate. In small microwave-safe bowl
place 1/2 cup butter or margarine.
Microwave at HIGH (100%) about 1
minute or until melted. Stir in 1 1/2
cups graham cracker crumbs, 6
tablespoons HERSHEY'S Cocoa and
1/3 cup confectioners' sugar until well
blended. Press onto bottom and up
sides of prepared pie plate.
Microwave at HIGH 1 to 1 1/2 minutes
or until blistered; *do not overcook.*
Cool completely before filling.

Chocolatetown Pie

9-inch unbaked pastry shell
1/2 cup butter or margarine,
  softened
2 eggs, beaten
2 teaspoons vanilla extract or
  2 tablespoons bourbon
1 cup sugar
1/2 cup all-purpose flour
1 cup HERSHEY'S Semi-Sweet
  Chocolate Chips or MINI
  CHIPS
1 cup chopped pecans or
  walnuts
Festive Whipped Cream
  (optional, recipe follows)

Prepare pastry shell; set aside. Heat
oven to 350°. In small mixer bowl
cream butter; add eggs and vanilla.
Combine sugar and flour; add to
creamed mixture. Stir in chocolate
chips and nuts; pour into unbaked
pastry shell. Bake 45 to 50 minutes or
until golden. Cool about 1 hour.
Serve warm with Festive Whipped
Cream, if desired. Garnish as
desired.   *8 to 10 servings*

Festive Whipped Cream

1/2 cup chilled whipping cream
2 tablespoons confectioners'
  sugar
1/4 teaspoon vanilla extract or
  1 teaspoon bourbon

In small mixer bowl combine all
ingredients; beat until stiff.
              About 1 cup topping

Chocolate Mousse Pie with Rum Cream Topping

Chocolate Mousse (recipe page 39)
8-inch baked pastry shell or 8-inch (6 ounces) packaged chocolate flavored crumb crust
1 cup chilled whipping cream
2 tablespoons confectioners' sugar
2 teaspoons light rum or ¼ teaspoon rum extract

Prepare Chocolate Mousse. Pour mixture into pastry shell. In small mixer bowl beat cream, confectioners' sugar and rum until stiff. Spread topping over mousse. Cover; chill at least 2 hours. Garnish as desired.   *6 to 8 servings*

Chocolate Cream Pie

1 package (3 ounces) cream cheese, softened
½ cup sugar
1 teaspoon vanilla extract
⅓ cup HERSHEY'S Cocoa
⅓ cup milk
1 container (8 ounces) frozen non-dairy whipped topping, thawed
8-inch (6 ounces) packaged graham crumb crust

In small mixer bowl combine cream cheese, sugar and vanilla until blended. Add cocoa alternately with milk, beating until smooth. Gradually fold in whipped topping until well combined. Spoon into crust. Cover; chill 4 to 6 hours or until set.
6 to 8 servings

Chocolate Mousse Pie with Rum Cream Topping

Cocoa Cloud Pie

2 packages (3 ounces each)
  cream cheese, softened
1 cup confectioners' sugar
2 teaspoons vanilla extract
1/2 cup HERSHEY'S Cocoa
1/4 cup milk
2 cups chilled whipping cream
  8-inch (6 ounces) packaged
  crumb crust

In large mixer bowl beat cream
cheese, confectioners' sugar and
vanilla until well blended. Add
cocoa alternately with milk, beating
until smooth. Gradually add
whipping cream, beating until stiff.
Spoon into crust. Cover; chill several
hours or overnight. Garnish as
desired.   *6 to 8 servings*

Peanut Butter Tarts

1 package (3 1/2 ounces) instant
  vanilla pudding and pie
  filling
1 1/2 cups milk, divided
1 cup REESE'S Peanut Butter Chips
6 (4-ounce package) single
  serve graham crusts
  Whipped topping
  Fresh fruit

In small mixer bowl blend pudding
mix and 1 cup milk; set aside. In top
of double boiler over hot, not boiling,
water melt peanut butter chips with
remaining 1/2 cup milk, stirring
constantly to blend. (OR in small
microwave-safe bowl place chips
and 1/2 cup milk. Microwave at HIGH
(100%) 45 seconds; stir. If necessary,
microwave at HIGH additional 15
seconds or until melted and smooth
when stirred.) Gradually add to

pudding, blending well. Spoon into
crusts. Cover; chill until set. Garnish
with whipped topping and fruit.
                              6 servings

Individual Chocolate Cream Pies

1 1/2 ounces (1/2 of 3-ounce
  package) cream cheese,
  softened
6 tablespoons sugar
1/2 teaspoon vanilla extract
2 1/2 tablespoons HERSHEY'S Cocoa
2 1/2 tablespoons milk
1 cup chilled whipping cream
6 (4-ounce package) single
  serve graham crusts
  Whipped topping
  HERSHEY'S MINI CHIPS Semi-
  Sweet Chocolate

In small mixer bowl beat cream
cheese, sugar and vanilla until well
blended. Add cocoa alternately with
milk, beating until smooth. In
separate bowl beat whipping cream
until stiff; fold into chocolate mixture.
Spoon into crusts. Cover; chill until
set. Garnish with whipped topping
and MINI CHIPS Chocolate.
                              6 servings

*From top to bottom: Cocoa Cloud Pie,
Peanut Butter Tarts and Individual
Chocolate Cream Pies*

*H*ershey's *Syrup Pie*

    9-inch baked pastry shell
 2 egg yolks
 1/3 cup cornstarch
 1/4 teaspoon salt
 1 3/4 cups milk
 1 cup HERSHEY'S Syrup
 1 teaspoon vanilla extract
    Syrup Whipped Topping
       (recipe follows)
    Fresh fruit

Microwave Directions: In medium microwave-safe bowl beat egg yolks. Add cornstarch, salt, milk and syrup; blend well. Microwave at MEDIUM-HIGH (70%) 6 to 8 minutes, stirring every 2 minutes with whisk, or until mixture is smooth and very thick. Stir in vanilla. Pour into baked pastry shell. Press plastic wrap directly onto surface; chill several hours or overnight. Garnish with Syrup Whipped Topping and fresh fruit.

6 to 8 servings

Syrup Whipped Topping
In small mixer bowl combine 1 cup chilled whipping cream, 1/2 cup HERSHEY'S Syrup, 2 tablespoons confectioners' sugar and 1/2 teaspoon vanilla extract. Beat just until cream holds definite shape; *do not overbeat.*

About 2 1/4 cups topping

Fudge Brownie Pie

2 eggs
1 cup sugar
1/2 cup butter or margarine, melted
1/2 cup all-purpose flour
1/3 cup HERSHEY'S Cocoa
1/4 teaspoon salt
1 teaspoon vanilla extract
1/2 cup chopped nuts (optional)
Ice Cream
Hot Fudge Sauce (recipe follows)

Heat oven to 350°. Lightly grease 8-inch pie plate. In small mixer bowl beat eggs; blend in sugar and butter. Combine flour, cocoa and salt; add to butter mixture. Stir in vanilla and nuts, if desired. Pour into prepared pie plate. Bake 25 to 30 minutes or until almost set. (Pie will not test done in center.) Cool; cut into wedges. Serve topped with scoop of ice cream and drizzled with Hot Fudge Sauce.   *6 to 8 servings*

Hot Fudge Sauce

3/4 cup sugar
1/2 cup HERSHEY'S Cocoa
1/2 cup plus 2 tablespoons (5-ounce can) evaporated milk
1/3 cup light corn syrup
1/3 cup butter or margarine
1 teaspoon vanilla extract

In small saucepan combine sugar and cocoa; blend in evaporated milk and corn syrup. Cook over medium heat, stirring constantly, until mixture boils; boil and stir 1 minute. Remove from heat; stir in butter and vanilla. Serve warm.
                    About 1 3/4 cups sauce

Microwave Directions: In medium microwave-safe bowl combine all sauce ingredients except butter and vanilla. Microwave at HIGH (100%) 1 to 3 minutes, stirring often, until mixture boils. Stir in butter and vanilla. Cool slightly; serve warm.

Banana Split Pie

Crumb-Nut Crust (recipe follows)
1¼ cups sugar
⅓ cup cornstarch
⅓ cup HERSHEY'S Cocoa
¼ teaspoon salt
2½ cups milk
2 egg yolks, slightly beaten
3 tablespoons butter or margarine
1 teaspoon vanilla extract
2 medium ripe bananas, sliced
Frozen whipped topping, thawed
Chopped peanuts
Additional banana slices
Maraschino cherries

Prepare Crumb-Nut Crust. In medium saucepan stir together sugar, cornstarch, cocoa and salt. Blend milk and egg yolks; gradually stir into sugar mixture. Cook over medium heat, stirring constantly, until mixture thickens and boils. Boil and stir over low heat 3 minutes. Remove from heat, blend in butter and vanilla. Press plastic wrap directly onto filling; cool about 20 minutes. Arrange banana slices over bottom of crust. Pour filling over bananas; press plastic wrap onto filling. Refrigerate 3 to 4 hours. Remove plastic wrap; top pie with dollops of whipped topping. Garnish with chopped peanuts, banana slices and maraschino cherries.   *8 servings*

Crumb-Nut Crust

1¼ cups graham cracker crumbs
⅓ cup butter or margarine, melted
¼ cup finely chopped peanuts

Heat oven to 350°. In medium bowl combine all ingredients; press evenly onto bottom and up sides of 9-inch pie plate. Bake 8 to 10 minutes; cool.

Chocolate Cheese Pie

Chocolate Cheese Pie

　1 package (8 ounces) cream
　　　cheese, softened
　1 package (3 ounces) cream
　　　cheese, softened
　3/4 cup sugar
　1 teaspoon vanilla extract
　1/4 cup HERSHEY'S Cocoa
　2 eggs
　1/2 cup whipping cream
　　　8-inch (6 ounces) packaged
　　　crumb crust
　　　Cherry pie or peach pie filling

Heat oven to 350°. In large mixer
bowl beat cream cheese, sugar and
vanilla until well blended. Blend in
cocoa, scraping sides of bowl and
beaters frequently. Add eggs; blend
well. Blend in whipping cream. Pour
into crust. Bake 35 to 40 minutes.
(Center will be soft but will set upon
cooling). Cool to room temperature.
Cover; chill several hours or
overnight. Serve with pie filling.
6 to 8 servings

Chocolate Pecan Pie

　　　9-inch unbaked pastry shell
　1 cup sugar
　1/3 cup HERSHEY'S Cocoa
　3 eggs, slightly beaten
　1 cup light corn syrup
　1 tablespoon butter or
　　　margarine, melted
　1 teaspoon vanilla extract
　1 cup pecan halves
　　　Whipped topping

Prepare pastry shell; set aside. Heat
oven to 350°. In medium bowl
combine sugar and cocoa. Add
eggs, corn syrup, butter and vanilla;
stir until well blended. Stir in pecans.
Pour into unbaked pastry shell. Bake
60 minutes. Cool completely. Garnish
with whipped topping.　*8 servings*

BREADS, MUFFINS & COFFEECAKES

Let the irresistible aroma of these breads and coffeecakes fill your kitchen.

Chocolate Chip Banana Bread (top) and Cocoa Oatmeal Muffins (recipes page 54)

53

Cocoa Oatmeal Muffins

  1 cup quick-cooking rolled oats
  1 cup buttermilk or sour milk*
 1/3 cup butter or margarine,
      softened
 1/2 cup packed light brown sugar
  1 egg
  1 cup all-purpose flour
 1/4 cup HERSHEY'S Cocoa
  1 teaspoon baking powder
  1 teaspoon salt
 1/2 teaspoon baking soda
  1 cup raisins
 1/2 cup chopped walnuts
      (optional)

Heat oven to 400°. Grease or paper-line muffin cups (2 1/2 inches in diameter). In small bowl stir together oats and buttermilk; let stand 20 minutes. In large bowl beat butter, sugar and egg until fluffy. Stir together flour, cocoa, baking powder, salt and baking soda; add to butter mixture alternately with oats mixture. Stir in raisins and walnuts, if desired. Fill prepared muffin cups 2/3 full with batter. Bake 18 to 20 minutes or until wooden pick inserted in center comes out clean.
About 14 muffins

*To sour milk: Use 1 tablespoon white vinegar plus milk to equal 1 cup.

Chocolate Chip Banana Bread

  2 cups all-purpose flour
  1 cup sugar
  1 teaspoon baking powder
 1/2 teaspoon baking soda
  1 teaspoon salt
  1 cup mashed ripe bananas
      (about 3 small)
 1/2 cup shortening
  2 eggs
  1 cup HERSHEY'S Semi-Sweet
      Chocolate Chips
 1/2 cup chopped walnuts

Heat oven to 350°. Grease bottoms only of two 8 1/2 x 4 1/2 x 2 1/2-inch loaf pans. In large mixer bowl combine all ingredients except chocolate chips and walnuts; blend well on medium speed. Stir in chips and walnuts. Pour into prepared pans. Bake 45 to 50 minutes or until wooden pick inserted in center comes out clean. Cool 10 minutes; remove from pans. Cool completely on wire rack.
2 loaves

Chocolate Almond Braided Coffeecake

 1/3 cup HERSHEY'S Semi-Sweet
      Chocolate Chips, melted
      and cooled
 1/3 cup sugar
 1/4 cup dairy sour cream
  2 tablespoons chopped, toasted
      almonds*
  1 can (8 ounces) refrigerated
      quick crescent dinner rolls

Heat oven to 350°. In small mixer bowl combine melted chocolate, sugar and sour cream; stir in almonds. On ungreased cookie sheet unroll dough into 2 long rectangles. Overlap long sides to form 13 x 7-inch rectangle; press perforations to seal. Spread chocolate mixture in 2-inch strip lengthwise down center of dough. Make cuts 1 inch apart on each side just to edge of filling. Fold strips at an angle across filling, alternating from side to side. Fold under ends to seal. Bake 20 to 25 minutes or until browned. Cool; cut into slices. Serve warm.
8 servings

*To toast almonds: Toast in shallow baking pan in 350° oven, stirring occasionally, 8 to 10 minutes or until golden brown.

Chocolate Dessert Waffles

1/2 cup HERSHEY'S Cocoa
1/4 cup butter or margarine, melted
3/4 cup sugar
2 eggs
2 teaspoons vanilla extract
1 cup all-purpose flour
1/2 teaspoon baking soda
1/2 teaspoon salt
1/2 cup buttermilk or sour milk*
1/2 cup chopped nuts (optional)
   Hot Fudge Sauce (recipe page 49)
   Strawberry Dessert Cream (recipe follows)

In small mixer bowl blend cocoa and butter until smooth; stir in sugar. Add eggs and vanilla; beat well. Combine flour, baking soda and salt; add alternately with buttermilk to cocoa mixture. Stir in nuts, if desired. Bake in waffle iron according to manufacturer's directions. Carefully remove waffle from iron. Serve warm with Hot Fudge Sauce and Strawberry Dessert Cream.
About ten 4-inch waffles

*To sour milk: Use 1 1/2 teaspoons white vinegar plus milk to equal 1/2 cup.

Strawberry Dessert Cream

In small mixer bowl beat 1 cup chilled whipping cream until stiff. Fold in 1/3 cup strawberry preserves and 3 drops red food color, if desired. *About 2 cups topping*

Mini Chips Blueberry Bread

2 packages (14.5 ounces each)
   blueberry nut quick bread
   mix
2 eggs, slightly beaten
3/4 cup buttermilk or sour milk*
1/2 cup vegetable oil
1 1/2 cups HERSHEY'S MINI CHIPS
   Semi-Sweet Chocolate
Mini Chips Glaze (recipe
   follows)

Heat oven to 350°. Grease and flour 12-cup Bundt pan. In large bowl combine bread mix, eggs, buttermilk and oil. Beat with spoon 1 minute. Stir in MINI CHIPS Chocolate. Pour into prepared pan. Bake 45 to 50 minutes or until wooden pick inserted in center comes out clean. Cool 10 minutes; remove from pan. Wrap tightly in foil. Cool completely. Glaze with Mini Chips Glaze.   *12 servings*

*To sour milk: Use 2 teaspoons white vinegar plus milk to equal 3/4 cup.

Loaf Version: Prepare half of batter as directed above using 1 package blueberry nut quick bread mix, 1 egg, 6 tablespoons buttermilk or sour milk, 1/4 cup vegetable oil and 3/4 cup MINI CHIPS Semi-Sweet Chocolate. Pour batter into greased and floured 9 × 5 × 3-inch loaf pan. Bake; cool as directed above.

1 loaf

Mini Chips Glaze

In small saucepan bring 2 tablespoons sugar and 2 tablespoons water to boil, stirring until sugar dissolves. Remove from heat; add 1/2 cup HERSHEY'S MINI CHIPS Semi-Sweet Chocolate. Stir with wire whisk until chips are melted and mixture is smooth; use immediately.

About 1/2 cup glaze

Mini Chips Blueberry Breakfast Cake

1 package (14.5 ounces)
   blueberry nut quick bread
   mix
1 cup dairy sour cream
1/4 cup water
1 egg
1/2 cup HERSHEY'S MINI CHIPS Semi-
   Sweet Chocolate
Topping (recipe follows)

Heat oven to 350°. Grease bottom only of 9-inch square baking pan. In medium bowl combine bread mix, sour cream, water, egg and MINI CHIPS Chocolate; stir until well moistened and blended. Spread into prepared pan. Sprinkle Topping over batter. Bake 40 to 45 minutes or until golden brown. Cool; cut into squares.   *9 servings*

Topping

In small bowl combine 1/4 cup all-purpose flour, 1/4 cup sugar and 2 tablespoons softened butter or margarine until crumbly. Stir in 1/4 cup HERSHEY'S MINI CHIPS Semi-Sweet Chocolate.

Mini Chips Blueberry Bread (top) and Mini Chips Blueberry Breakfast Cake

Mini Chips Surprise Muffins

1 package (16.1 ounces) nut
    quick bread mix
1 egg, slightly beaten
1 cup milk
1/4 cup vegetable oil
1 cup HERSHEY'S MINI CHIPS Semi-
    Sweet Chocolate
1/3 cup fruit preserves, any flavor

Heat oven to 400°. Grease or paper-line 18 muffin cups (2 1/2 inches in diameter). In large bowl combine bread mix, egg, milk and oil. Beat with spoon 1 minute. Stir in MINI CHIPS Chocolate. Fill muffin cups 1/4 full with batter. Spoon about 1/2 teaspoon preserves onto center of batter. Fill muffin cups 3/4 full with batter. Bake 20 to 22 minutes or until lightly browned. Serve warm.

About 1 1/2 dozen muffins

Mini Chips Surprise Muffins

Easy Chocolate Zucchini Cake

1 package (16.1 ounces) nut
    quick bread mix
1/2 cup granulated sugar
1 teaspoon ground cinnamon
3/4 cup vegetable oil
3 eggs, slightly beaten
1 1/2 cups shredded zucchini
1 cup HERSHEY'S Semi-Sweet
    Chocolate Chips
    Confectioners' sugar (optional)

Heat oven to 350°. Grease and flour 9-inch square baking pan. In large bowl combine bread mix, granulated sugar, cinnamon, oil and eggs; mix until well blended. Stir in zucchini and chocolate chips; pour into prepared pan. Bake 40 to 45 minutes or until wooden pick inserted in center comes out clean. Cool. Sprinkle confectioners' sugar over top, if desired. Cover; refrigerate leftovers.

9 servings

Mini Chips Pancakes

1 carton (16 ounces) frozen
    pancake batter, thawed
1/2 cup HERSHEY'S MINI CHIPS Semi-
    Sweet Chocolate
    Fruit syrup or pancake syrup

Lightly grease griddle; heat to 375°. In small bowl combine pancake batter and MINI CHIPS Chocolate. Pour about 2 tablespoons batter onto hot griddle. Turn when surface is bubbly; cook until lightly browned. Serve warm with syrup.

About 14 four-inch pancakes

Chocolate Upside Down Coffeecake

¾ cup apple jelly
1 package (16 ounces) pound cake mix
1 cup HERSHEY'S Milk Chocolate Chips, divided

Heat oven to 325°. Grease and flour 9-inch square baking pan. Spread jelly evenly onto bottom of prepared pan. Prepare cake batter according to package directions. Stir in ½ cup milk chocolate chips. Pour batter over jelly layer, spreading gently and evenly. Sprinkle remaining ½ cup chips over top. Bake 50 to 55 minutes or until cake springs back when touched lightly. Cool 5 minutes in pan; invert onto serving plate. Cool at least 15 minutes; serve warm.

About 9 servings

Cocoa-Nut Bread

2¼ cups all-purpose flour
1½ cups sugar
⅓ cup HERSHEY'S Cocoa
3½ teaspoons baking powder
1 teaspoon salt
1 egg
1¼ cups milk
½ cup vegetable oil
1 cup finely chopped nuts

Heat oven to 350°. Grease and flour 9 x 5 x 3-inch loaf pan. In large bowl combine all ingredients except nuts. Beat with spoon 30 seconds; stir in nuts. Pour into prepared pan. Bake 65 to 70 minutes or until wooden pick inserted in center comes out clean. Cool 10 minutes; remove from pan. Wrap tightly in foil. Cool completely.

1 loaf

Mini Chips Cinnamon Crescents

Mini Chips Cinnamon Crescents

1 can (8 ounces) refrigerated quick crescent dinner rolls
Ground cinnamon
½ cup HERSHEY'S MINI CHIPS Semi-Sweet Chocolate
Confectioners' sugar

Heat oven to 375°. On ungreased cookie sheet unroll dough to form 8 triangles. Lightly sprinkle cinnamon and 1 tablespoon MINI CHIPS Chocolate on top of each. Gently press into dough to adhere. Starting at shortest side of triangle, roll dough to opposite point. Bake 10 to 12 minutes or until golden brown. Sprinkle confectioners' sugar over top. Serve warm. *8 crescents*

CANDIES & SNACKS

Easiest-ever candies for holiday gift giving, plus plenty of great treats for anytime snacking.

Clockwise from far left: Easy Rocky Road, Pastel-Coated Cocoa Bonbons, Easy Double Decker Fudge (recipes page 62) and Coconut Honey Bars (recipe page 64)

Pastel-Coated Cocoa Bonbons

2 packages (3 ounces each)
    cream cheese, softened
2 cups confectioners' sugar
1/2 cup HERSHEY'S Cocoa
2 tablespoons butter, melted
1 teaspoon vanilla extract
    Pastel Coating (recipe follows)

In small mixer bowl beat cream cheese. Add confectioners' sugar, cocoa, butter and vanilla; blend well. Cover; chill several hours or until firm enough to handle. Shape into 1-inch balls; place on wax paper-covered tray. Refrigerate, uncovered, 3 to 4 hours or until dry. Using long fork dip cold centers into very warm Pastel Coating. Quickly remove. Place on wax paper-covered tray; swirl coating on top of bonbon. Refrigerate until firm. Store in airtight container in refrigerator.

2 dozen bonbons

Pastel Coating

6 tablespoons butter
3 cups confectioners' sugar
1/4 cup milk
1 teaspoon vanilla extract
    Red or green food color

Microwave Directions: In medium microwave-safe bowl combine all ingredients except food color. Microwave at HIGH (100%) 1 to 1 1/2 minutes or until smooth when stirred. Tint pastel pink or green with several drops food color.

Easy Rocky Road

2 cups (12-ounce package)
    HERSHEY'S Semi-Sweet
    Chocolate Chips
1/4 cup butter or margarine
2 tablespoons shortening
3 cups miniature marshmallows
1/2 cup coarsely chopped nuts

Microwave Directions: Butter 8-inch square pan. In large microwave-safe bowl place chocolate chips, butter and shortening; microwave at MEDIUM (50%) 5 to 7 minutes or until chips are melted and mixture is smooth when stirred. Add marshmallows and nuts; blend well. Spread evenly into prepared pan. Cover; chill until firm. Cut into 2-inch squares. *16 squares*

Easy Double Decker Fudge

1 cup REESE'S Peanut Butter Chips
1 can (14 ounces) sweetened
    condensed milk, divided
2 tablespoons butter or
    margarine, softened
1 cup HERSHEY'S Semi-Sweet
    Chocolate Chips
1 teaspoon vanilla extract,
    divided

Microwave Directions: Line 9-inch square pan or 9 x 5 x 3-inch loaf pan with foil; lightly butter foil. In medium microwave-safe bowl, place peanut butter chips, 2/3 cup sweetened condensed milk and butter. In second medium microwave-safe bowl, place chocolate chips and remaining sweetened condensed milk. Microwave bowl with peanut butter chips at HIGH (100%) 1 minute or until chips are melted and mixture is smooth when stirred; stir in 1/2 teaspoon vanilla. Immediately pour and spread evenly into prepared pan. Microwave bowl with chocolate chips at HIGH 1 minute or until chips are melted and mixture is smooth when stirred; stir in remaining 1/2 teaspoon vanilla. Immediately pour and spread over peanut butter layer; cool. Cover; refrigerate until firm. Cut into 1-inch squares. Store in airtight container in refrigerator.

About 2 dozen squares

Chocolate-Marshmallow Treats

2 cups (12-ounce package)
  HERSHEY'S Semi-Sweet
  Chocolate Chips
2 tablespoons shortening
12 large marshmallows
1 1/2 cups pecan halves

In top of double boiler over hot, not boiling, water melt chocolate chips and shortening, stirring until smooth. Remove from heat. Set aside; cool mixture to 85°F. Cut marshmallows in half horizontally; place on wax paper and flatten slightly. Set aside. To form base for treats make 24 clusters by arranging pecans on wax paper-covered tray in groups of five, placing flat side of pecan halves down and ends touching in center. Into center of each cluster of pecans spoon 1/2 teaspoon melted chocolate mixture. Use fork to dip marshmallow halves in melted mixture; place one half over each set of pecan clusters, pressing down slightly. Top with pecan half. Cool completely. Store, covered, in refrigerator.   *2 dozen snacks*

Microwave Directions: In 1-quart microwave-safe bowl place chocolate chips and shortening. Microwave at HIGH (100%) 1 1/2 to 2 minutes, stirring once, until chips are melted and mixture is smooth when stirred. Proceed as above.

Chocolate-Marshmallow Treats

Chocolate Dipped Snacks

1/2 cup HERSHEY'S Milk Chocolate
  Chips
1/2 cup HERSHEY'S Semi-Sweet
  Chocolate Chips
1 tablespoon shortening
  Potato chips, cookies, dried
  apricots or miniature pretzels

Microwave Directions: In small microwave-safe bowl place milk chocolate chips, semi-sweet chocolate chips and shortening. Microwave at HIGH (100%) 1 to 1 1/2 minutes or just until chips are melted and mixture is smooth when stirred. Cool slightly. Dip 2/3 of each snack or fruit into chocolate mixture. Shake gently to remove excess chocolate. Place on wax paper-covered tray. Chill, uncovered, about 30 minutes or until chocolate is firm. Store in airtight container in cool, dry place.
                    About 1/2 cup coating

Fast Chocolate-Pecan Fudge

1/2 cup butter or margarine
3/4 cup HERSHEY'S Cocoa
4 cups confectioners' sugar
1 teaspoon vanilla extract
1/2 cup evaporated milk
1 cup pecan pieces
Pecan halves (optional)

Microwave Directions: Line 8-inch square pan with foil. In medium microwave-safe bowl place butter. Microwave at HIGH (100%) 1 to 1 1/2 minutes or until melted. Add cocoa; stir until smooth. Stir in confectioners' sugar and vanilla; blend well (mixture will be dry and crumbly). Stir in evaporated milk. Microwave at HIGH 1 minute; stir. Microwave additional 1 minute or until mixture is hot. Beat with wooden spoon until smooth; add pecans. Pour into prepared pan. Cool. Cover; chill until firm. Cut into 1-inch squares. Garnish with pecan halves, if desired. Cover; store in refrigerator.

About 4 dozen squares

Coconut Honey Bars

1/3 cup butter or margarine
1/3 cup packed light brown sugar
1/3 cup honey
1/2 teaspoon vanilla extract
2 cups quick-cooking rolled oats
1 1/3 cups flaked coconut
1/2 cup raisins
1 cup REESE'S Peanut Butter Chips

Heat oven to 400°. Line 8-inch square baking pan with foil; grease foil. In large saucepan melt butter; remove from heat. Add remaining ingredients; stir until blended. Press mixture into prepared pan. Bake 15 to 20 minutes or just until golden brown. Cool completely; cut into bars. *About 2 dozen bars*

Mint 'n Chocolate Fudge

1/2 cup butter or margarine
3/4 cup HERSHEY'S Cocoa
4 cups confectioners' sugar
1 teaspoon vanilla extract
1/2 cup evaporated milk
Pastel Mint Topping (recipe follows)

Microwave Directions: Line 8-inch square pan with foil. In medium microwave-safe bowl place butter. Microwave at HIGH (100%) 1 to 1 1/2 minutes or until melted. Add cocoa; stir until smooth. Stir in confectioners' sugar and vanilla; blend well (mixture will be dry and crumbly). Stir in evaporated milk. Microwave at HIGH 1 to 2 minutes or until mixture is hot. Beat with wire whisk until smooth. Immediately pour into prepared pan. Cover; chill until firm. Spread Pastel Mint Topping evenly over fudge; chill until firm. Cut into 1-inch squares. Cover; store in refrigerator.

About 4 dozen squares

Pastel Mint Topping

In small mixer bowl beat 3 tablespoons softened butter or margarine, 1 tablespoon water and 1/8 to 1/4 teaspoon mint extract until blended. Gradually add 1 1/2 cups confectioners' sugar and 2 drops green or red food color. Beat until smooth.

From top to bottom: Cherries 'n Chocolate Fudge (recipe page 67), Fast Chocolate-Pecan Fudge and Mint 'n Chocolate Fudge

Mocha Truffles

1/4 cup whipping cream
3 tablespoons sugar
3 tablespoons butter
1 1/2 teaspoons powdered instant coffee
1/2 cup HERSHEY'S Semi-Sweet Chocolate Chips
1/2 teaspoon vanilla extract
Chopped nuts or HERSHEY'S Semi-Sweet Baking Chocolate, grated

In small saucepan combine whipping cream, sugar, butter and instant coffee; cook over low heat, stirring constantly, just until mixture boils. Remove from heat; immediately add chocolate chips. Stir until chips are melted and mixture is smooth when stirred; add vanilla. Pour into small bowl; chill, stirring occasionally, until mixture begins to set. Cover; chill several hours or overnight to allow mixture to ripen and harden. Form small amounts of mixture into 1/2-inch balls, working quickly to prevent melting; roll in nuts or chocolate. Cover; store in refrigerator. Serve cold.
About 1 1/2 dozen truffles

Chocolate Pralines

1 1/2 cups granulated sugar
1 1/2 cups packed light brown sugar
6 tablespoons HERSHEY'S Cocoa
1 cup light cream
6 tablespoons butter
1 teaspoon vanilla extract
2 cups coarsely broken pecans

Line 2 cookie sheets with wax paper. In heavy 3-quart saucepan combine granulated sugar, brown sugar, cocoa and light cream. Cook over medium heat, stirring constantly, until mixture boils. Reduce heat to low; cook, stirring constantly, to 234°F. (soft-ball stage) or until syrup, when dropped into very cold water, forms soft ball which flattens when removed from water. (Bulb of candy thermometer should not rest on bottom of saucepan.) Remove from heat. Add butter and vanilla. *Do not stir.* Cool at room temperature to 160°F. Add pecans. Beat with wooden spoon just until mixture begins to thicken, *about 1 to 2 minutes*, but is still glossy. Quickly drop by teaspoonfuls onto prepared cookie sheets. Cool. Store tightly covered or wrap individually in plastic wrap.
About 3 dozen candies

Chocolate Surprise Truffles

1/2 cup unsalted butter, softened
2 1/2 cups confectioners' sugar
1/2 cup HERSHEY'S Cocoa
1/4 cup whipping cream
1 1/2 teaspoons vanilla extract
Centers: After-dinner mints, whole candied cherries, whole almonds, pecan or walnut halves
Coatings: Confectioners' sugar, flaked coconut, chopped nuts

In large mixer bowl cream butter. In separate bowl combine confectioners' sugar and cocoa; add to butter mixture alternately with whipping cream and vanilla, blending well. Chill until firm. Shape small amount of mixture around desired center; roll into 1-inch balls. Drop into desired coating, turning until well covered. Refrigerate until firm. *About 3 dozen truffles*

Variation: Add 1/2 teaspoon rum extract; decrease vanilla to 1 teaspoon.

Cherries 'n Chocolate Fudge

1 can (14 ounces) sweetened
    condensed milk
2 cups (12-ounce package)
    HERSHEY'S Semi-Sweet
    Chocolate Chips
1/2 cup coarsely chopped
    almonds
1/2 cup chopped candied
    cherries
1 teaspoon almond extract
    Candied cherry halves
    (optional)

Line 8-inch square pan with foil. In medium microwave-safe bowl combine sweetened condensed milk and chocolate chips; stir lightly. Microwave at HIGH (100%) 1 1/2 to 2 minutes or until chips are melted and mixture is smooth when stirred. Stir in almonds, chopped cherries and almond extract. Spread evenly in prepared pan. Cover; chill until firm. Cut into 1-inch squares. Garnish with cherry halves, if desired. Cover; store in refrigerator.

About 4 dozen squares

Chocolate Dipped Fruit

1 cup HERSHEY'S Semi-Sweet
    Chocolate Chips
1 tablespoon shortening (not
    butter, margarine or oil)
    Assorted fresh fruit, washed
    and chilled

In top of double boiler over hot, not boiling, water melt chocolate chips and shortening; stir until smooth. Allow mixture to cool slightly. Dip fruit or fruit slices about 2/3 of the way into chocolate mixture. Shake gently to remove excess chocolate. Place on wax paper-covered tray. Chill, uncovered, about 30 minutes or until chocolate is firm.

About 1/2 cup coating

Fudge Caramels

Fudge Caramels

2 cups sugar
2/3 cup HERSHEY'S Cocoa
1/8 teaspoon salt
1 cup light corn syrup
1 cup evaporated milk
1/2 cup water
1/4 cup butter or margarine
1 teaspoon vanilla extract

Butter 9-inch square pan; set aside. In heavy 3-quart saucepan combine sugar, cocoa, salt and corn syrup; stir in evaporated milk and water. Cook over medium heat, stirring constantly, until mixture boils. Cook, stirring frequently, to 245°F on a candy thermometer (firm-ball stage) or until syrup, when dropped into very cold water, forms a firm ball that does not flatten when removed from water. Remove from heat; stir in butter and vanilla, blending well. Pour into prepared pan; cool. With buttered scissors cut into 1-inch squares. Wrap individually.

About 6 dozen candies

In large mixer bowl beat cream cheese and milk until fluffy. Add confectioners' sugar, cocoa and vanilla; blend well. Stir in nuts, if desired. Cover; chill several hours or until firm enough to handle. To form centers shape into 1-inch balls. Place on wax paper-covered tray. Refrigerate, uncovered, 3 to 4 hours or until dry. Using long fork, dip cold centers into Peanut Butter coating. (To remove excess coating, slide fork across rim of pan and tap a few times.) Place on wax paper-covered tray; swirl coating on top of bonbon. If coating becomes too thick, reheat over hot water. OR reheat in microwave at HIGH (100%) 30 seconds. Refrigerate, uncovered, 1 hour. Store in airtight container in refrigerator.

About 10 dozen bonbons

Peanut Butter Coating

In top of double boiler over hot, not boiling, water melt 3¹/₃ cups (two 10-ounce packages) REESE'S Peanut Butter Chips and ¹/₄ cup shortening (not butter, margarine or oil), stirring constantly to blend. Set aside; cool slightly.

Microwave Directions: Make centers as directed. In 2-quart microwave-safe bowl place peanut butter chips and shortening. Microwave at HIGH (100%) 1 to 2 minutes, stirring once, or just until chips are melted and mixture is smooth when stirred. Coat and store bonbons as directed.

Peanutty-Cocoa Bonbons

2 packages (3 ounces each) cream cheese, softened
1 tablespoon milk
4 cups confectioners' sugar
¹/₃ cup HERSHEY'S Cocoa
1 teaspoon vanilla extract
1 cup finely chopped nuts (optional)
Peanut Butter Coating (recipe follows)

*C*hocolate Truffles

¾ cup butter
¾ cup HERSHEY'S Cocoa
1 can (14 ounces) sweetened
  condensed milk
1 tablespoon vanilla extract
  Cocoa or confectioners' sugar

In heavy saucepan over low heat melt butter. Add cocoa; stir until smooth. Blend in sweetened condensed milk; stir constantly until mixture is thick, smooth and glossy, about 4 minutes. Remove from heat; stir in vanilla. Chill 3 to 4 hours or until firm. Shape into 1¼-inch balls; roll in cocoa or confectioners' sugar. Chill until firm, 1 to 2 hours. Store, covered, in refrigerator.
About 2½ dozen candies

VARIATIONS
Nut Truffles: Add ¾ cup coarsely chopped toasted pecans to chocolate mixture when adding vanilla. (To toast pecans: Toast ¾ cup pecan halves in shallow baking pan in 350° oven, stirring occasionally, 6 to 8 minutes or until golden brown. Cool.)

Rum Nut Truffles: Decrease vanilla to 1 teaspoon. Stir in 2 to 3 tablespoons rum or 1 teaspoon rum extract and ¾ cup coarsely chopped toasted nuts.

Espresso Truffles: Decrease vanilla to 1 teaspoon. Stir in 1¼ teaspoons instant espresso coffee with vanilla. Roll balls in cocoa or chopped nuts.

Nut-Coated Truffles: Roll balls in chopped nuts.

Cookies & Cookie Bars

Here's all kinds of cookies to choose from— all made delicious with chocolate.

Five Layer Bars (left) and Cocoa Cherry Drops (recipes page 72)

Cocoa Cherry Drops

1/2 cup plus 2 tablespoons butter
    or margarine
1 cup sugar
1 egg
1 teaspoon vanilla extract
1 1/4 cups all-purpose flour
6 tablespoons HERSHEY'S Cocoa
1/2 teaspoon baking soda
1/2 teaspoon salt
1 cup chopped maraschino
    cherries, well drained
1/2 cup chopped walnuts
    Walnut pieces (optional)

Heat oven to 350°. In large mixer bowl cream butter and sugar. Beat in egg and vanilla. Combine flour, cocoa, baking soda and salt; blend into creamed mixture. Stir in cherries and chopped walnuts. Drop by rounded teaspoonfuls onto ungreased cookie sheet. Press walnut piece into each cookie, if desired. Bake 10 to 12 minutes or until set. Cool slightly; remove from cookie sheet to wire rack. Cool completely.
About 4 dozen cookies

Five Layer Bars

3/4 cup butter or margarine
1 3/4 cups graham cracker crumbs
1/4 cup HERSHEY'S Cocoa
2 tablespoons sugar
1 can (14 ounces) sweetened
    condensed milk
1 cup HERSHEY'S Semi-Sweet
    Chocolate Chips
1 cup raisins or chopped dried
    apricots or miniature
    marshmallows
1 cup chopped nuts

Heat oven to 350°. In 13 x 9 x 2-inch baking pan melt butter in oven. Combine crumbs, cocoa and sugar; sprinkle over butter. Pour sweetened condensed milk evenly over crumbs. Sprinkle chocolate chips and raisins over sweetened condensed milk. Sprinkle nuts on top; press down firmly. Bake 25 to 30 minutes or until lightly browned. Cool completely; cover with aluminum foil. Let stand at room temperature about 8 hours before cutting into bars.
About 3 dozen bars

VARIATION
Golden Bars: Substitute 1 cup REESE'S Peanut Butter Chips for chocolate chips. Sprinkle 1 cup golden raisins or chopped dried apricots over chips. Proceed as above.

Chewy Chocolate Macaroons

1 package (14 ounces) flaked
    coconut (about 5 1/3 cups)
1/2 cup HERSHEY'S Cocoa
1 can (14 ounces) sweetened
    condensed milk
2 teaspoons vanilla extract
    Red candied cherries, halved

Heat oven to 350°. In large bowl thoroughly combine coconut and cocoa; stir in sweetened condensed milk and vanilla. Drop by rounded teaspoonfuls onto generously greased cookie sheet. Press cherry half into each cookie. Bake 8 to 10 minutes or until almost set. Immediately remove from cookie sheet to wire rack. Cool completely. Store loosely covered at room temperature.
About 4 dozen cookies

Buried Cherry Cookies

Chocolate Frosting (recipe follows)
$1/2$ cup butter or margarine
1 cup sugar
1 egg
$1 1/2$ teaspoons vanilla extract
$1 1/2$ cups all-purpose flour
$1/3$ cup HERSHEY'S Cocoa
$1/4$ teaspoon baking powder
$1/4$ teaspoon baking soda
$1/4$ teaspoon salt
1 jar (10 ounces) small maraschino cherries (about 44)

Prepare Chocolate Frosting; set aside. Heat oven to 350°. In large mixer bowl cream butter, sugar, egg and vanilla until light and fluffy. Combine flour, cocoa, baking powder, baking soda and salt; gradually add to creamed mixture until well blended. Shape dough into 1-inch balls. Place about 2 inches apart on ungreased cookie sheet. Press thumb gently in center of each cookie. Drain cherries; place one cherry in center of each cookie. Bake 10 minutes or until edges are set; remove from cookie sheet to wire rack. Spoon scant teaspoonful frosting over cherry, spreading to cover cherry.

About 3 $1/2$ dozen cookies

Chocolate Frosting

$2/3$ cup sweetened condensed milk
$1/2$ cup HERSHEY'S Semi-Sweet Chocolate Chips

In small saucepan combine sweetened condensed milk and chocolate chips. Stir constantly over low heat until chips are melted and mixture is smooth, about 5 minutes. Remove from heat; cool thoroughly.

No-Bake Cocoa Haystacks

1 1/2 cups sugar
1/2 cup butter or margarine
1/2 cup milk
1/2 cup HERSHEY'S Cocoa
1 teaspoon vanilla extract
3 1/2 cups quick-cooking rolled oats
1 cup flaked coconut
1/2 cup chopped nuts

In medium saucepan combine sugar, butter, milk and cocoa. Cook over medium heat, stirring constantly, until mixture comes to a full boil; remove from heat. Stir in remaining ingredients. Immediately drop by rounded teaspoonfuls onto wax paper. Cool completely. Store in cool, dry place.

About 4 dozen cookies

Spiced Chip Cookies

1 package (18.25 or 18.5 ounces) spice cake mix
1 cup quick-cooking rolled oats
3/4 cup butter or margarine, softened
2 eggs
2 cups (11.5-ounce package) HERSHEY'S Milk Chocolate Chips
1/2 cup coarsely chopped nuts

Heat oven to 350°. In large mixer bowl combine cake mix, oats, butter and eggs; mix well. Stir in milk chocolate chips and nuts. Drop by rounded teaspoonfuls onto ungreased cookie sheet. Bake 10 to 12 minutes or until very lightly browned. Cool slightly; remove from cookie sheet to wire rack. Cool completely.

About 4 dozen cookies

Cut Out Chocolate Cookies

1/2 cup butter or margarine
3/4 cup sugar
1 egg
1 teaspoon vanilla extract
1 1/2 cups all-purpose flour
1/3 cup HERSHEY'S Cocoa
1/2 teaspoon baking powder
1/2 teaspoon baking soda
1/4 teaspoon salt
Satiny Chocolate Glaze or Vanilla Glaze (recipes follow)

In large mixer bowl cream butter, sugar, egg and vanilla until light and fluffy. Combine flour, cocoa, baking powder, baking soda and salt; add to butter mixture, blending well. Chill dough about 1 hour or until firm enough to roll. Heat oven to 325°. On lightly floured board or between 2 pieces of wax paper, roll small portions of dough to 1/4-inch thickness. Cut into desired shapes with cookie cutters; place on ungreased cookie sheet. Bake 5 to 7 minutes or until no indentation remains when touched. Cool slightly; remove from cookie sheet to wire rack. Cool completely. Frost with Satiny Chocolate Glaze or Vanilla Glaze. *About 3 dozen cookies*

Cut Out Chocolate Cookies

Satiny Chocolate Glaze

      2 tablespoons butter or
        margarine
      3 tablespoons HERSHEY'S Cocoa
      2 tablespoons water
    ½ teaspoon vanilla extract
      1 cup confectioners' sugar

In small saucepan over low heat,
melt butter. Add cocoa and water.
Cook, stirring constantly, until mixture
thickens; *do not boil*. Remove from
heat; add vanilla. Gradually add
confectioners' sugar, beating with
wire whisk until smooth. Add
additional water, ½ teaspoon at a
time, until desired consistency.

About ¾ cup glaze

Vanilla Glaze

      3 tablespoons butter or
        margarine
      2 cups confectioners' sugar
      1 teaspoon vanilla extract
      2 to 3 tablespoons milk
      2 to 4 drops food color (optional)

In small saucepan over low heat,
melt butter. Remove from heat; blend
in confectioners' sugar and vanilla.
Gradually add milk, beating with
wire whisk until smooth. Blend in food
color, if desired.

About 1 cup glaze

English Toffee Bars

English Toffee Bars

    2 cups all-purpose flour
    1 cup packed light brown sugar
1/2 cup butter
    1 cup pecan halves
    Toffee Topping (recipe follows)
    1 cup HERSHEY'S Milk Chocolate
    Chips

Heat oven to 350°. In large mixer bowl combine flour, sugar and butter; mix until fine crumbs form. (A few large crumbs may remain.) Press into ungreased 13 x 9 x 2-inch baking pan. Sprinkle pecans over crust. Drizzle Toffee Topping evenly over pecans and crust. Bake 20 to 22 minutes or until topping is bubbly and golden. Remove from oven. Immediately sprinkle chocolate chips over top; press gently onto surface. Cool completely. Cut into bars.   *About 3 dozen bars*

Toffee Topping

In small saucepan combine 2/3 cup butter and 1/3 cup packed light brown sugar. Cook over medium heat, stirring constantly, until mixture comes to boil; boil and stir 30 seconds. Use immediately.

Butter Pecan Squares

1/2 cup butter, softened
1/2 cup packed light brown sugar
   1 egg
   1 teaspoon vanilla extract
3/4 cup all-purpose flour
   2 cups HERSHEY'S Milk Chocolate
    Chips, divided
3/4 cup chopped pecans, divided

Heat oven to 350°. Grease 8- or 9-inch square baking pan. In small mixer bowl cream butter, sugar, egg and vanilla until light and fluffy. Blend in flour. Stir in 1 cup milk chocolate chips and 1/2 cup pecans. Spread into prepared pan. Bake 25 to 30 minutes or until lightly browned. Remove from oven. Immediately sprinkle remaining 1 cup chips over surface. Let stand 5 to 10 minutes or until chips soften; spread evenly. Immediately sprinkle remaining 1/4 cup pecans over top; press gently onto chocolate. Cool completely. Cut into squares.   *About 16 squares*

Butter Pecan Squares

Drizzle Topped Brownies

Drizzle Topped Brownies

1 1/4 cups all-purpose biscuit baking
    mix
 1 cup sugar
 1/2 cup HERSHEY'S Cocoa
 1/2 cup butter or margarine,
    melted
 2 eggs
 1 teaspoon vanilla extract
 1 cup HERSHEY'S Semi-Sweet
    Chocolate Chips or MINI
    CHIPS
    Quick Vanilla Glaze (recipe
    follows)

Heat oven to 350°. Grease 8- or 9-inch square baking pan. In medium bowl combine baking mix, sugar and cocoa; mix with spoon or fork until thoroughly blended. Add butter, eggs and vanilla, mixing well. Stir in chocolate chips. Spread into prepared pan. Bake 25 to 30 minutes or until wooden pick inserted in center comes out clean. Cool completely. Drizzle Quick Vanilla Glaze over cooled brownies. Cut into bars. *About 20 brownies*

Quick Vanilla Glaze
In small bowl combine 1/2 cup confectioners' sugar, 1 tablespoon water and 1/4 teaspoon vanilla extract; blend well.

Signature Brownies

 1 package (15 ounces) golden
    sugar cookie mix
 1/2 cup HERSHEY'S Cocoa
 1/2 cup HERSHEY'S Syrup
 1/4 cup butter or margarine,
    melted
 1 egg
 1/2 cup coarsely chopped nuts
    No-Cook Fudge Frosting
    (recipe follows)

Heat oven to 350°. Grease 8- or 9-inch square baking pan. In medium bowl combine cookie mix (and enclosed flavor packet) and cocoa. Stir in syrup, butter and egg, blending well. Stir in nuts. Spread into prepared pan. Bake 25 to 30 minutes or until wooden pick inserted in center comes out clean. Cool completely. Frost with No-Cook Fudge Frosting. Cut into bars. *About 20 brownies*

No-Cook Fudge Frosting
In small bowl combine 2 cups confectioners' sugar, 1/2 cup HERSHEY'S Syrup, 1/4 cup HERSHEY'S Cocoa, 1/4 cup melted butter or margarine and 1/2 teaspoon vanilla extract; blend well. Use immediately.

Chocolate Teddy Bears

²/₃ cup butter or margarine
1 cup sugar
2 teaspoons vanilla extract
2 eggs
2¹/₂ cups all-purpose flour
¹/₂ cup HERSHEY'S Cocoa
¹/₂ teaspoon baking soda
¹/₄ teaspoon salt

In large mixer bowl cream butter, sugar and vanilla until light and fluffy. Add eggs; blend well. Combine flour, cocoa, baking soda and salt; gradually add to creamed mixture, blending thoroughly. Chill until dough is firm enough to handle. Heat oven to 350°.

To shape teddy bears: For each cookie, form a portion of the dough into 1 large ball for body (1 to 1¹/₂ inches), 1 medium-size ball for head (³/₄ to 1 inch), 4 small balls for arms and legs (¹/₂ inch), 2 smaller balls for ears, 1 tiny ball for nose and 4 tiny balls for paws (optional). On ungreased cookie sheet flatten large ball slightly for body. Attach medium-size ball for head by overlapping slightly onto body. Place balls for arms, legs and ears, and a tiny ball on head for nose. Arrange other tiny balls atop ends of legs and arms for paws, if desired. With wooden pick, draw eyes and mouth; pierce small hole at top of cookie for use as hanging ornament, if desired. Bake 6 to 8 minutes or until set. Cool 1 minute; remove from cookie sheet to wire rack. Cool completely. Store in covered container. If cookies will be used as ornaments, allow to dry on wire rack at least 6 hours before hanging. Decorate with ribbon or pull ribbon through hole for hanging, if desired.   *About 14 cookies*

Peanut Butter Chips and Jelly Bars

1 1/2 cups all-purpose flour
1/2 cup sugar
3/4 teaspoon baking powder
1/2 cup butter or margarine
1 egg, beaten
3/4 cup grape jelly
1 cup REESE'S Peanut Butter Chips, divided

Heat oven to 375°. Grease 9-inch square baking pan. In medium bowl combine flour, sugar and baking powder; cut in butter with pastry blender or fork to form coarse crumbs. Add egg; blend well. Reserve half of mixture; press remaining mixture onto bottom of prepared pan. Spread jelly evenly over crust. Sprinkle 1/2 cup peanut butter chips over jelly. Combine remaining crumb mixture with remaining 1/2 cup chips; sprinkle over top. Bake 25 to 30 minutes or until lightly browned. Cool completely. Cut into bars.

About 1 1/2 dozen bars

Chocolate Crinkle Cookies

2 cups sugar
3/4 cup vegetable oil
3/4 cup HERSHEY'S Cocoa
4 eggs
2 teaspoons vanilla extract
2 1/3 cups all-purpose flour
2 teaspoons baking powder
1/2 teaspoon salt
Confectioners' sugar

In large mixer bowl combine sugar and oil; add cocoa, blending well. Beat in eggs and vanilla. Combine flour, baking powder and salt; add to cocoa mixture, blending well. Cover; chill at least 6 hours. Heat oven to 350°. Shape dough into 1-inch balls; roll in confectioners' sugar. Place 2 inches apart on greased cookie sheet. Bake 12 to 14 minutes or until almost no indentation remains when touched. Remove from cookie sheet to wire rack. Cool completely.

About 4 dozen cookies

Peanut Butter Chips and Jelly Bars

BEVERAGES

Rich cocoas to warm you in winter, plus frothy favorites to cool you off in summer.

From left to right: Irish Cocoa, Cocoa-Banana Shake and Hot Cocoa (recipes page 82)

Irish Cocoa

6 tablespoons sugar
3 tablespoons HERSHEY'S Cocoa
    Dash salt
1/4 cup hot water
3 cups milk
6 tablespoons Irish whiskey
1/2 cup chilled whipping cream,
    whipped

In medium saucepan combine sugar, cocoa and salt; stir in water. Cook over medium heat, stirring constantly, until mixture boils. Boil and stir 2 minutes. Add milk; stir and heat to serving temperature. *Do not boil.* Remove from heat. Pour 1 tablespoon whiskey in each cup or goblet. Fill cup with hot cocoa; stir to blend. Serve hot, topped with whipped cream.

About six 6-ounce servings

Cocoa-Banana Shake

1 ripe, medium banana
1/4 cup HERSHEY'S Cocoa
1/4 cup honey
1/4 cup hot water
2 cups cold milk
1 cup vanilla ice cream

Slice banana into blender container. Add cocoa, honey and water; cover and blend until smooth. Add milk; cover and blend. Add ice cream; cover and blend until smooth. Serve immediately.

About four 8-ounce servings

Hot Cocoa

1/2 cup sugar
1/4 cup HERSHEY'S Cocoa
    Dash salt
1/3 cup hot water
4 cups (1 quart) milk
3/4 teaspoon vanilla extract
    Sweetened Whipped Cream
    (optional, recipe page 88)

In medium saucepan combine sugar, cocoa and salt; blend in water. Cook over medium heat, stirring constantly, until mixture boils. Boil and stir 2 minutes. Add milk; stir and heat to serving temperature. *Do not boil.* Remove from heat; add vanilla. Beat with rotary beater or wire whisk until foamy. Serve hot, topped with Sweetened Whipped Cream, if desired.

About six 6-ounce servings

VARIATIONS

Spiced Cocoa: Add 1/8 teaspoon ground cinnamon and 1/8 teaspoon ground nutmeg with vanilla.

Citrus Cocoa: Add 1/2 teaspoon orange extract or 2 to 3 tablespoons orange liqueur with vanilla.

Swiss Mocha: Add 2 to 2 1/2 teaspoons powdered instant coffee with vanilla.

Mint Cocoa: Add 1/2 teaspoon mint extract, or 3 tablespoons crushed hard peppermint candy, or 2 to 3 tablespoons white creme de menthe with vanilla.

Cocoa au Lait: Omit whipped cream. Spoon 2 tablespoons softened vanilla ice cream on top of each cup of cocoa at serving time.

Slim-Trim Cocoa: Omit sugar. Combine cocoa, salt and water; substitute skim milk. Proceed as above. With vanilla, stir in sugar substitute with sweetening equivalence of 1/2 cup sugar.

Microwave Single Serving: In 8-ounce microwave-safe mug, combine 2 heaping teaspoons sugar and 1 heaping teaspoon HERSHEY'S Cocoa. Add 2 teaspoons cold milk; stir until smooth. Fill mug with milk; microwave at HIGH (100%) 1 to 1 1/2 minutes or just until hot. Stir to blend before serving.

Chocolate Strawberry Cooler

1/2 cup sliced strawberries
2 tablespoons sugar
1 tablespoon HERSHEY'S Cocoa
1 cup milk, divided
1/2 cup cold club soda, freshly opened
 Ice cream or whipped cream
2 fresh strawberries (optional)

In blender container combine sliced strawberries, sugar, cocoa and 1/2 cup milk; cover and blend until smooth. Add remaining 1/2 cup milk and club soda; cover and blend. Pour into 2 glasses. Garnish with ice cream or whipped cream and strawberry, if desired. Serve immediately.

About two 8-ounce servings

Chocolate Strawberry Cooler

*D*ouble Chocolate Malt

1/2 cup cold milk
1/4 cup HERSHEY'S Syrup
  2 tablespoons chocolate malted
    milk powder
  2 cups vanilla ice cream,
    softened

In blender container place milk,
syrup and malted milk powder.
Cover; blend. Add ice cream. Cover;
blend until smooth. Serve
immediately.
About three 6-ounce servings

VARIATION
Triple Chocolate Malt: Substitute
chocolate ice cream for vanilla ice
cream.

*H*ot Cocoa For A Crowd

1 1/2 cups sugar
1 1/4 cups HERSHEY'S Cocoa
  1/2 teaspoon salt
  3/4 cup hot water
   4 quarts (1 gallon) milk
   1 tablespoon vanilla extract

In 6-quart saucepan combine sugar,
cocoa and salt; gradually add hot
water. Cook over medium heat,
stirring constantly, until mixture boils.
Boil and stir 2 minutes. Add milk;
heat to serving temperature, stirring
occasionally. *Do not boil.* Remove
from heat; add vanilla. Serve hot.
About twenty-two 6-ounce servings

*H*ot Merry Mocha

6 tablespoons HERSHEY'S Cocoa
1 to 2 tablespoons powdered
  instant coffee
1/8 teaspoon salt
6 cups hot water
1 can (14 ounces) sweetened
  condensed milk
  Sweetened Whipped Cream
  (optional, recipe page 88)

In 4-quart saucepan combine
cocoa, instant coffee and salt; stir in
water. Cook over medium heat,
stirring occasionally, until mixture
boils. Stir in sweetened condensed
milk; heat thoroughly. *Do not boil.*
Beat with rotary beater or wire whisk
until foamy. Serve hot, topped with
Sweetened Whipped Cream, if
desired.
About ten 6-ounce servings

VARIATION
Minted Hot Chocolate: Follow
directions above omitting instant
coffee. Stir in 1/4 to 1/2 teaspoon mint
extract before beating. Serve with
candy cane for stirrer, if desired.

*C*appuccino Cooler

1 1/2 cups cold coffee
1 1/2 cups chocolate ice cream
  1/4 cup HERSHEY'S Syrup
    Crushed ice
    Whipped cream

In blender container place coffee,
ice cream and syrup. Cover; blend
until smooth. Serve immediately over
crushed ice. Garnish with whipped
cream.
About four 6-ounce servings

Hot Cocoa Mix

2 cups nonfat dry milk powder
3/4 cup sugar
1/2 cup HERSHEY'S Cocoa
1/2 cup powdered non-dairy
    creamer
Dash salt

In large bowl combine all
ingredients; blend well. Store mix in
tightly covered container.

3³/4 cups mix
(about fifteen 6-ounce servings)

Single serving: Place 1/4 cup mix in
heatproof cup or mug; stir in 3/4 cup
boiling water. Serve hot, topped with
marshmallows, if desired.

Choco Peanut Butter Shake

3/4 cup cold milk
1/4 cup creamy peanut butter
3 tablespoons HERSHEY'S Cocoa
1 tablespoon marshmallow
    creme
2 cups vanilla ice cream

In blender container place milk,
peanut butter, cocoa and
marshmallow creme. Cover; blend.
Add ice cream. Cover; blend until
smooth. Serve immediately.

About three 6-ounce servings

Spiced Mocha (from mix)

Spiced Mocha Mix

1 cup sugar
1 cup nonfat dry milk powder
1/2 cup powdered non-dairy
    creamer
1/2 cup HERSHEY'S Cocoa
3 tablespoons powdered instant
    coffee
1/2 teaspoon ground allspice
1/4 teaspoon ground cinnamon
Dash salt

In large bowl combine all
ingredients. Store in airtight container.

2¹/2 cups mix (12 to 14 servings)

For Single Serving: Place 3
tablespoons mix in mug or cup; add
3/4 cup boiling water. Stir until mix is
dissolved. Top with marshmallows, if
desired. Serve immediately.

EXTRAS

Delicious sauces and frostings plus the luscious dessert recipes pictured on the front cover.

From left to right: Fudge Frosting, Quick Hot Fudge Sauce and Chocolate Whipped Cream (recipes page 88)

Fudge Frosting

1 cup sugar
¼ cup HERSHEY'S Cocoa
½ cup milk
¼ cup butter or margarine
2 tablespoons light corn syrup
Dash salt
1½ cups confectioners' sugar
1 teaspoon vanilla extract

In medium saucepan combine sugar and cocoa. Stir in milk, butter, corn syrup and salt. Cook over medium heat, stirring constantly, until mixture comes to a full boil. Boil, stirring occasionally, 3 minutes. Remove from heat; cool to lukewarm. In small mixer bowl place confectioners' sugar; stir in chocolate mixture and vanilla. Beat until spreading consistency.
About 2 cups frosting

Sweetened Whipped Cream

1 cup chilled whipping cream
1 to 2 tablespoons
    confectioners' sugar
½ teaspoon vanilla extract

In small mixer bowl combine cream, confectioners' sugar and vanilla; beat until stiff. Serve cold.
About 2 cups topping

Chocolate Whipped Cream

In small mixer bowl combine ½ cup sugar and ¼ cup HERSHEY'S Cocoa. Add 1 cup chilled whipping cream and 1 teaspoon vanilla extract; beat until stiff. Serve cold.
About 2 cups topping

Quick Hot Fudge Sauce

2 tablespoons butter or
    margarine
⅓ cup HERSHEY'S Cocoa
1 can (14 ounces) sweetened
    condensed milk
2 tablespoons water
1 teaspoon vanilla extract

In heavy 2-quart saucepan combine all ingredients except vanilla. Cook over medium heat, stirring constantly with whisk, until sauce is smooth and slightly thickened, about 5 minutes. Remove from heat; stir in vanilla. Serve warm over ice cream or desserts.   *About 1½ cups sauce*

Microwave Directions: In medium microwave-safe bowl place butter. Microwave at HIGH (100%) 30 to 45 seconds or until melted; stir in cocoa until smooth. Blend in sweetened condensed milk and water. Microwave at HIGH 1 minute; stir. Microwave at HIGH 1 to 2 additional minutes, stirring with whisk after each minute, or until mixture is smooth and warm. Stir in vanilla. Serve as directed.

Chocolate Peanut Butter Sauce

½ cup HERSHEY'S Chocolate
    Fudge Topping
½ cup HERSHEY'S Syrup
¼ cup creamy peanut butter

In small saucepan place all ingredients. Cook over low heat, stirring constantly, until mixture is warm. Serve immediately over ice cream or other desserts.
About 1¼ cups sauce

Chocolate Sour Cream Frosting

1/2 cup butter or margarine
1/2 cup HERSHEY'S Cocoa
3 cups confectioners' sugar
1/2 cup dairy sour cream
2 teaspoons vanilla extract

In small saucepan over low heat melt butter. Add cocoa and stir constantly until mixture is smooth and slightly thickened. Transfer to small mixer bowl; cool slightly. Add confectioners' sugar alternately with sour cream; beat to spreading consistency. Stir in vanilla.

About 2 1/2 cups frosting

Cocoa Glaze

1 cup whipping cream
1 tablespoon light corn syrup
1 cup HERSHEY'S Cocoa
1 cup sugar
2 tablespoons butter or
    margarine
1 tablespoon vanilla extract

In heavy 2-quart saucepan stir together cream and corn syrup. Sift cocoa and sugar together; stir into cream mixture. Add butter. Cook over low heat, stirring constantly, 6 to 8 minutes or until butter melts and mixture is smooth; *do not boil.* Remove from heat; stir in vanilla. Use glaze while warm.

About 2 cups glaze

Note: Glaze can be stored in airtight container in refrigerator up to 2 weeks. Reheat over low heat, stirring constantly.

Fudgey Chocolate Fondue

1/2 cup butter or margarine
1/2 cup HERSHEY'S Cocoa
3/4 cup sugar
1/2 cup evaporated milk or light
    cream
1 teaspoon vanilla extract

In small saucepan over low heat melt butter. Remove from heat; immediately stir in cocoa. Add sugar and evaporated milk; cook over low heat, stirring constantly, until sugar is dissolved and mixture is smooth. Remove from heat; stir in vanilla. Serve warm with selection of fruit, marshmallows or small pieces of cake or cookies.

About 1 1/2 cups fondue

Fudgey Chocolate Fondue

Peanut Butter Sauce

1 cup REESE'S Peanut Butter Chips
1/3 cup milk
1/4 cup whipping cream
1/4 teaspoon vanilla extract

In small saucepan place peanut butter chips, milk and whipping cream. Cook over low heat, stirring constantly, until chips are melted and mixture is smooth. Remove from heat; stir in vanilla. Serve warm. Cover; refrigerate leftover sauce.

About 1 cup sauce

To reheat: Place sauce in small saucepan. Stir constantly over low heat until warm. Add additional milk or whipping cream for desired consistency.

Creamy Chocolate Frosting

3 bars (3 ounces) HERSHEY'S Unsweetened Baking Chocolate
1 cup miniature marshmallows
1/2 cup butter or margarine, softened
1/3 cup milk
2 1/2 cups confectioners' sugar
1/2 teaspoon vanilla extract

In top of double boiler over hot, not boiling, water melt baking chocolate. Add marshmallows; stir frequently until marshmallows are melted. Pour mixture into small mixer bowl. Beat in butter and milk until mixture is smooth. Add confectioners' sugar and vanilla; beat to desired consistency.

About 2 1/2 cups frosting

Easy Bittersweet Chocolate Sauce

2 cups (12-ounce package) HERSHEY'S Semi-Sweet Chocolate Chips
2 bars (2 ounces) HERSHEY'S Unsweetened Baking Chocolate, chopped
1 cup whipping cream
1 1/2 teaspoons vanilla extract

In top of double boiler over hot, not boiling, water place chocolate chips, baking chocolate and whipping cream. Cook, stirring frequently, until chocolate is melted and mixture is smooth. Remove from heat; stir in vanilla. Serve warm. Cover; refrigerate leftover sauce.

About 2 cups sauce

To reheat: Place sauce in small saucepan. Stir constantly over low heat until warm.

Chocolate and Vanilla Yule Log

4 eggs, separated
1/2 cup plus 1/3 cup sugar, divided
1 teaspoon vanilla extract
1/2 cup all-purpose flour
1/4 cup HERSHEY'S Cocoa
1/2 teaspoon baking powder
1/4 teaspoon baking soda
1/8 teaspoon salt
1/3 cup water
  Vanilla Cream Filling (recipe follows)
  Chocolate Glaze (recipe follows)
  Vanilla Leaves (recipe follows)

Heat oven to 375°. Line 15 1/2 x 10 1/2 x 1-inch jelly roll pan with foil; generously grease foil. In large mixer bowl beat egg whites until soft peaks form; gradually add 1/2 cup sugar and beat until stiff peaks form. Set aside.

In small mixer bowl beat egg yolks and vanilla on high speed about 3 minutes; gradually add remaining 1/3 cup sugar. Continue beating 2 additional minutes until mixture is thick and lemon-colored. Combine flour, cocoa, baking powder, baking soda and salt; gently fold into egg yolk mixture alternately with water just until mixture is smooth. Gradually fold chocolate mixture into egg whites; spread batter evenly into prepared pan. Bake 12 to 15 minutes or until top springs back when touched lightly in center. Immediately loosen cake from edges of pan; invert onto linen towel sprinkled with confectioners' sugar. Carefully peel off foil. Immediately roll cake in towel starting from narrow end; place on wire rack. Cool completely. Prepare Vanilla Cream Filling. Unroll cake; remove towel. Spread with filling; reroll cake. Glaze with Chocolate Glaze. Cover; refrigerate until just before serving. Garnish with Vanilla Leaves.

10 to 12 servings

Vanilla Cream Filling

  1/2 teaspoon unflavored gelatin
  1 tablespoon cold water
  2/3 cup HERSHEY'S Vanilla Milk
      Chips
  1/4 cup milk
  1 teaspoon vanilla extract
  1 cup chilled whipping cream

Microwave Directions: In small cup sprinkle gelatin over cold water; let stand several minutes to soften. In small microwave-safe bowl microwave vanilla chips and milk at HIGH (100%) 30 seconds to 1 minute, stirring vigorously after 30 seconds, until chips are melted when stirred. Add gelatin mixture and vanilla extract; stir until gelatin is dissolved. Cool to room temperature. In cold small mixer bowl beat whipping

cream until stiff; carefully fold into vanilla mixture. Chill 10 minutes or until filling begins to set.

About 3 cups filling

Chocolate Glaze

  2 tablespoons butter or
      margarine
  2 tablespoons HERSHEY'S Cocoa
  2 tablespoons water
  1 cup confectioners' sugar
  1/2 teaspoon vanilla extract

In small saucepan over low heat melt butter; add cocoa and water, stirring until smooth and slightly thickened. *Do not boil.* Remove from heat; cool slightly. Gradually blend in sugar and vanilla; beat with wire whisk until smooth and slightly thickened. *About 3/4 cup glaze*

Vanilla Leaves

  Non-toxic leaves (rose or
      lemon leaves)
  1/2 cup HERSHEY'S Vanilla Milk
      Chips
  1 teaspoon shortening

Microwave Directions: Thoroughly wash and dry several leaves. In small microwave-safe bowl microwave vanilla chips and shortening at HIGH (100%) 30 seconds to 1 minute, stirring vigorously after 30 seconds, until chips are melted when stirred. With small, soft-bristled pastry brush, brush melted vanilla mixture onto backs of leaves; place on wax paper. Refrigerate until very firm. Carefully peel green leaves from vanilla leaves; refrigerate until ready to use.

Cranberry Orange Ricotta Cheese Brownies

Filling (recipe follows)
1/2 cup butter or margarine, melted
3/4 cup sugar
1 teaspoon vanilla extract
2 eggs
3/4 cup all-purpose flour
1/2 cup HERSHEY'S Cocoa
1/2 teaspoon baking powder
1/2 teaspoon salt

Prepare Filling; set aside. Heat oven to 350°. Grease 9-inch square baking pan. In small bowl combine melted butter, sugar and vanilla; add eggs, beating well. Combine flour, cocoa, baking powder and salt; add to butter mixture, mixing thoroughly. Spread half of chocolate batter in prepared pan. Spread Filling over top. Drop remaining chocolate batter by 1/2 teaspoonfuls onto cheese mixture. Bake 40 to 45 minutes or until wooden pick inserted in center comes out clean. Cool completely. Cut into squares. Store leftovers in refrigerator.

About 16 squares

Filling

1 cup ricotta cheese
3 tablespoons whole-berry cranberry sauce
1/4 cup sugar
1 egg
2 tablespoons cornstarch
1/4 to 1/2 teaspoon grated orange peel

In small mixer bowl beat ricotta cheese, cranberry sauce, sugar, egg and cornstarch until smooth. Stir in orange peel.

Chocolate Festival Cheesecake

Chocolate Crumb Crust (recipe follows)
3 packages (8 ounces each) cream cheese, softened
1 1/4 cups sugar
1/4 cup HERSHEY'S Cocoa
1/2 cup dairy sour cream
2 teaspoons vanilla extract
2 tablespoons all-purpose flour
3 eggs
Assorted fresh fruit, sliced (optional)
Sweetened whipped cream or whipped topping (optional)

Prepare Chocolate Crumb Crust; set aside. Heat oven to 450°. In large mixer bowl combine cream cheese, sugar, cocoa, sour cream and vanilla; beat on medium speed with electric mixer until smooth. Add flour and eggs; beat well. Pour into prepared crust. Bake 10 minutes. Without opening oven door, decrease temperature to 250°; continue baking 30 minutes. (Cheesecake may not appear set in middle.) Cool 30 minutes. Loosen cheesecake from rim of pan; cool to room temperature. Chill several hours or overnight; remove rim of pan. Garnish with sliced fruit and whipped cream, if desired.

10 to 12 servings

Chocolate Crumb Crust

1 1/4 cups vanilla wafer crumbs (about 30 wafers, crushed)
1/3 cup confectioners' sugar
1/3 cup HERSHEY'S Cocoa
1/4 cup butter or margarine, melted

Heat oven to 350°. In small bowl combine crumbs, sugar and cocoa; blend in melted butter. Press mixture onto bottom and 1/2 inch up side of 9-inch springform pan. Bake 8 to 10 minutes. Cool.

Rich Chocolate Mini-Cakes

2/3 cup all-purpose flour
1/2 cup sugar
3 tablespoons HERSHEY'S Cocoa
1/2 teaspoon baking powder
1/4 teaspoon baking soda
1/4 teaspoon salt
1/2 cup water
3 tablespoons vegetable oil
1 teaspoon vanilla extract
Chocolate Glaze (recipe follows)
Vanilla Drizzle (recipe follows)

Heat oven to 350°. Lightly grease 24 small muffin cups (1 3/4 inches in diameter). In medium bowl combine flour, sugar, cocoa, baking powder, baking soda and salt. Add water, oil and vanilla; stir or whisk until batter is smooth and blended. (Batter will be thin.) Spoon batter in prepared cups filling 2/3 full. Bake 12 to 14 minutes or until top springs back when touched lightly in center. Cool in pans on wire rack 3 minutes; invert onto rack. Cool completely. Prepare Chocolate Glaze; dip rounded portion into glaze or spread glaze on tops. Place on wax-paper-covered tray; chill 10 minutes to set glaze. Prepare Vanilla Drizzle; drizzle onto mini-cakes. Decorate as desired.
About 2 dozen mini-cakes

Chocolate Glaze

2 tablespoons butter or margarine
2 tablespoons HERSHEY'S Cocoa
2 tablespoons water
1 cup confectioners' sugar
1/2 teaspoon vanilla extract

In small saucepan over low heat melt butter; add cocoa and water, stirring until smooth and slightly thickened. *Do not boil.* Remove from heat; cool slightly. Gradually blend in sugar and vanilla; beat with wire whisk until smooth and slightly thickened.   *About 3/4 cup glaze*

Vanilla Drizzle

1/2 cup HERSHEY'S Vanilla Milk Chips
1 tablespoon shortening

Microwave Directions: In small microwave-safe bowl microwave vanilla chips and shortening at HIGH (100%) 30 seconds; stir until smooth. If necessary, microwave at HIGH additional 15 seconds or just until chips are melted and smooth when stirred.

Milk Chocolate Pots de Creme

2 cups (11.5-oz. package) HERSHEY'S Milk Chocolate Chips
1/2 cup light cream
1/2 teaspoon vanilla extract
Sweetened whipped cream (page 88) or whipped topping (optional)

In medium microwave-safe bowl place milk chocolate chips and light cream. Microwave at HIGH (100%) 1 1/2 minutes; stir. If necessary, microwave at HIGH an additional 15 seconds at a time, stirring after each heating, until chocolate is melted and mixture is smooth when stirred. Stir in vanilla. Pour into demitasse cups or very small souffle dishes. Cover; refrigerate until firm. Serve cold with sweetened whipped cream, if desired.   *6 to 8 servings*

INDEX